Common Sense about Police Review

Common Sense
about Police Review

Douglas W. Perez

 Temple University Press   *Philadelphia*

Temple University Press, Philadelphia 19122
Copyright © 1994 by Temple University. All rights reserved
Published 1994
Printed in the United States of America

The paper used in this publication meets the minimum requirements of
American National Standard for Information Sciences—Permanence of Paper
for Printed Library Materials, ANSI Z39.48-1984♾

Library of Congress Cataloging-in-Publication Data
Perez, Douglas Werner.
    Common sense about police review / Douglas W. Perez.
      p.   cm.
    Includes bibliographical references and index.
    ISBN 1-56639-132-6
    1. Police—United States—Complaints against.   2. Police administration—
United States.   I. Title.
HV8141.P36   1994
363.2'3—dc20   93-11192

For my girls,
Betsy, Elizabeth, and Annie

Contents

Acknowledgments

This study was completed with support from a Comprehensive Employment and Training Act (CETA) project grant developed by Jim Newman in Oakland, California, and from the Skyline College Department of Social Sciences and Creative Arts in San Bruno, California, headed by Paula Anderson. Over the course of fifteen years, their backing helped to keep alive what has always been a controversial endeavor. The politically sensitive nature of police review being what it is, their support from outside the police review environment has been critical.

Several chiefs of police and civilian review system leaders have opened up their systems to the scrutiny of the project. In doing so they have indicated not only a confidence in their own systems but also an interest in the development of new knowledge. They have, at some political risk, allowed access to confidential files, procedures, and deliberations so that I might develop a complete understanding of police review. They include Dashel Butler, Jim Casey, Earnest Clements, Joseph McNamara, Pete Meredith, Fred O'Hearn, Kit Perrow, Sally Power, Richard Rainey, Joe Rodriguez, O'Dell Sylvester, and Willie Walton. Of particular importance has been the help of Chief George Hart of the Oakland Police Department. As is true for the departments of all these professionals, Oakland is very lucky to have a chief law enforcement executive who is not only open to criticism but also interested in positive change.

Within the organizations studied, numerous professionals operating in internal affairs sections, in city offices, and in civilian review mechanisms have given their time and ideas to the project. They include Robert Bailey, Bob Cancilla, Larry Carroll, Don Casimere, Joe Colletti, Nolan Darnell, Rich Ehle, Stephanie Fleming, Roy Fox, John Gackowski, Peter Hagberg, Doug Hambleton, Mike Langer, Bill Moulder, Doug Sciberling, Jim Simonson, Mike Stamp, Norm Stamper, and James Stewart. These people have included this study in their day-to-day operations. They have opened windows to police review realities never before shared with "outsiders" like me.

As I trust this study amply illustrates, beat cops, police union leaders, police attorneys, American Civil Liberties Union (ACLU) attorneys, reporters, and police commissioners in cities throughout the country have offered their cooperation. Some important contributions have come from Ed Compano, John Crew, Phil Doran, Larry Estrada, Rachel Ginsburg, Fred Lopez, Kevin Skully, Hadwick Thompson, Robert Valladon, and Bill Wallace. Whatever insights the study may have are the direct products of the openness, honesty, and intelligence of all the aforementioned professionals.

Several "intellectual dilettantes" who neither study in the field of police review nor have any experience in its practical side have aided the project immeasurably with their insights. Reading drafts, discussing findings, and bringing an external perspective to the work, these people have helped on numerous occasions to keep the project from losing its focus and direction. They include Paula Anderson, Dan Carter, Wes Donohower, Bill Geller, John Kirchmeier, Betsy Kutzner, Jim Kutzner, David Leonard, David Richman, and Bill Zumwalt. Selma Monsky and Steve Rosenstone of Berkeley helped with the important task of survey research tool development.

Jerry Skolnick originally suggested that I conduct a comparative study of police review systems in 1977. Bob Kagan showed me a problem with the organization of the original research and then helped me to solve it. Wayne Kerstetter, Carl Klockars, and Werner Peterson have been most helpful with suggestions, great and small, that have focused the project and its analysis.

Sandy Muir, who first suggested I study the police twenty years ago, has been the shadow of the project from its inception. He has been flawless in his analysis and undying in his enthusiasm. He is the finest teacher I have ever known. As such, he mixes criticism and applause, direction and suggestion, learning and teaching. Would that everyone had such a dynamic and insightful teacher, friend, and colleague.

Most important, I must thank Betsy, my wife. She has edited

drafts, discussed conceptual frameworks, analyzed specific organizations, reorganized the work's presentation, and done a thousand other tasks as "editor in chief." Yet my debt to her goes deeper, for this work took more than a decade to produce. At times it was "supported" by nothing more than the Perez family household. Betsy's patience and undying faith in me and in the importance of the project made it all happen. If I wrote a hundred more books, no one could ever be so important to the fruition of a work. To her go my respect, my gratitude, and my love.

Common Sense about Police Review

Introduction

In Boston a young man is shot by police under mysterious circumstances. In Los Angeles a motorist is beaten by a group of officers after a high-speed chase. In Milwaukee a mass murderer kills a young boy after police refuse to come to the boy's aid. In New York hundreds of police officers swinging clubs wade into a crowd and injure over one hundred people. In Detroit plainclothes detectives beat a motorist to death with flashlights.

The script that follows is familiar. It has been played out repeatedly in the cities of America over the course of the past few decades. Police officers, often white, are accused of misconduct aimed at citizens who are often black or Latino. Whether the actions of the police are legally justified becomes obscured. The press jumps on the issue of police malpractice. Local civil liberties organizations, ethnic minority group leaders, and politicians call for an end to police violence and misbehavior.

The local police department investigates the allegations of misconduct. Its internal review system finds the actions of the officers to be "legal and proper." Occasionally, the police find fault with their peers. But the discipline handed out does not satisfy those outside the law enforcement subculture, who call for the institution of civilian review of police conduct. Only with outside scrutiny, they argue, will the police be effectively held accountable for their actions.

The police respond that protestations ignore the difficulty of policing the streets of America. The local police union asserts that civilian review will mean an end to the ability of officers to do their jobs. Pointing to the history of political interference with the police, police administrators predict a return to an era of widespread corruption.

In this charged atmosphere, local leaders are asked to evaluate the fairness, objectivity, and effectiveness of their police review mechanisms. They are asked to make a measured analysis of how civilian review would impact police operations. As often as not, such discussions are disconcerting to everyone: to the police organization, to the individual police officer, to the citizens who feel victimized by police brutality, and to the community in general.

This book is a comparative study of police review systems. It attempts a realistic analysis of the problem of holding a powerful group of individuals accountable for their actions. The discussion endeavors to avoid the emotion and sensationalism that normally surround the police review debate. It draws on a growing field of literature and on recently completed survey research of police officer and citizen complainant attitudes. (For a discussion of the research involved, see Appendix A.) The study compares internal, external (civilian), and hybrid forms of review. It analyzes three model systems, those operated by the police exclusively, by civilians outside law enforcement, and by a combination of the two.

The topic of police review involves stubborn, intractable interest groups. These groups have made the debate one that at times borders on the absurd. Because of the emotionally charged rhetoric involved, discussions about police review systems usually degenerate into arguments, arguments that involve several distinctive sides.

After seventeen years of studying the issues involved and interacting with spokespersons for each side, it is my contention that it is time for a realistic, objective, agendaless appraisal of police review systems. This appraisal compares internal review and civilian review systems. Analysis must necessarily begin by casting aside the silly, irrational, and almost hysterical arguments that each side has brought to the civilian review debate for decades.

PARADOXES IN THE POLICE REVIEW DEBATE

In an effort to bring some common sense to the discussion, one must ignore the bizarre assertions of some representatives of law enforcement, such as that of J. Edgar Hoover, that civilian review is "communist inspired" (FBI Bulletins

2

1970; Reiner 1985). Concomitantly, one must reject the rhetoric of the 1960s, which often called for civilian review to be instituted in the name of ending the "systematic murder of Black people" by the police (Foner 1970).

This is not to say that there are no Communists among civilian review advocates. Nor does it mean that the police have never murdered a black person. It means that rhetoric about grand conspiracies gets us nowhere. It obscures the realistic arguments that each side of the debate has to offer.

On one side of the argument there are police executives, police unions, police officers, and the "law and order" lobby. Most of these actors have historically rejected the idea of civilian review out of hand. Most law enforcement professionals confidently assert that internal control of the police is the only way to manage the problem of police misbehavior. The following tenets support this assertion: (1) supervisors must have authority commensurate with their responsibility, (2) professionally trained police investigators are best equipped to discover the truth in a complaint investigation, (3) a genuine police professionalism will be nurtured by requiring the police to take disciplinary responsibility for themselves, and (4) the police must remain above the political fray in order to insure their freedom from corrupting influences. These are all solid arguments in favor of internal review.

Yet the central theme of law enforcement's defense against the idea of civilian review has always been an irrational paradox, at best. Everywhere that law enforcement has fought against civilian review the police have asserted that people who have never experienced the police officer's lot *cannot* review police conduct fairly. According to the argument, this is due to the civilian's ignorance of the police perspective.

Because of this problem of perspective, the police argue that they should be left to police themselves. Now, anyone involved in law enforcement who possesses an ounce of common sense realizes that those outside the subculture will not accept this. It is axiomatic to American principles of limited government that no one be left to judge him- or herself. Today's modern police are well aware of this important political principle. How then can the police believe that their demand to police themselves could (or should) be acceptable to those outside the subculture?

3

The answer is that they don't believe it, not really. The argument is just part of the verbal jousting involved in the largely intuitive battle the police have always fought to avoid civilian review. On occasion, when the findings of internal systems seem to be prejudiced against them, police unions themselves even call for "independent investigations" into alleged misconduct (*Burlington Free Press*, 17 February 1993). Furthermore, because they have been embroiled in this argument, and not in rational debate, the overwhelming majority of police officers and administrators are ignorant about civilian review.

It is easy to prove that the police do not believe their own argument. Consider a police disciplinary system to be a miniature criminal justice system. It sets up rules and regulations, prohibits certain types of behavior, and prescribes punishments for those who transgress its code of conduct. It provides for the reception, investigation, and adjudication of complaints of errant behavior that it receives from alleged victims. It then attempts to bring an objective viewpoint to bear on decisions of guilt or innocence.

The object of these actions is twofold: First, the system retroactively punishes those who have transgressed, and second, it deters not only those guilty of misconduct but also every other member of the policed population from misbehaving in the future. This is the model both of traditional, internal, punishment-oriented police review systems and of the criminal justice system, in toto.

Of course, it is no secret that the police tend to be cynical about the criminal justice system's attempts to implement this model. Most police officers and administrators believe that the system must "get tougher" or lose its war against crime. But, by and large, they are firm believers in the theoretical efficacy of this model. Most police officers and administrators believe that if operated properly, without interference from progressive politicians, permissive courts, or liberal interest groups, the criminal justice system will effectively punish the guilty and deter errant behavior.

Suppose the idea were postulated to the law enforcement community that those accused of criminal behavior be allowed to "police themselves." Or what if it were suggested that unless

4

someone has personally experienced being involved in criminal activity, being arrested and jailed, he or she could never "understand that experience" (surely a believable premise)? Would these ideas be acceptable to anyone in law enforcement? Of course not. Yet the police subculture somehow expects the rest of society to accept this same line of argument when it disputes civilian review.

But there are two sides to any debate. Those who call for tenacious, punitive sanctioning systems to bring an end to police misbehavior are equally guilty of arguing past a paradox. In fact, there are several paradoxes central to the viewpoint of those in favor of civilian review. When these proponents of civilian review use these incongruous arguments, they find that these ideas tend to get in the way of good, solid rationalizations.

The following arguments support civilian review in a logical, rational way: (1) complaint systems operated at police buildings deter some (perhaps many) citizens from filing legitimate complaints, (2) civilian interviewers make many complainants feel more comfortable and free to air their grievances, (3) a non–police officer perspective promotes fairness, and (4) the community's values and goals should help to determine police behavior patterns.

But these powerful arguments suffer from being advanced alongside arguments that are intrinsically irrational. First there is the paradoxical treatment that civilian review proponents give to the "blue curtain of silence." This blue curtain stifles police officers when they are asked to discuss their own misconduct or that of fellow officers. Blue curtain believers posit that outside the confines of the locker room police officers never reveal the misdeeds of other cops.

This code of silence has been noted by virtually every student of police behavior who has ever written about disciplinary systems. There can be no doubt that there exists in the police the propensity to protect themselves and their peers from external attack. (Berkley 1969; Goldsmith 1991; Petterson 1991; Ricker 1991; U.S. Civil Rights Commission 1981). Yet in arguments favoring civilian review, the code of silence idea is turned on its head and used in a peculiar way. The fact that the police will not share their transgressions with other-than-police people is given

5

as proof positive that other-than-police people should be used to investigate citizens' complaints. It is positively uncanny how often one runs across this argument in the rhetoric and literature favoring civilian review (Goldsmith 1991; NYCLU 1990; *New York Times*, 29 July 1992; Petterson 1991; Terrill 1990).

It may well be true that accused police officers will not *often* be moved to "rat" on themselves if interrogated by fellow police officers. But to anyone who believes in the blue curtain, it is axiomatic that they will not *ever* confess their guilt to civilians. And if this is so, how can we expect a civilianized investigatory system to conduct thorough investigations?

A second line of argument is equally paradoxical and equally dysfunctional. It is often posited that what is needed to curb police misconduct is tougher sanctioning systems. This line of reasoning rejects informal and peer oriented solutions. It asserts that police review systems should possess expansive investigatory powers with which to pursue malpractice and that they should invoke severe punishment when officers are found guilty of misconduct.

When the police police themselves, the argument goes, this tenacity and thoroughness is missing: Giving more power to an external police regulatory system will translate into achieving more deterrence; and more deterrence means less police abuse. Advocates have argued for almost sixty years that this will be the impact of civilian review.

There is a logic problem here, again related to the analogy between the police review system and the criminal justice system. We have known for some time that more police power does not translate into less crime (Moore and Kelling 1983; Steer 1985). Why, then, expect anything different from a police review system? As Robert Reiner states:

> If the law and order lobby err in postulating the rational deterrent model with regard to policing crime (more police power = greater deterrence = less crime), the civil liberties lobby adopt the same model for policing the police. It is amazing that all the insights of the "new" radical criminology drop by the wayside when it comes to considering police wrongdoing. But sauce for the crook should be sauce for the constable. (1985)

It should be noted that each of these arguments has a place in this debate. The perspective and experiences of the police officer on the street ought to have some influence over police review system decision making. Concomitantly, civilian investigators may indeed have an important role to play in police review. And getting tough with errant cops has its place as part of the strategy that might be imposed by a rationally constructed review system.

But as an absolute position, none of these ideas is persuasive. Such ideas applied rigidly by their champions only help to polarize the civilian review debate further. When they carry such inconsistent arguments into battle, both the police "defenders" and the civilian review "attackers" limit the usefulness of their positions, and in doing so, they sometimes make their causes appear silly and frivolous.

There is more to frustrate the police review analyst than this set of paradoxes, however, for the study of the policing of the police is fertile ground for the development of an understanding between two usually adversarial groups: the law and order lobby and the civil liberties lobby.

In the midst of the study of police review, law and order advocates should (ideally) develop a personal understanding of the principles of due process. Here they might find an appreciation for the reasons the criminal justice system is replete with procedural safeguards. In police review systems, police officers are the suspects. As such, they are afforded due process rights, which include the right to representation, the right to refrain from self-incrimination (in some places), the right to the presumption of innocence, and so on. Those on the law enforcement side of the debate ought to better understand the procedural niceties of the criminal justice system when law enforcement officers must defend themselves in an adversarial system. They might better accept the idea that some substantively guilty individuals are set free because critical notions of fairness are important for the system to maintain its integrity in the long run.

Similarly, it is within the police review debate that civil libertarians should develop an appreciation for the concern that the police have always had about substantive responsibility. Civil libertarians want police review systems to get tough and "find the bastards guilty." Yet systems set up for doing so will occasionally let those who are substantively guilty go free. If they realize this, civilian review proponents might better understand the frustrations of the average cop as well as the average citizen when they critique the criminal justice system for letting "criminals walk the streets."

Those who wish to make the police more accountable for their actions through the civilianization of review mechanisms pursue a laudable goal. They must understand, however, that this idea is in some ways threatening, in some ways genuinely "revolutionary" to people whose careers have taken them into law enforcement. Their concepts must be presented logically; their discussion must be rational. They must be willing to acknowledge police officers' general honesty and commitment to justice.

By the same token, those in law enforcement must understand that they are dealing with people who are bombarded with seemingly endless stories of police greed, corruption, and brutality. They must try to realize that police assertions that "all is well" are not believable. No amount of explanation will convince those outside the field of law enforcement that abuses do not occur or that these abuses are often dealt with sternly by internal systems.

Because of the volatile nature of the police review debate, one must balance the concerns of the police, the community, complaining citizens, and accused officers. This book discusses the operations of three archetypical police review mechanisms. It evaluates their potential for balancing the aforementioned interests. It attempts to generate an understanding of administrative review that I hope transcends the world of police officers. It constructs an understanding of the trade-offs inherent in the operation of police review systems of all kinds.

POLICE ACCOUNTABILITY

The police are both political and legal actors. Because of this, the police review debate outlines the balances that are basic to any consideration of administrative accountability. Rigorous review must be tempered with a concern for the counterproductive effects of overzealousness. Similarly, the maintenance of the administrative integrity of the police organization must be weighed against the need for openness in the review processes. The public's right to have input in the operation of its own governmental administration must be compared to the pragmatic, educated expertise of the professional.

Lord John Acton made the consummate statement about the behavior of powerful individuals when he observed that "power tends to corrupt, and absolute power corrupts absolutely." In a more pragmatic vein, Edmund Burke stated that the exercise of power cannot parallel its control. To attempt "to exercise and to control together is contradictory and impossible" (Burke 1790). Taken together, these two statements lay the groundwork for understanding mechanisms that attempt to hold actors responsible to others for their exercise of power.

Modern representative democracy is only the latest step in humankind's long struggle to free the many from the oligarchical exercise of power by the few. But popular democracy has severe limitations. However one may admire the institutions that accomplish democratic tasks, these institutions do not necessarily guarantee that the individual will be free from the arbitrary exercise of power by the many. While legislative institutions were developed to hold the few accountable for what they did to the many (Madison [1789] 1961), legal institutions had to be created to hold the many accountable for what they might do to the few (Dahl 1989; Mill 1961).

In theory, legislative accountability obtains in a representative democracy through the operations of suffrage, the free press, and universal education. The actions of legislators are supposedly monitored by the public. Through the ballot box, educated popular opinion is changed into policy by these closely monitored representatives. However loosely one may feel the connection operates, legislators are responsible to "the people."

Judicial accountability is of a different order. Judges are bound by codified law and, most important, by "higher principles" of equity, fairness, and professional conduct. Their first allegiance is to the Constitution and to its basic principles. Holding the judiciary accountable to "the law" is an attempt to curb the tyranny of the majority.

Of course, the idea that the legislator is accountable to the   9 people and the judge is accountable to the law can be overstated. It is not a pure distinction. Legislators do consider the law and the Constitution when they act (de Tocqueville 1968). And legislators do hold each other to professional standards of conduct. Then too, judges consider the political ramifications of their decisions. To state that their actions are completely independent of politics would be foolish.

Yet these two actors do present accountability problems of different sorts. If only in emphasis, legislators and judges must develop working styles that adapt to existing accountability mechanisms in different ways. To some extent, legislative and judicial accountability are at odds with each other; and when one concerns oneself with the police, one must focus on its combined form, "administrative accountability."

Administrative accountability is more complex than is either legislative or judicial accountability. Administrators apply the law as defined by the legislature and as interpreted by the judiciary. The administrator's prime task is, in a sense, to apply laws and regulations that have been defined and refined elsewhere. He or she must do so in an objective, nondiscriminatory manner.

Administrative performance should thus be subject to review on the basis of substantive legal correctness. As with the judge, the administrator must be held accountable to formal objective legal standards of competence. Indeed, the elimination of caprice is the very basis from which the need to codify rules develops. The "culprit . . . is the arbitrary decision . . . based upon improper criterion that do not relate in any rational way to organizational ends. The paradigm arbitrary decision is one that is based upon particularistic criteria such as friendship, ascriptive criteria such as race, or upon caprice, whim, or prejudice" (Jowell 1973).

Yet like the legislator, the administrator must also react to his or her constituency. Administrators must consider the will of the citizens they contact. They must use discretionary latitude to make the law meaningful, realistic, humane, and responsive to the needs of citizens. In short, the administrator must employ Benjamin Cardozo's so-called "method of sociology" by importing equity, social welfare, and public policy concerns into decisions (Cardozo 1921).

Police officers are administrators. They administer the criminal law as defined by legislators and as interpreted by the judiciary. The street cop functions in a great many more capacities than that of administrator of course. The cop on the beat can be seen as a politician (Jefferson 1990; Muir 1977), as a generalized social service agent (Wilson 1972), or as a judicial actor (Davis 1969). The police officer's part in determining how the criminal law will be applied to people on the street, however, places the cop in an administrative role. This position is analogous to that of the welfare worker, Federal Aviation Administration commissioner, or parole board member.

Every affirmative action that a police officer takes must be legal in a strict, judicial sense. For all the leeway that it must allow the officer, an accountability mechanism aimed at reviewing police conduct must hold the officer strictly answerable to the law. If a police officer beats a suspect, thus committing "assault under color of authority," it can be no defense that "the guy was a bad actor" and "deserved it."

Equally important, police officers must be able to use the laws of the land to shield themselves. If police actions are legal, they must be found to be proper by a review system. It would be extremely problematic for the street cop to be held in error by a review mechanism if he or she acted in a legal manner. Even if a localized constituency wanted police officers to deemphasize the enforcement of certain violations of the law, a review system could not ethically find officers guilty for disregarding this desire and enforcing the law.

For example, on "fraternity row" near college campuses, local undergraduates often feel that underaged drinking laws should be applied in a lax manner. Suppose an officer were to make an arrest for underaged drinking in such an area. A fair police review mechanism should not find the beat cop guilty of misconduct because the officer was not reacting to the feelings of the local constituency. To do so would be unfair to the individual police officer.

Police work, of course, is often labeled as "law enforcement," and the major focus of police training concerns the law enforcement tasks of the police. Yet only a small part of the police officer's job truly involves positive enforcement of the law (Geller 1985; Hunt 1972; Reiner 1985; Reiss 1971; Skolnick 1966;

Wilson 1972). Much more prevalent in the police officer's workaday life is maintaining order, in general.

The function of maintaining order in society is so important that some argue it is the police officers' primary task (Garmire 1982; Kelling 1985). The police accomplish this task in various ways, many unrelated to the formal application of the criminal law. The police and other administrators use semilegal and nonlegal methods to maintain order. Young toughs may be physically intimidated away from a late-night convenience store. Barroom brawlers may be told to "go home and sober up or else!" Standing on shaky legal ground, police officers will often pronounce, "If we have to come back again tonight, somebody's going to jail."

This often happens because the law is unresponsive to the practical realities of human problems. As Hunt (1972) and others note, there is a "broad range of practical and effective ways of dealing with suspects which the policeman knows to be technically improper but considers morally justified." Thus another problem for police review mechanisms is how to handle such semilegal behavior.

Equally important, police officers as legislators reacting to their constituencies often do not enforce the codified dictates of the law in the interests of justice and equity. It is altogether proper that police officers do this in some cases (Selznick 1969). The street police officer may verbally chastise a first-time shoplifter rather than make an arrest. He or she may settle a family fight by advising one party or the other to leave the house and go next-door. The police may avail a drunk of a taxi ride rather than a night in jail. Or the cop may well give teenagers the kind of behavioral lecture that absent parents might have provided. The police, applying the "attitude test," more often than not avoid making arrests when they perceive that the interests of justice and equity will be thus served. In these and many similar ways, the police maintain order in society without resorting to enforcement of the law. They cleave to the dictates of the situation. They hear, evaluate, and respond to their constituency in a commonsensical fashion. Theirs is a "democratic" endeavor.

The nature of police work is equally democratic because citizens initiate the majority of encounters and control the work load of the police. This observation has been confirmed by several studies that followed police officers and drew statistical pictures of how police activity was initiated (Goldstein 1990; Lundman 1980; Reiss 1971). Policies and individual incidents are controlled by community involvement in police operations. And this is how it should be. As Reiss (1985) notes, "There must be ways that local constituencies can make the police responsive to their needs and problems if we are to have *their* as well as *our* respect for the rule of law." Thus, as legislators do, the police must react to a constituency that can have a significant impact on their daily work environment (Uglow 1988). Yet their job is more complex. The police must also act legally and be answerable to the law.

For police officers to do either of these things to excess would be catastrophic. If officers reacted totally to their constituencies, without regard for the dictates of the law, the result would be an end to law itself. The consequent form of legal administration would be an arbitrary sort of "khadi justice" (Ehrmann 1976). (The Khadi decides cases individually, without reference to set principles or precedent.) This form of justice would underwrite all sorts of prejudicial behavior on the part of society's agents. In terms of the previous discussion, it would involve the tyranny of the masses being invoked against the interests of the few.

Yet were the police to attempt to apply the rigid constructs of the law universally, a perhaps more abhorrent chaos would ensue. If everyone who was technically "arrestable" were taken into custody, the courts and jails of America would be swamped with bodies and cases (Berkley 1969; Black 1972; Wilson 1972). What is more, the impact on individual freedom of such "full enforcement" of the law would be a price that few would be willing to pay.

Administrative and police accountability mechanisms, then, must balance several concerns. They must weigh the interests of the majority against those of the individual and the rights of the many against those of the few. And this is precisely the balance that must be struck by the beat cop on the street every night (Manning 1977; Moore and Stephens 1991).

The crux of the police officer's problem is weighing the individual's liberty against the social necessities of regulation. The

13

street cop's daily dilemma is the basic dilemma of social life, so beautifully presented by John Stuart Mill (1961): "What then is the rightful limit to the sovereignty of the individual over himself? Where does the authority of society begin? How much of human life should be assigned to individuality, and how much to society?"

The most basic balance that a police accountability system must strike is this: It must allow the police great latitude within which to work and yet require that they cleave to the dictates of the formal legal system. It is neither an easy nor a particularly clear balance to keep. It is as difficult to weigh as are the scales of justice themselves.

Because they must answer to both the public and to the law, because they are so conspicuous, and because they must so often resort to other-than legal tactics, the police are the repository of most complaints about the legal system. As Paul Chevigny illustrates, "For legislators and judges the police are a godsend, because all of the acts of oppression that must be performed in this society to keep it running smoothly are pushed upon the police. The police get the blame, and the officials stay free of the stigma of approving their highhanded acts" (1969).

THE FOCUS OF THE STUDY

As with any complex problem, holding the police accountable for their actions involves balancing a variety of organizational and societal interests. The street police officer must be allowed a great deal of room in pursuing the charge of maintaining order and enforcing the law. Beat cops must feel free to use force when it is required, to arrest when it is necessary, and to become involved in the lives of the people on their beats. Concomitantly, in the interests of justice, the cop must be able to mediate and counsel rather than take official action. Society demands no less of its police agents than the prudent exercise of a high degree of administrative discretion.

Therefore, accountability systems must do several things at once. They must rigorously investigate alleged police abuses and deter future malpractice. They must bridge the gap between police and citizen in determining the directions of police policy.

They must exonerate police officers when they have acted properly and legally. None of these tasks can be sacrificed in favor of another. All of society would suffer if an accountability scheme ignored any of these charges.

Any monitoring process will necessarily concern itself with two methods of behavior control: regulation and socialization. The external regulation of human behavior, for an administrative organization, is the easiest method to implement. It involves defining rules in a prospective manner, organizing adjudicative procedures, and enforcing sanctions. It is a relatively low-cost enterprise. It can protect the organization from criticism and develop a perceptual legitimacy in the external environment (Durkheim 1933).

Regulation can often be very ineffective in actually influencing behavior in a prospective manner, however. Any formalized process can be subverted, cheated, and abused by the population policed. In the case of policing the police, the subjects of the regulatory mechanism who might be moved to subvert it are themselves experts in the application of such systems. Presumably their subversion efforts will be quite effective. Thus such formal regulatory mechanisms are of limited utility when applied to expert regulators.

Self-sanctioning, self-regulating control mechanisms, on the other hand, are extremely effective in controlling human behavior. When social values, individual desires, professional standards of competence, subcultural expectations, and organizational goals are congruent, accountability is internalized.

This process is known, of course, as socialization (Merton 1957). It is far more effective at influencing behavior than is regulation. Police officers will go to great lengths, even risk injury and death, to cleave to principles they hold dear. They will brave gunfire, swim flood-ravaged rivers, enter burning buildings, in order to save the lives of strangers. They will do this because they believe it is their moral imperative.

Yet the same officers will often rationalize ignoring a regulatory mechanism's pronouncements. When told to behave in a certain way by a system that is "just" a review mechanism, these powerful actors may balk at conformity. They may reject the legitimacy of an accountability scheme that is centered out-

side their peer group. Like any occupational group, police officers effectively illustrate the limitations of regulation and the
strengths of socialization.

But socialization has its drawbacks. It is extremely problematic to attempt to fashion artificial links between individual,
subcultural, organizational, and societal values and goals. Multiple goals make "desired behavior" difficult to define. Individual
personalities and collective behavior patterns can inhibit the in-
culcation of new values and norms of conduct. Thus, for all of
their effectiveness, socialization processes are difficult and
costly to manipulate. When self-sanctioning mechanisms fail,
they leave the police organization vulnerable to criticism. They
are simply not as legally defensible as are regulatory systems.

Police accountability, then, must develop from a compromise
between externally imposed sanctioning systems and internalized, "professional" norms of conduct. Police review systems
must balance the concerns of several interest groups and weigh
the expertise of the professional against the desires of the citizenry. The analysis of such systems is therefore complicated,
because it cannot prioritize the interests of police officers, complainants, politicians, or neighborhoods. It cannot "choose" between these interests; it must hold them all in a delicate balance.

THE PROBLEMS
OF POLICE REVIEW

1 The Nature of Police Malpractice

This discussion begins with a consideration of what constitutes police malpractice. To be able to analyze police review systems one must first paint a picture of the raw material that these systems process reactively. In doing so, one also develops an understanding of those types of behavior that review systems attempt to deter prospectively.

This discussion reviews the history of police malpractice, spends some time with classification schemes, and then treats the specifics of review organization caseloads. It presents outlines of two examples of police misconduct investigations and considers them throughout the remainder of the work. Because they are rather spectacular in their impact, the Detroit and Los Angeles malpractice incidents provide guides for analysis. They illustrate organizational problems for review systems, political realities that affect accountability, leadership styles that are pointedly diverse, and external review dynamics that transcend the control of the police.

THE HISTORY OF POLICE MALPRACTICE

Those who have studied the matter have come to the conclusion that there has been a concern over the fiscal corruption of the police as long as there have been police (Lane 1967; Lee 1971; Pringle 1955; Walker 1977). Police malpractice includes more than monetary corruption, however. It has now come to include the daily abuse of authority and the excessive use of force.

When formal police organizations were in their infancy, there was little concern over the use of excessive force, the harassment of citizens, or abuse of discretionary decision-making powers. As Roger Lane notes in his study of the early days of 19

Boston's police department, "No members of the government in 1837 voiced . . . suspicion of police as possible oppressors" (1967: 38).

A cavalier attitude existed toward the few protests that were launched against police violence. According to Lane, the Boston City Council rejected the charge of one complainant, which related to a beating and denial of bail, stating, "It may happen that the complainants belong to a class not often exposed to the treatment they are likely to meet within a watch house or jail" (1967: 35).

Over time, rising standards of public order, originally aimed at criminality, violence, and riot by citizens, began to be applied to police conduct. The enforcers of law and maintainers of order themselves became subjects of concern. By the turn of the century, the policing of the police had become a problem. The issue of abuse by police was to receive sporadic publicity over the first half of the twentieth century. Beside occasional press coverage, police malpractice was uncovered in numerous riot commission studies. Commissions found the police guilty of misconduct in East St. Louis, Illinois, in 1917 (U.S. Congress. House. 1918), in Chicago in 1919 (Chicago Commission on Race Relations 1922), in New York in 1935 (Mayor's Commission on Conditions in Harlem 1935), and in Detroit in 1943 (Governor's Committee to Investigate Riots Occurring in Detroit 1943), to name several prominent incidents. In 1931 the commonplace nature of station house and curbside abuses by the police was noted by the Wickersham Commission: "The third degree . . . that is, the use of physical brutality or other forms of cruelty to obtain involuntary confessions . . . is widespread. . . . Physical brutality, illegal detention, and refusal to allow access to counsel to the prisoner is common. . . . Brutality and violence in making an arrest also were employed at times" (1931: 4).

Such routine abuses began to catch the eye of the federal judiciary. The United States Supreme Court, first with some reluctance and later with some degree of zeal (Schlesinger 1977, Stephens 1973), began to attempt to control the excesses of the police. The Court issued landmark opinions in cases involving interrogations and confessions of guilt, access to counsel, search and seizure, and electronic surveillance. In *Mapp v. Ohio* (1961),

20

it issued its most important decree. That case applied the federal exclusionary rule to the states (see Table of Court Cases).

But is was not until the 1960s that police abuse became truly topical throughout all of American society. This era saw the expansion of both black and student protests. On several occasions, reacting to the unfolding events of the period, police officers rioted in the streets. Command structures deteriorated to such an extent that individual police officers vented their frustrations on innocent civilians. Police riots occurred in Los Angeles in 1967, in Berkeley on numerous occasions, at Columbia University in 1968 (Stark 1972), and at the Chicago Democratic National Convention in 1968 (Mailer 1968).

The events in Chicago, more than any other single occurrence, educated the majority of Americans about the existence and gravity of the problem of police abuse. Before that moment in 1968, most Americans thought that accusations of police abuse were the self-serving, irrational rhetoric of criminals and political extremists. It is not an exaggeration to say that after the convention, average, middle-American citizens would never again feel the same about their police and about police review.

When the war in Vietnam ended and the public's interest in the Watergate scandal subsided, concerns about police abuses seemed to dissolve, along with so many issues that had seemed critically important during the 1960s. For ten years people in America hardly heard mention of the topic of police malpractice. That did not mean, of course, that local scandals and debates over review systems no longer existed. In the decade of the 1980s, over thirty civilianized review systems of various kinds were put into place throughout the country. Most were instituted as a direct result of police-abuse scandals (Walker and Bumphus 1991).

Police malpractice and its dramatic nature became topical again at the end of the 1980s. The media coverage of the 1988 police riot in New York City's Tompkins Square gave people evidence of the volatile nature of the issue of police misconduct. The Tompkins Square incident involved hundreds of police officers, and fifty-two civilians were injured seriously enough in the riot to require medical attention. One hundred twenty-one citizens eventually filed complaints against the police. When less than a dozen officers were found guilty of misconduct, after two years of investigations, the community reacted vehemently (NYCLU 1990).

At the national level, the incident involving the beating of Rodney King by police on 3 March 1991 in Los Angeles once again brought to center stage issues that would necessitate serious consideration of police review (*Time*, 1 April 1991). On the heels of that incident, Sacramento, Boston, Milwaukee, San Jose, and St. Louis all held debates over civilianized review. Once again, the media coverage that followed the events in Los Angeles had helped to bring to the surface issues that had been simmering not so far below. The death of a Detroit man at the hands of several police officers in November 1992 threw additional fuel on the fire. The move to civilianize police review was given added political support owing to these spectacular incidents of police abuse.

It is important to remember that such incidents have *always* been the basis for change in the field of police review (Goldsmith 1988; Guyot 1991; Petterson 1991), and they will be discussed more fully later in the book. This study has not discovered any examples of police review being debated without the influence of emotion and opportunism produced through crisis. And "the *ad hoc* response to 'yesterday's battle' poses the danger not only that police will be ill-equipped to fight 'tomorrow's battle' but that incremental steps will be taken in the heat of the moment that would have been avoided following rational appraisal" (Waddington 1991).

To evaluate adequately the occurrences of police abuse and the systems necessary to deal with them, one must first understand what that term entails.

WHAT IS POLICE MALPRACTICE?

A good definition of police misconduct can be found in Richard Lundman's *Police Behavior*: "Misconduct by police patrol officers includes abuse of discretion, corruption, and use of unnecessary force" (1980). Because it is an important, albeit separate, topic from the focus of this book, what follows is only a brief discussion of corruption.

Police corruption is an illegal use of organizational power for personal gain. The personal nature of the gain distinguishes corruption from brutality, perjury, illegal search, or other law violations committed in the pursuit of such legitimate organizational goals as fighting crime. . . . Police corruption inverts the formal goals of the police organization. It is a use of organizational power to encourage and create crime rather than to deter it. (Sherman 1978)

The kinds of activities that are considered specifically herein are corruption of authority, kickbacks, shakedowns, protection of illegal activities, "fixes," direct criminal activities, and internal payoffs (Barker and Roebuck 1973; Carter 1990). These are termed "organizational corruption." While external review mechanisms may not be necessary for handling individual corruption, they are absolutely essential for dealing with organizational corruption.

It is important to differentiate between corruption *in* police organizations and corruption *by* police organizations. The former involves deviant behavior by individuals or small groups of officers. It is the sort of behavior that can be investigated and reformed by administrative mechanisms within the organization itself.

Corruption *by* police organizations convolutes the entire mission of the organization. It sometimes involves entire police departmental command structures, local politicians, and even prosecutors. To objectively evaluate such organizational corruption, external, state, or even federal agencies and perspectives are necessary. Because organizational corruption is not a part of the normal work load of citizens' complaints systems, it will only be referred to tangentially.

Our concern is the sort of police malpractice that generates the common citizen's complaint, that which involves the day-to-day operations of systems that must receive, investigate, and adjudicate such complaints. The use of excessive force and the abuse of discretion are two standard classifications of behavior labeled here as "police malpractice." These classifications constitute the bulk of the work load of police review systems and the overwhelming majority of citizens' complaint cases.

The use of excessive force, or "police brutality," is perhaps 23 more topical and important than are all other forms of police malpractice combined. There is a critical, threshold difficulty in defining excessive force. As Egon Bittner cogently illustrates:

> The frequently heard talk about the lawful use of force by the police is practically meaningless and, because no one knows what is meant by it, so is the talk about the use of minimum force. . . . In fact, the only instructions any policeman ever receives in this respect consist of sermonizing that he should be humane and circumspect, and that he must not desist from what he has undertaken merely because its accomplishment may call for coercive means. . . . Our expectation that policemen will use force, coupled by our refusals to state clearly what we mean by it (aside from sanctimonious homilies), smacks of more than a bit of perversity. (1990)

Parallel to concerns about formulating formal rules for police work in general, this inability to successfully define excessive force in a meaningful way is the premiere limitation of review of police conduct. Absent specific standards with which to gauge behavior, either retrospectively or prospectively, it is problematic for any morally defensible system to review the actions of the individual police officer.

Police use of excessive force is also an important topic because of the amount of physical abuse that occurs, or that people believe occurs, on the streets of America. A study on the subject found that 25 percent of a cross section of residents of the Bronx, New York, indicated that they had witnessed police harassment or brutality during an arrest (Davis 1990). Whether or not such abuse was "genuine," this figure indicates that a number of people believe that abuse is a serious problem. In a remark about the amount of abuse in the same city, Mike Meyers of the New York Civil Liberties Union said, "There is an epidemic of police officer violence and misconduct in New York City" (ACLU 1991).

Excessive force is used quite often on the most disenfranchised members of society *precisely because of their position in the social order* (Betz 1985; Box 1983; Chigwada 1991; Whitaker and Phillips 1983). Allen Wagner's study of complaint demographics in the inner city is illustrative. Blacks made up 41 percent of the population base of his study area, yet they filed 67

24

percent of the complaints against the police. Furthermore, almost 25 percent of those who complained were unemployed (Wagner 1980).

Middle-class and upper-class people, however, are not the subjects of police abuse very often because they do not interact as frequently with the police in situations that involve potential violence. Also, these classes are victimized by the police less frequently because their higher social standing makes it easier for them to cause trouble for the individual officer and for the police department (Bouza 1990).

The second general category of police malpractice, "the abuse of discretion," is a topic that, to many, is less threatening, less volatile, than is the excessive use of force. Nevertheless, as administrators, police officers make daily decisions about when and how to apply the law and their nonlegal police powers. In making these judgments, the police can become guilty of verbal abuse, harassment, discrimination, and failure to take action. They can also abuse their positions of trust through thievery.

Allegations of "verbal abuse" is a common category in complaints lodged against the police. It includes racial slurs, as well as general discourtesy. After what many consider to be the progress of the 1960s, there is evidence that in law enforcement, as in American society in general, racial discrimination and prejudice are making a comeback. The Christopher Commission (1991) in Los Angeles, for example, found police officers openly using racially derogatory language in communications on their car-to-car computer screens.

While racial slurs are the exception rather than the rule in many areas, they still take up a significant percentage of the caseloads of review systems. Verbal abuse of citizens by police is commonplace everywhere. It is the singularly most-reported type of complaint-generating behavior; 41.5 percent of citizens' complaints nationwide fall into this category (Dugan and Breda 1991: 38).

Another problem that people often report is "harassment" by the police. It normally takes the form of illegal detentions of suspects and illegal searches by police. Police officers can rationalize all sorts of illegal tactics in the pursuit of suspects. Illegal stops and searches are a common harassment tool used to force particular individuals off one's beat. John Dugan and Daniel Breda found that the "abuse of authority" category of their schema (which corresponds to harassment here) makes up 12.7 percent of today's cases (1991). Police review organizations use different sets of categories, such statistics, therefore, are approximations that pull together different schema.

To complicate matters, harassment is often supported by local constituencies. Communities seldom want the police to use excessive force, discrimination, or verbal abuse as tactics against any of their citizens, but it is quite clear to the beat cop that harassment of certain types of individuals is perfectly acceptable to many people. In the past, members of a police officer's constituency may have rationalized police harassment of hippies, blacks, Chicanos, Puerto Ricans, and so on. Today, it is the gang member or suspected drug dealer that is the target. Police officers receive daily feedback from average citizens who support certain forms of harassment that they feel is acceptable for police to impose on such "deviant" types.

Tangential to these other forms of police misbehavior are "discrimination" complaints. Studies conducted in San Diego, Philadelphia, Denver, and New York indicate that minority peoples believe that discrimination in law enforcement is widespread (Bayley and Mendelsohn 1968; Lohman and Misner 1966; NYCLU 1990; *New York Times*, 8 July 1992).

"Failure to take action" is also an important problem according to information from citizens' complaints. In the interest of justice, it is crucial that street cops feel free to exercise their discretionary decision-making authority *not* to arrest. But the exercise of discretion often offends members of the public. James Davis found in his study of the Bronx that the dissatisfaction of people with the police was most directly related to their failure to take action, not to the use of force, harassment, or even verbal abuse (1990). Martin Luther King, Jr., once labeled the lack of police service being delivered in the ghetto as the number-one law enforcement–related problem for minority peoples (Berkley 1969).

Finally, "missing property," a polite way of categorizing police theft, is a category found in most administrative complaint-handling systems. Of course, theft involves individual corruption,

26

but it is the kind of corruption that need not necessarily be investigated from outside the police organization. Since theft by police is reported by citizens, unlike some forms of corruption, it is considered in the list of daily citizens' complaints.

It is difficult to evaluate the authenticity of claims that officers have stolen from citizens, usually arrestees. In a "missing property" complaint, citizen-complainant says one thing and the police officer says another. No other evidence exists. In this instance, no sort of review mechanism can discern the truth of the matter.

Complaints of police theft might be the most damaging problem for police review. Because it can be argued that decisions to arrest or to use force are decisions of judgment—sometimes they are made in the heat of the moment—they are subject to debate and distortion, and they involve matters of degree. But theft is a problem of a different order. It is *malum in se,* an offense that is evil or wrong from its own nature. It is the sort of behavior that does not involve degrees that may be debated. For the trusted public servant, no scale of culpability exists regarding theft (Delattre 1989).

This brief summary of the types of daily police malpractice with which all of the review systems concern themselves may be indicative of the nature of police abuses. But one must take care when considering whether complaint statistics indicate the gravity of these problems. According to the data reviewed, citizens rarely file complaints against the police. In Oakland, California, for example, only 250 complaints are filed in an average year. This city of 360,000 people has a police department of 700 officers. In Berkeley, California, the civilian system receives about 100 complaints per year from its population of 104,000 people. In Kansas City, Missouri, the civilian monitor system also receives about one complaint per 1,000 citizens each year (420 complaints for 428,000 people). In New York City, only 3,379 complaints were filed in 1991. This city of 10 million people has a police department of 30,000 officers. The numbers appear quite small compared to the numbers of police-citizen interactions that occur in a year. In New York, for example, there are an estimated 10,450,000 contacts between police and citizens in any given year (Andrews 1985).

To check these numbers, one might extrapolate Davis's findings about perceived abusive behavior, taken from a cross section of New Yorkers. Although this endeavor is obviously replete with methodological problems, one can conclude that there may be hundreds of thousands of unreported instances in which citizens believe that the police have used excessive force. While one should not make too much of this enterprise, it does seem to confirm frequent assertions that it is inconceivable that so few citizens' complaints are generated. It is often argued that those complaints that are received indicate only the "tip of the iceberg."

Comparisons of complainant demographics for analytical purposes are impossible to make in most jurisdictions. For largely political reasons, most police review systems eschew making statistical compilations of data about race and sex. In order to avoid charges of discriminatory complaint-handling, personnel are usually prohibited from noting the race and sex of complainants. However, in the jurisdictions where such demographics are kept a predictable pattern emerges. Men complain more often than women, relative to their numbers in the overall population (OCCB 1986, 1987, 1989, 1990). This finding might be expected with respect to how many more men in America are arrested than are women. It might also be explained by the difference between how police officers interact with men and women and, concomitantly, how men and women treat police officers. In addition, ethnic minorities complain more often than do whites. In New York, for example, blacks make up 24 percent of the population and file 44.8 percent of the citizens' complaints. Hispanics make up 19.9 percent of the city and file 25.1 percent of the complaints (NYCCIB 1989).

One can also analyze complaint patterns from the perspective of the police officers accused of misbehavior. According to some statistics, the average police officer will receive between two and four complaints during the course of his or her career. In San Francisco, where it may seem that the propensity of the citizenry to complain is great, complaints per officer may rise much higher. In areas such as suburban departments, complaint numbers may be much lower.

Comparing numbers across jurisdictions is extremely problematic, however. This may be because of differences in citizen perceptions of police officer conduct, variations in media coverage (or a lack of coverage), malpractice, extreme diversity in the socioeconomic makeup of the local population, and so forth. People who are more educated, more economically secure, more socially elevated in station, and more adept at dealing with powerful governmental actors tend to complain less.

Other factors influence complaint statistics. Differences in complaint input structures can affect complaint numbers greatly. Some review systems allow a great deal of latitude within which to deal with complaints informally. In such locations, such as in Los Angeles during the 1980s, complaint numbers appear inordinately low, because only those complaints that cannot be dealt with informally turn into statistics for review. By the same token, in San Francisco, where no such latitude exists for the review mechanism, the lack of available informal processes tends to help produce inordinately high rates of complaint filing.

Three more concepts should be considered. First, most police officers receive one or fewer complaints each year, though a small percentage receive two in a given year. An extremely small minority of officers receive complaints at a rate greater than this (Honolulu Police Commission 1989). With few exceptions, reports of police officer malpractice make their way into the review system sporadically.

Second, the overwhelming majority of complaints filed against the police are shared among the majority of officers. In other words, very few individual police officers receive large numbers of complaints. The Christopher Commission in Los Angeles, for example, found that only forty-four officers had received six or more allegations from 1986 to 1990 (Christopher Commission 1991). The officers, considered extreme deviants by the commission's analysts, were receiving about one complaint each year, but the rest of the more than eight thousand officers in the department were receiving fewer than that. The statistical analysis of Oakland's numbers indicate a similar pattern. This is important data. It flies in the face of conventional wisdom.

Outside the field of law enforcement people generally believe that significant numbers of police officers receive large numbers of complaints. Instead, this study has found that most officers, even errant officers, seldom exhibit patterns that any review system would define as systematic. It is natural to cleave to the idea that a few "rotten apples" get most of the complaints, that a review system only need weed out those few "bad cops" and all will be well. Unfortunately, these ideas do not square with the realities of the reports of police misconduct. Individual patterns and career histories are far more complex than such simple analysis implies.

Third, most cops receive citizens' complaints in their first few years of service. This seems to be critically important for police officer learning. Where seniority is related to complaint reception, it has been observed that young cops, particularly with experience levels of between two and six years, receive the vast majority of citizens' complaints. This study tracked Oakland statistics for twenty years. These data indicate that at about six years of seniority, the average police officer's propensity to receive complaints tapers off to insignificance. In New York City, a similar pattern has been found. Younger officers generally are the ones who create the work load for police review systems. Thus, for reasons analyzed later, police officers exhibit a tendency to "grow out of" receiving complaints.

With this brief background, this study considers two police misconduct scandals and how they have helped us to frame this discussion's questions for analysis.

TWO CASES IN POINT

Two particular incidents of police misconduct occurred in Detroit, Michigan, and Los Angeles, California, during this study: In Detroit detectives beat a man to death, and in Los Angeles police were involved in the now-famous Rodney King beating incident. Each action created an unusual amount of publicity, and both illustrate the operations of internal review processes under very different leadership. They can tell a great deal about the strengths and weaknesses of the kind of in-house review mechanisms that operate in most jurisdictions.

On 5 November 1992, in Detroit, Malice Green was beaten to death by police detectives outside of a "suspected crack house" (*Detroit Free Press*, 7 November 1992). The man was beaten on the head repeatedly while he was sitting in his car. Four additional officers, a sergeant, and numerous witnesses were also present. Detroit's chief of police launched an immediate, all-night investigation into the incident. On the morning of 6 November, less than a day later, the chief held a news conference, during which he "angrily announced the suspension of all seven officers without pay and called the attack a 'disgrace'" (*Detroit Free Press*, 7 November 1992).

The Detroit chief pressed for the filing of criminal complaints against all the police officers involved. He rigorously pursued an internal investigation, which was completed in a month. At the end of the internal hearing held about the incident, he fired four of the officers (*Detroit Free Press*, 12 December 1992). He took swift and strong administrative action, ignoring the pace of the criminal prosecutions. Internal investigatory hearings took just one month to accomplish. The chief sent messages to all of the police officers of Detroit, and indirectly to the community, stating that such behavior was unacceptable. The burden of proof of their innocence was placed clearly on the errant police officers. Their suspension *without pay*, in particular, was an indication of the seriousness of the matter and the presumptions of the Detroit chief.

The Los Angeles incident followed a different path. For a number of years, the city's police officer corps had developed a tacitly understood practice among street officers with respect to vehicle stops. According to police officer interviews, the rules of the game were that any motorist who did not immediately pull over to the side of the road when the police presented their red lights would be beaten. Sometimes this rule was applied to people who were guilty of criminal behavior, sometimes to people who led the police on high-speed chases. But at other times, the police officers used this unspoken rule even when motorists simply did not see the police lights.

In Los Angeles, on an evening in spring 1991, the driver of a vehicle involved in a high-speed chase was beaten by three officers at the scene of the eventual stop. A large group of other officers watched as this event took place. The group of fourteen spectators included a sergeant and several members of the California Highway Patrol. Although the police officers did not know it then, a citizen nearby had videotaped the beating. The 31 tape was forwarded to local media sources, and it was broadcast on national television (*Los Angeles Times*, 5 March 1991). The local grand jury subsequently indicted four police officers who were most directly involved, including the sergeant. The chief suspended the four, *with pay, after their indictments*. The fate of the others awaited the action of internal hearings. While the hearings resulted in disciplinary action against several of the officers who looked on, it took months for them to reach completion (no less than three, and in some cases more than twelve). Despite the political importance of what became the King "incident," no effort was made to hasten the proceedings with an eye toward sending signals from the police department to either the community in general or the police officers on the street. (The discipline handed out is discussed later.) Furthermore, disciplinary hearings for those charged with criminal acts were postponed until after several trials at the state and federal level were concluded. At this writing, fall 1993, or two and one-half years after the incident, disciplinary hearings within the department are still under way. (*Burlington Free Press*, 2 September 1993).

Initially, the Los Angeles chief fired no one. In fact, only because of media probing about the King incident and their investigation of violence by the Los Angeles police in general, did the chief respond. He took a public relations approach to the incident and attempted to sell the idea that the officers of the Los Angeles Police Department were, by and large, an honest group. In doing so, he tried to deflect criticism and focus from the incident itself. The chief obtained the support of local conservative politicians when the police commission of the city began asking for changes and for answers to questions about the pattern of violence. Essentially, the Los Angeles chief attempted to change the incident into a citywide referendum on whether people were "pro" or "anti" police (*Time* 1 April 1991).

The differences in these two tragic events illustrate interesting lessons. In Detroit, the police chief reacted quickly and harshly to the allegations that some of his officers were guilty of misconduct. In Los Angeles, the administrative and legal systems appeared to have forced the chief into taking action against his troops. On one hand, an efficient, rapid internal investigation in Detroit resulted in officers being fired in a timely fashion.

They then had to fight if they wished to get their jobs back. The Los Angeles officers, on the other hand, were in a position to obtain legal advice in order to *keep* their jobs.

While the specifics of these cases are unusual, especially in terms of the numbers of individuals involved, the actions of police executives are not. These examples serve the purposes of this analysis well because they were politically volatile enough to generate community interest and comment. (The overwhelming majority of citizen complaint cases, of course, do not develop such interest.)

The issues involved in these two cases raise a number of questions about civilian review of police malpractice. Would civilianizing the investigations process in Detroit still have enabled the investigators to conduct such a thorough investigation and to complete it quickly? Would police officers have discussed the abusive behavior of other officers as freely with investigators from outside their organization as they did with internal review people? Would an open, civilianized hearing process have let the Detroit officers off easier? Did the anticipated reaction of the Civil Service Commission allow the chief to fire the officers and thus "appear" tough? Was the Detroit chief allowed latitude because he knew that the civilianized review of these civil servants might cause the department to give these cops their jobs back anyway?

Regarding Los Angeles events, How should the policy formulation process have dealt with the preexisting police violence problem? Was additional training in order? Would the King beating have been avoided by a chief who sent out a "no nonsense" message about such behavior? Would the politics of the specific incident have been different had the chief taken immediate and decisive action, as did the Detroit chief? Would an internal investigation completed in thirty days, as opposed to three months, have changed the volatility of the case? Would civilianization of the review process have changed the chief's responsiveness to the press and to the public in Los Angeles? I shall draw on these important, central questions often as I analyze what should be included in an effective police review mechanism.

SUMMATION

I have sketched a picture of the typical input of complaints or problems with which a police review system must deal. The police use of excessive force, as I have noted, is certainly the most volatile and topical type of police malpractice, nevertheless, I have also discussed several other forms that police malpractice takes. Because the demographics of complaint input numbers vary with the population being policed and with the type of police organization, an understanding of this reality will help to underline an important limitation to this study, discussed later on: that police review systems are not transferrable from one location to another. The system operative in a relatively calm jurisdiction, which takes complaints about police officers' attitudes seriously, may not be workable in an area where review systems deal with caseloads that include compelling numbers of force and individual corruption allegations. The significant cases of the events involving police in Detroit and Los Angeles have served to focus attention on the proper functioning of review systems, and perhaps on the limitations of such systems as well.

2 The Limits of Reform

Any analysis of a contemporary social problem must include a consideration of the limits of reform. The American police officer attempts to do a difficult, stressful job in a violent, divided society, handcuffed, in some sense, by numerous political, legal, and organizational restrictions. Systems meant to hold the police accountable will be limited by these realities. No system, within or without the law enforcement subculture, will be able to solve all of the problems of police malpractice.

In this chapter the discussion of administrative review systems is couched within a realistic understanding of what such systems cannot do. As such, a four-fold method is presented here. I discuss some of the causes of genuine police misbehavior; consider the kinds of misconceptions and expectations that create the perception of malpractice among the citizenry; outline the severe limitations that nonadministrative mechanisms encounter when attempting to affect police behavior; and, finally, discuss legal limits placed on police review mechanisms by the courts and by legislatures.

WHY THE POLICE MISBEHAVE

It is tempting for some to rationalize that police malpractice occurs because certain types of people are drawn to and selected for the job. Some want to believe that "bad people in uniform" cause malpractice. Would that this problem (and life in general) were so simple to understand. In fact, contemporary scholars assert that modern police recruits bring the same psychological profiles and expectations to the job as those possessed by the general population (Bayley and Mendelsohn 1968; Bouza 1990; Box 1983; Leuci 1989; Reiner 1985). Thus "average" people become members of the police subculture and are then subject to all of the stresses that entails. Police malpractice, in a real sense, is created by several dynamics that impact these average men and women who are trying to accomplish their multiple, "impossible" tasks.

This discussion, like any discussion of the sociology of the police, must begin by noting that the American cop polices an increasingly violent society. It is not necessary or productive to delve into the numbers of this reality but only to acknowledge that such increasing levels of violence will create more violent situations for the police to solve, and more violent solutions.

As distasteful and uncivilized as it may appear to some, those who maintain order in any society must be prepared to quell the use of force with equal or superior force. This is a central reality of police work. Those who would argue that the police can control violence without ever resorting to the use of force, and there are those who believe this, simply do not understand life on the American street. It must be understood that a violent society will produce violent police.

A growing anonymity divides American society. Neighbors, even coworkers, no longer know each other well. Informal behavioral controls and dispute resolution channels become increasingly unworkable as anonymity manifests itself in a lack of interdependence between people (Toffler 1971). This means that people will more often consult the police to resolve disputes. Concomitantly, those disputes will be of a more polarized nature due to ever-increasing alienation and uncertainty. Over time, the police must solve more disputes involving people with less social homogeneity between them (Vick 1982).

Equally important to police behavior is the officers' reaction to the ostracism they face by the American public. The average citizen's distrust of government manifests itself often in a visible, overt disgust for police. This is constantly apparent to the American street cop (Banton 1964). A reflection of both of these dynamics is that, while police training and education has changed markedly in the past several decades, the populace still clings to the "dumb flatfoot" image about the beat cop. As Albert Reiss, Jr. and David Bordua put it, "The American . . . public seems unwilling to accord the police status either in the European sense of status honor as representatives of the state or in the more typically American sense of prestige based on the claim of occupational competence" (1967: 25).

This dynamic produces citizen-police tensions in two ways. The presence of distrust and disdain for the police can cause citizens to be overly aggressive, condescending, rude, and even assaultive toward the police (Kieselhorst 1974). And the police can react to this ostracism with self-righteous indignation. As Hubbard Buckner points out:

> A police officer is the target of more hostility, most of which he personally did not earn, than is the occupant of any other position I can think of in society. It seems so senseless to the officer. He knows he does good things, and when he arrests people, he thinks it is usually for their own good or for the good of society. To be greeted with hostility in many situations does not square with this self-conception, so the officer assumes that the moral character and social control of the hostile person is in some sense defective. (1967: 333)

Hostility and violence aimed at the police is, of course, only part of the problem. American cops see themselves as the subjects of discriminatory treatment as a group. They "come to look upon themselves as an oppressed minority, subject to the same kind of prejudice as other minorities" (Lipset 1974: 103). This idea sounds foreign, even silly, to many. But the police officer's feelings of oppression are very real and very important. The public assumes the cop to be authoritarian in personality type, not too smart, a "gun nut," politically conservative, brutal, insensitive, bigoted, and so forth. Any or all of these may of course be true of a given police officer. But when the young street cop sees the public treat these assumptions as fact, the cop is offended and can react vehemently (Bouza 1990).

William Westley sums it up when he says that

> the policeman's world is spawned of degradation, corruption, and insecurity. He sees men as ill-willed, exploitative, mean, and dirty; himself a victim of injustice, misunderstood and defiled. He tends to meet those portions of the public which are acting contrary to the law or using the law to further their own ends. He is exposed to public immorality. He becomes cynical. His is a society emphasizing the crooked, the weak, and the unscrupulous. Accordingly, his

37

morality is one of expediency and his self-conception one of a mar-
tyr. (1970: 98)

All of this plays on the cop and the citizen alike and can lead
to a rationalization on the part of police officers that extralegal
means are acceptable to achieve morally defensible ends. But the
rationalization goes further. Like the citizen who cheats on his
or her income tax because "all of those people in Washington are
crooks too," the cop will tend to become involved more easily in
misconduct of all sorts due to living in such an anomic situation
(Durkheim 1933; Sherman 1974).

Thus American cultural dynamics help to produce a strong,
counterculture among the police. They cleave to the support of
their fellows for psychic sustenance. The police then will often
view minority cultures as hostile, the legal culture as out of
touch with reality, and society in general as unresponsive to
their plight (Los Angeles Daily News, 19 July 1991). This in turn
pushes the police into a "siege mentality," wherein they view
their culture as being surrounded by hostile forces (Los Angeles
Times, 10 July 1991).

The subculture thus created is a self-sustaining mechanism.
Its presumptions are transferred to rookies as they first hit the
street. The subculture's "nobody understands us" perspective is
underwritten even by police executive leadership. Witness several statements made by former chief Daryl Gates of the Los
Angeles Police Department, surrounding the Rodney King example. Gates's assertions that his department was "not getting public support" and that he personally was under attack from critics
who "hate me" bears the mark of this sort of siege mentality
(Time, 1 April 1991).

A final note about the concept of limited government. Anglo-
American administrative and judicial institutions place significant obstacles in the path of the police. These obstacles restrict
the actions of police officers severely when compared to the
carte blanche afforded police in many other countries. The
American judicial system questions the police officer's investigative skills and competence. It stresses the possibility of error
on the part of the street cop. The process rejects "informal fact

finding processes as definitive of factual guilt, and . . . [insists] on formal, adjudicative, adversary fact finding processes in which the factual case against the accused is publicly heard by an impartial tribunal" (Packer 1968: 163). The police in America will often go a step further to state that the system even questions their integrity (Fletcher 1990).

The police react to this lack of professional respect with a cynicism toward the very legal system that they represent. Going outside the system to "get the job done" has almost become a requirement of the job in the subcultural wisdom of American policing. What Edwin Delattre labels "noble cause corruption" develops as a consequence (1989). When he or she is focusing on the morally justifiable ends of protecting life and property, maintaining order, and serving the public, the street cop can become involved in all sorts of questionable behavior (Box 1983; Donner 1989; Rubenstein 1973). This "Dirty Harry" problem involves a conscious choice that "the morally good end warrants or justifies an ethically, politically, or legally dangerous means to its achievement" (Klockars 1985: 55).

In fact, the cop's concern for the plight of the victims of crime and substantive guilt is considered by some academics as emblematic of confusion about the criminal justice system. "The trouble is that police confuse factual guilt with legal guilt, and soon become discouraged when their 'good pinches' do not result in conviction and serious punishment" (Betz 1985: 177). This assertion rings true in that the police do become discouraged. But it completely misses the point about substantive guilt, for police practitioners, unlike lawyers and other legal actors, interact with victims every day. Empathizing with the plight of victims, the average cop would counter that it is the legal profession that is "confused," not the police. It is the legal profession's focus on legal guilt to the exclusion of factual guilt that is problematic, not the cop's empathy for victims. Coerced confessions, illegal searches, verbal and physical harassment all are products of these dynamics.

Without attempting to be synoptic, I propose that these are some of the dynamics operative within American culture and within the police subculture that create genuine misbehavior. 39

THE IMPACT OF VIOLENCE ON THE POLICE

In America, as elsewhere, the young and the disadvantaged are those most often in contact with the police. Their indignation over the inequities of the criminal justice system and of society in general creates extreme tension between them and the police. These people see that police officers arrest many more minority people than whites (per capita). They perceive that their demographic groups are more often harassed by the police (Davis 1990). They witness different standards of prosecution for white-collar or political crimes than they see applied to street crimes. This all tugs at their egalitarian values.

Police officers are the most visible symbol of a governmental and social system that is somehow responsible for the gap between egalitarian values and the reality of stratified American society. Feelings of resentment toward authority in general, especially among those most disenfranchised by contemporary society, run high. The police then often suffer the brunt of these explosive feelings that have been produced out of an increasingly unequal socioeconomic situation (Phillips 1989).

A second set of problems exists. The entertainment media have instilled in the American populace a notion that police work is one continuous violent confrontation between the good guys of the law and the bad criminals. In reality, there is little violence in police work (Bouza 1990; Major 1991; *San Francisco Chronicle*, 6 July 1978). Yet *potential* violence is of tremendous significance to the cop on the beat. Increases in gun usage, gang activity, citizen-on-citizen assaults, and violent crime statistics generally create a paranoia about violence among the police. Police academies and in-service training systems consciously project a fear for officers' safety that is supposed to help protect them from routinizing the job to the point of becoming careless. Rookies are bombarded with input from experts, attempting to implant in them an awareness of their own vulnerability.

The new police officer is taught to be constantly on guard for what Jerome Skolnick has labeled the "symbolic assailant." Cops learn "to identify certain kinds of people as symbolic assailants, that is, as persons who use gestures, language, and attire that the policeman has come to identify as a prelude to violence" (Skolnick 1967: 3). This practice lessens street cops' uncertainty by helping to make them safe from surprise attack.

Such self-preservation techniques are logically defensible from the police perspective, but they produce citizen perceptions of police paranoia, authoritarianism, and discourtesy. Moreover, unlike any other judicial actor, social welfare agent, or organizational decision maker, the police officer on the street is pressured by time constraints. Often decisions must be made in a fraction of a second. So while all human beings tend to form stereotypical images of groups, individuals, and situations, the cop is moved to do so quickly and with a particular urgency (Bittner 1990; Bouza 1990; Yarmey 1990).

The ever-present threat of violence requires the cop to develop a "perceptual shorthand" that quickly identifies assailants and violent situations (Skolnick 1967). But under the pressure of time, using minimum amounts of information, police officers make mistakes. They make more mistakes, more often, than do other administrators. Given the potential arsenal of weapons that the police possess, it is understandable that police officers' mistakes generate significant numbers of citizens' complaints and ill will in general. Most citizens are not accustomed to considering themselves as symbolic assailants. They therefore view the police officer's self-protective actions as excessive. In the citizen's mind, there is great disparity between the gravity of the average police-citizen interaction and the amount of aggressiveness exhibited by the police.

No review system will lessen the tendency for police officers to be wary of the potentiality of violence on the street, nor should a system attempt to do so. To inhibit such decision making would be to place the police officer in a precarious position and to thwart the interests of society. Therefore, the police are particularly difficult agents to attempt to hold accountable.

To make this all worse, the types of interactions that generate apprehension in the police officer are precisely those types of incidents that are most frequently faced by street cops. Family quarrels, barroom brawls, traffic stops, and juvenile crowd situations are all commonplace in police work. These sorts of situations may be perceived as normal, everyday occurrences by citizens. They are, however, potentially violent confrontations, of the utmost gravity in the eyes of police officers (Major 1991).

Although this treatment of the impact of violence on the police experience has been brief, one cannot overemphasize the importance of this phenomenon. Its influence within the subculture is ubiquitous, yet this preoccupation with violence is almost always unwarranted. It imposes significant limitations on the ability of any police review system to lessen the number of citizens' complaints it receives or to develop better police-community relations in general. A review system can only take note of these dynamics. It cannot do away with them.

Coercive Force

It is obvious that police officers are a very powerful group of individuals. They are licensed by society to put their hands on people, arrest them, handcuff them, transport them, use physical force when it is necessary, and even to use lethal force, under certain circumstances. This exercise of power is central to their image and role.

Egon Bittner writes in his now-famous study, *The Functions of the Police in Modern Society,* that "the role of the police is best understood as a mechanism for the distribution of non-negotiable coercive force employed in accordance with the dictates of an intuitive grasp of situational exigencies" (1970: 56). This statement relates to several important points in this discussion. It touches on the idea that what the police do is a sort of "fly by the seat of the pants," "sixth sense" oriented craft (Cohen and Feldberg 1991; Skolnick 1967: 182). This is important because it outlines a critical problem that police accountability mechanisms have: how to hold accountable a group of individuals who possess this kind of practical knowledge (or "street sense," in the cop's vernacular), when those outside the police experience do not and cannot possess it.

Bittner touches on the "non-negotiable coercive power" of the police. It is obvious to even the casual observer that those who exercise such coercive power, especially in a liberal society, are resented by the policed populace. This resentment, of course, produces both citizens' complaints and attempts to attach rigid civilian controls to police policy formulation systems. As William Muir, Jr. sums up, the exercise of coercive power "seems on first acquaintance mean and barbaric. . . . The human qualities which appear to be required for the practice of coercion seem incompatible with any civilized notion of the good" (Muir 1977: 48).

The coercive power transaction affects police accountability mechanisms in two ways. First, the citizen's notions of the police officer's ability to coerce tend to generate indignation and conflict on the part of the public. These feelings at times manifest themselves in a general contempt for the police, in attempts to exercise civilian control over the police, or in specific complaints about police behavior. Second, the street cop often sees the indignation of the citizen as unwarranted, ignorant, and self-serving. Officers see the citizens' complaint process as just one more way "the system" victimizes them. They react with self-righteous indignation when civilians seek either to control police policy or to grieve about particular incidents. Police cooperation with a review process and their faith in its fairness will be problematic at best. An external review system, in particular, has to deal with a significant perceptual gap between police and community understandings of the nature of police power.

Paramilitarism

An additional point of discussion is that of militarism. Police departments are organized along what are commonly called "paramilitary" lines. Strict chains of command, uniform dress codes, personal grooming standards, and formal inspections characterize most urban and suburban police organizations in America. This method of structuring is rationalized in several ways by police administrators. Of course, uniforms make the police easily recognizable by citizens in need of assistance, and uniformity is meant to instill discipline in the troops. It is also meant to define strictly the lines of authority and responsibly in the police organization (Reiss and Bordua 1967; Wilson 1968).

Militarism is an important topic for this discussion because   43

there are so many drawbacks to its operations. Police departments' requirements that grown people get haircuts and shine
their shoes is demeaning both to police officers and to the supervisors who must require this and is hardly commensurate with
the responsibilities and powers that both the street cop and his
or her supervisor possess. This obsession with uniformity and
conservative appearance often seems petty to the street cop.
("Don't they have better things to worry about?")

Perhaps more important is the gestapo image that militarism
creates. Citizens often append the gestapo label to their complaints about the police. Ramsey Clark takes it one step further.
He feels that the paramilitary psychology of police personnel,
"based on force and fear," actually increases the amount of police-directed violence in America (Clark 1970). And Skolnick
points out that this paramilitary focus also tends to produce a
martial concept of order among the police. "Internal regulations
based on martial principles suggest external cognitions based on
similar principles." (Skolnick 1967: 11). Thus militarism can
foster an overemphasis on law enforcement, to the exclusion of
less formal, more humane, more "community-oriented" ways of
handling situations.

In Tony Jefferson's view, paramilitarism puts a "premium on
decisiveness, firm interventions and toughness, the sense of being the cavalry to whom beleaguered divisions turn to for help."
A cult of masculinity and a preoccupation with violence combines with a system that recruits "keen young men anxious to
prove themselves through active involvement, and a training
programme that covers everything except what really matters—
the trouble-free prevention of disorder" (Jefferson 1990: 127).

This is all bad for police-community relations. The solidarity
that the paramilitary experience provides may help to soothe the
individual police officer psyche from the painful costs of isolation from society. But it provides fertile ground in which antipolice cynicism grows in the civilian population. It is productive
of problems for police accountability mechanisms at all levels.

Setting Organizational Goals

Police organizations suffer from problems unique to
social welfare organizations. Specifically, confusion about goals

and means is critical. Much of what the police do is non-legal, and therefore not subject to the provisions of penal codes or review before the bar (Manning 1977; Reiner 1985; Whitaker and Phillips 1983). In order to hold police officers accountable for activities that do not relate to "law enforcement," regulations must be developed that are both legally acceptable and organizationally sound. Those who develop such rules must first determine the organizational goals toward which specific regulations aim. For most, it is assumed that the organizational mission of the police is known. In fact, the goals of the police are often multiple, conflicting, and vague. And because they are, confusion can be created for the organization, for the police officer, and for review systems.

What is the mission of the police? Is it to enforce the law? To maintain order? To protect lives and property? Is it to be of service, generally, to the community? Is it to protect the existing political power structure from those who would oppose it? It can be argued that each of these is a traditional function of the police. Yet each is inconsistent with the others under certain circumstances (Goldstein 1990).

An example of this goal confusion, and its consequent accountability problems, is illustrated by an altercation that occurred during the course of this research between the Hell's Angels motorcycle gang and some members of the Oakland Police Department. The incident, widely covered by local media, involved the destruction of the gang's clubhouse after several dozen gang members assaulted two police officers on the street in front of the establishment. The officers had to be hospitalized, and thus the thirty officers involved had "reason," in their view, to become upset at the gang members. But the $2,000 damage done to the clubhouse by rampaging police officers resulted in an internal investigation and the firing of six officers.

Important to this discussion of the incident, however, is the public outrage *at the firing of the officers*. Significant numbers of citizens protested to the press and to the police that the Oakland chief had overreacted in firing the officers involved. As one caller put it, "How could the chief fire those officers? . . . You know how those gang people live!"

The outrage of the community against the firing of the police officers involved was edifying. Some members of the public,   45 along with some officers on the force, rationalized the actions of the errant officers as necessary because of the violent nature of the motorcycle gang's members. The gang saw the polices' actions in breaking up their headquarters and destroying their property as an illustration of police power. The chief's actions in firing those officers responsible made some officers and some citizens feel as if the chief was not behind his troops. The propensity for many citizens to side in this way with errant police officers has been documented by other authors (Moore and Stephens 1991; Ricker 1991; Skolnick and Bayley 1986). (It is an important dynamic to remember when I later consider the potentialities of civilian review.)

Thus the presumed deterrent effect (on violent or criminal behavior in the city) of allowing the police to harass certain members of society is seen by some citizens as being a legitimate function of the police; indiscriminantly observing the rights of all citizens is somehow rationalized as of secondary importance. If some officers, and more important, some citizens, rationalize overt vandalism by the police, it is clear that contrasting signals regarding goal orientations are often received by the individual police officer. Developing criterion by which review systems should evaluate police conduct is therefore difficult at best. Can standards of conduct be developed to which the cop may be rigorously held, when the political climate sometimes asks the police to be oppressive? Will that standard survive the scrutiny of police administrators, citizens, and street cops alike?

Finally, I must note that for the majority of their tasks, rules are irrelevant to the police (Schuck 1983). Police work, as any street cop will tell you, is mostly common sense. Rules cannot be developed that will be definitive of "the one way" police officers should act. As James Q. Wilson points out:

> No very useful—certainly no complete—set of instructions can be devised for what the officer should do with say quarreling lovers. Defining a policy in such matters is difficult not because the police have not given much thought to the matter or because they do not know how they should be handled, but because so much depends on the particular circumstances of time, place, event and personality. Psychiatrists do not use "how to do it" manuals and they have the advantage of dealing with people at leisure, over protracted periods of time and periods of relative calm. (1968: 65)

Even thousands of pages of penal codes and case law cannot effectively limit the police officer's discretion by delineating the "correct" way to handle domestic disturbances, barroom brawls, juvenile gang confrontations, and so forth. Two points must then be made about police work and rules. Related to the incident discussion, it may not be possible to define rules for the police; and, related to police subcultural dynamics, even if it were possible to do so, the rules may have a limited impact on police behavior. According to Schuck (1983:15), "Norms that pervade the peer subculture of police officers on the beat not only constrain but sometimes overwhelm the impact of the legal rules with which agency supervisors and courts seek to control their behavior."

This discussion of the causes of police misbehavior and perceived misbehavior may be condensed into two general observations. First, all of the aforementioned environmental factors are causally related to police misbehavior. It must be understood that police abuse "is not an individual problem but a problem of the occupation and its organization, something in the nature of policework itself" (Stoddard 1983: 334). An appreciation of this fact may help to clarify the multiple limitations that impact police accountability at different levels.

Second, the nature of police work is such that it will naturally tend to create police-community tensions. As Bittner notes, "The policeman is always opposed to some articulated or articulable human interest. . . . Even if one were to suppose that they never err in judging legitimacy—a farfetched supposition, indeed—it would still remain the case that police work can, with very few exceptions, accomplish something *for* somebody only by proceeding *against* someone else" (1970: 96). Because of this, the police will generate a large number of complaints that come from the "losers" in daily police interactions. Whether substantively correct or not, with respect to legality and appropriateness of police actions, these complaints are problematic for a police review mechanism.

Police work and police organizations exhibit administrative problems common to all complex organizations and all public agencies. There are, however, significant differences between the police officer's working experience and that of other administrators. Both the cop and the citizen bring a certain amount of hostility and misunderstanding to the police-citizen interaction because of cultural dynamics, which promote preconceived notions of police behavior. American police work in a violent, hostile atmosphere, and they are constantly involved in coercive power relationships, both as victims and as victimizers. Their working environment requires a swiftness in decision making unknown to other public agents. The beat cop is effectively isolated from the citizenry policed by all of these dynamics, which are further complicated by the paramilitary organization of police systems.

This treatment of the limits of reform began with an outline of some of the constraints that operate through the use of internalized, socializing mechanisms in controlling police misbehavior. Now the discussion turns to a consideration of the limitations of external sanctioning mechanisms. Before I focus exclusively on administrative review systems, I consider other, nonadministrative, genuinely "external," forms of review.

EXTRA-ADMINISTRATIVE LIMITATIONS

What limits the potentiality of judicial review of police abuses? Why are grand juries not found vigorously pursuing malpractice? What have recent developments in the area of civil litigation done to influence police accountability? How effective is the power of the press in influencing police behavior? Why aren't legislatures as interested in police misbehavior as they often are in other forms of corruption? Each of these extra-administrative entities has been suggested as a potentially effective accountability mechanism. Each, however, has significant drawbacks.

In theory, a multiplicity of agencies and institutions stand poised to operate as accountability mechanisms with respect to police misconduct. "The grand juries, prosecutors, judges, the FBI, legislative bodies, investigative organizations, the press, and civil litigation [are all] vehicles for holding the police accountable for their actions, in addition to the internal inquiries undertaken by police agencies" (Bouza 1990: 253). Yet each of these systems of actors has its drawbacks. Even taken together they possess only an indirect potential for holding the police answerable for specific misdeeds.

Civil Litigation

As avenues of citizen reparation, both state and federal judicial systems are available for people to achieve redress of police-related grievances. The abused citizen may sue an errant police officer in state court and seek common law tort remedies. In federal court, the citizen may sue law enforcement officers for violations of his or her federal civil rights. Specifically, Section 1983 of the Federal Civil Rights Act is the chief vehicle for federal action. In a response to the 1991 Rodney King incident in Los Angeles, several efforts to further strengthen the potential impact of this type of action were introduced in the 102d Congress. Aimed at "patterns or practices" that deny citizens their constitutional privileges and immunities, these pieces of legislation might open up further civil avenues for citizen redress (U.S. Congress. House. 1991a, 1991b). In fact, federal civil actions against police officers under Section 1983 have risen dramatically.

Generally, however, civil litigation has not yet developed its potential as an accountability mechanism. Progress is being made in this area, but the number of successful actions brought each year is still small (U.S. Civil Rights Commission 1981). Although they theoretically encourage such litigation, federal authorities, in particular, are opposed to utilizing such avenues in lieu of local vehicles. A former assistant attorney general elaborates, "It is neither proper nor feasible for the federal government to become the law enforcement body of first resort. . . . We want to encourage local authorities to police themselves, to develop sound administrative and state procedure to deter, to detect and to discipline police misconduct at the local level" (U.S. Civil Rights Commission 1981: 116). In point of fact, "federal courts do not like to interfere with the enforcement of state laws" (Chevigny 1969: 255).

A further block to plaintiffs' actions against the police has been constructed by the ruling of the U.S. Supreme Court in *Graham vs. Conner*. This case holds that officers who act in good faith "to maintain or restore discipline" will prevail in civil litigation "where there is no evidence of improper intent" (Brown 1992).

In the area of state litigation, similar dynamics obtain. Num-   49 bers of actions are up significantly, as in the federal area (Schmidt 1985). But the limitations on the process are many. Again, successful suits are still few in number. Furthermore, most civil cases are based on claims of false arrest, malicious prosecution, and assault. The first two claims are negated if the citizen is convicted of the offense. Additionally, if a citizen claims assault, his or her ability to collect damages can be severely limited by the common police practice of cover-charging. Cover-charging involves charging citizens with resisting arrest or assaulting an officer when the citizen has been beaten (Bittner 1990; Chevigny 1969). This effectively does two things: It creates an automatic rationalization for police violence, and it adds a charge to be bargained away in exchange for citizen cooperation with the police. Cooperation takes the form of not filing suit (Chevigny 1969).

The civil damage avenue, then, is effectively limited to situations in which criminal charges are dropped or are never brought. More specifically, the damage route requires the citizen to take the initiative in obtaining legal aid and committing personal resources. Many of the citizens perhaps most often abused by the police do not have the resources to commit. This speaks to the pragmatic limitations of any courtroom procedure as an avenue for redress. Those citizens often abused do not, when on the witness stand, appear to have a veracity comparable to the average police officer. The officer's demeanor, language, posture, and legal expertise all limit the ability of any citizen, but especially those of lower socioeconomic status, to make an effective argument. Finally, tort remedies are limited because civilians must prove that they possess a social standing, financial security, and, generally, a "respectable" reputation that could be injured by illegal police activity. Many citizens who are abused simply have no such reputation to be damaged.

The Effectiveness of Prosecutors

In civil litigation matters, the citizen's problems are compounded by the search for counsel. As Karol Heppe of the Police Misconduct Lawyer Referral Service states, "we have found hundreds of attorneys who will turn down cases because they don't wish to instigate actions against governmental bodies" (ACLU 1991). This same political reality appears below, when I consider the limitations of other accountability mechanisms.

The judicial system can also hold the police accountable for their actions in the criminal arena. Prosecutors can choose to vigorously pursue abusive police officers through applying criminal statutes to situations involving police misconduct. Prosecutors may also choose not to prosecute civilians when they have been illegally handled by the police. Each power has been argued as having great potential impact on police behavior.

The effectiveness of the public prosecutor in holding the police accountable, however, is even more limited than are civil tort remedies (Moss 1977). In reality, prosecutors are not independent of the police. The prosecutor depends on the police for investigative help. Since prosecutors are evaluated by their conviction rates and their investigative staffs are always very limited, they must consistently cooperate with the police. As Robert Olson notes, "Because the public prosecutor must cooperate closely with the police force, he can ill afford to alienate the agency which detects criminal conduct he is charged to combat" (Olson 1969: 928). Thus the nepotistic expectations that most people hold for police internal review mechanisms are equally applicable to prosecutorial review (Guyot 1991; Schwartz 1970).

Aside from these practical concerns, prosecutors must also consider the political ramifications of rigorously pursuing police abuses. Public prosecutors usually are elected officials. Especially in urban areas, they must take cognizance of the political power of police unions, and they must realize that a significant segment of the population would consider the prosecution of police officers as an attack on "law and order" (Olson 1969). Thus the aggressive pursuit of malpractice could mean political suicide for the public prosecutor. Also, those "average" citizens who populate juries for the purposes of hearing criminal cases are known for supporting their local police. The Rodney King case in Los Angeles was not an isolated incident (*Los Angeles Times*, 2–5 May 1992). By and large, juries are reluctant to find police officers guilty of criminal misconduct. Local prosecutors know this and believe that time and money can be wasted in criminal actions brought against their local cops.

The Exclusionary Rule

The exclusionary rule leaves an additional avenue open to the prosecutor and to the courts to indirectly review police practices. By excluding evidence obtained through illegal searches and seizures, coerced confessions, illegally conducted lineups, unauthorized wire-tapping, and so forth, the judicial system might have influence on police operations. The avowed purpose of the rule is "to deter, [to] compel respect for the constitutional guarantee in the only effectively available way— by removing the incentive to disregard it" (See Table of Cases, *Elkins v. U.S.*). In theory, the police, wishing to obtain convictions, will pay close attention to the application of the exclusionary rule and cleave to the "judicial instructions" that it imports.

But the pragmatic operations of the American legal system are such that police do not and cannot learn from the exclusion of evidence. Decisions relating to the admissibility of evidence make up only one of a multiplicity of concerns that affect courtroom dynamics. Because of this, the police usually do not know why a case was dropped. They almost never learn when their behavior has led to a questionable confession or search being excluded. And even when exclusionary decisions are made in open court and the police are present, "trial judges do not explain clearly to officers why their evidence is being excluded, nor do they suggest to the officer how such mistakes may be avoided in the future" (Spiotto 1973). Direct learning from the operation of the rule, then, is minimal. Moreover, as Justice Byron White notes, "Although the rule is thought to deter unlawful police activity . . . if applied indiscriminantly it may well have the opposite effect of generating disrespect for the law and the administration of justice" (*Stone v. Powell*). Once again this emphasizes how police cynicism is exacerbated by the procedurally motivated decisions of the judiciary.

The exclusionary rule has other limitations. It only relates to the acceptance of evidence at the bar. It thus does not afford any redress to the overwhelming majority of people who are victimized by police malpractice, because it does not apply to police actions that are not aimed at prosecution and conviction. It does not affect the types of verbal abuse, racial discrimination, brutality, and harassment that constitute the bulk of what citizens find offensive in police conduct.

Federal Law Enforcement Agencies

Some have suggested that other agencies be used as mechanisms to oversee police accountability. Two agencies removed from the local police political situation, the Federal Bureau of Investigation (FBI) and the Department of Justice (DOJ), have been proposed, but their limitations are almost insurmountable. Aside from the aforementioned local versus federal arguments with respect to other avenues, the FBI holds the same sort of day-to-day cooperative relationship with local law enforcement as does the prosecutor. In fact, "The FBI testified that it investigated 3,000 charges of police brutality last year, yet the bureau sent only 40 to 50 cases to grand jury" (Ricker 1991: 48). It is simply unrealistic to expect the FBI to have any substantial impact on the everyday sort of malpractice discussed here. For the DOJ, the same holds true. Even fewer cases referred to the DOJ are filed and prosecuted. One study found 50 cases out of 12,000 presented to a grand jury, and only 16 resultant convictions (Ricker 1991).

Grand Juries

Grand juries are another part of the judicial system that should be effective accountability mechanisms. Grand juries neither require the direct cooperation of the police nor do they depend politically on good police morale. Therefore, they ought to develop a "watchdog" mentality toward the police that the public prosecutor's office does not have. In practice, however, grand juries have neither the time, the expertise, nor the inclination to pursue day-to-day police malpractice. With respect to the prosecutorial function, the grand jury "functions with rare exceptions simply as an extension of the prosecutor's office. The prosecutor who presents a case to the grand jury effectively dominates the proceedings" (Packer 1968).

Ironically, the dynamics that surround the indictment process 53 have developed the grand jury's role into exactly the opposite of its theoretically intended function. Instead of monitoring police abuse, the grand jury is used most often as a scapegoat for the public prosecutor. As Michael Tigar and Madeline Levy conclude:

> The grand jury performs its historic function, sifting evidence to determine whether a crime has been committed, in very few cases. Most district attorneys send only controversial cases to the grand jury—for example, a case involving alleged police misconduct, in which the D.A. can present a less-than-credible case for indictment; the grand jury can return "no bill" (fail to indict) and the decision has an air of impartiality nonetheless. (1974: 297)

The second function of the grand jury is to conduct public investigations and issue presentments. This occurs so rarely, however, as to be a relatively ineffective tool for monitoring day-to-day police abuses. And while grand juries do investigate corruption occasionally, they have no investigative staff. They must therefore depend on the public prosecutor and the police for most of their information.

Legislative Regulation of Police Misconduct

This discussion has been concerned thus far with the limits of judicial branch regulation of police behavior, but legislative policing of the police is a practice that has almost never been seriously considered. In theory, the tools available to legislatures and legislators are quite powerful. According to Walter Gellhorn, "Legislatures themselves engage in very considerable policing of administration, and have done so forcefully. They have some powerful weapons. Investigations, appropriations pressures, 'watch dog committees,' and the like have kept law makers closely in touch with law administrators" (1966: 136).

But limitations on legislative control are many. Some legislators put pressure on administrators irrespective of the merits of a client's case. This can create more maladministration than it cures. When this "customer is always right" dynamic becomes manifest, administrators can become cynical and unresponsive to individualized legislative appeals. The expertise of the administrator makes it relatively easy for him or her to ignore the occasional message, especially from an inexperienced legislator.

More important political realities make legislative control, of the police in particular, an unrealistic expectation. As noted above, it is considered political suicide in many places to question police practices. As George Berkley observes, "Not only do city councils decline to oversee police operations, but they recurrently refuse to approve any proposal that would antagonize the police department or its membership" (1969: 154). In Boston for example, the city's political elite have been resisting pressure to formulate civilianized review processes for a number of years because of a fear that such actions might upset the police. In fact, in some places, "the police may exert more influence on the legislatures than the legislatures do on the police" (Boston Globe, 3 August 1991).

It is not politically reasonable, then, to expect any effective legislative control of police misconduct. "Research indicates that specific legislative proposals to control police discretion are virtually nonexistent. Nor have concerns about police discretion arisen as part of other legislation" (Pinkele and Louthan 1985: 20).

The Media

What remains is a brief evaluation of the potential that one nongovernmental institution has for influencing police malpractice, the press, or the "fourth branch" of government. Arthur Niederhoffer writes that "police departments are extremely sensitive to the powers of the press, perceiving it as the barometer of public opinion" (1969: 234). Police executives normally serving in their capacities at the pleasure of local political elites attach particular importance to media coverage. Budgetary allotments, intragovernmental cooperation, and the general administrative integrity of the police organization can all be adversely affected by poor press.

There are, however, several practical problems with this idea of the power of the press. The American press is not normally critical of the police. The press and the police tend to be interdependent, and the police often grant favors, especially in terms of access to information, in exchange for favorable treatment (Uglow 1988). In a study of press coverage of the police, Benjamin Stalzer (1961) found that the press was, if anything, sympathetic toward the police.

While the press will not usually pursue police abuses of the daily sort, the occasional truly ignominious case of malpractice does tend to be covered extensively (Barry 1983; Johnston 1983; Skolnick and McCoy 1985). The police know this and are generally disgruntled over the sensational nature of such coverage (Wilson 1972; Skolnick and McCoy 1985). This fact leads to a second problem with press-generated accountability. The street cop gives little credence to press coverage. Unlike the police administrator, police officers on the street do not feel that it is necessary to concern themselves with media-generated images. Niederhoffer's (1969 234) study of police cynicism found that 95 percent of young patrol officers and 75 percent of all patrol officers felt that newspapers "in general seem to enjoy giving an unfavorable slant to news concerning the police and prominently play up police misdeeds rather than virtues." Thus, though observers believe the press to be demonstrably pro police, the street officer does not see it that way. And, as a part of the officer's cynical view of life on the street, the cop will tend to ignore the pronouncements of the press.

Finally, with respect to the press, the public's interest in any topic will wane over time. While those in a community may focus for short periods of time on a scandal, they will eventually lose interest and turn to other issues. This makes police misbehavior less sellable for the press. "Once the public interest flags, they [the press] turn to other news rather than probe the system" (Guyot 1991: 191).

Few nonadministrative methods of monitoring police abuses have significant potential for being as effective as administrative systems. They, at best, can have an indirect effect on police behavior. Some of these extra-administrative organs help to develop an understanding in police leadership circles that the task of controlling errant behavior must be taken seriously. They can thus help to enlighten some police administrators and local politicians who have not developed sincerely rigorous systems of review out of their own concern for police accountability. With the exception of civil litigation, none of these potential watch-dogs has developed any significant impact on police behavior.

LEGAL LIMITATIONS

This section describes procedural limitations on review systems. These include case law decisions, police officers' bills of rights, civil service rules and procedures, and some interesting developments in the area of criminal discovery. First is a treatment of those judicial due process requirements that are applicable to police discipline.

As with the citizen-suspect, the police officer accused of abusive behavior is allowed certain rights under the norms of limited government. These police officer rights operate to impede the effectiveness of reactive police review processes. They are, perhaps, no more important than the limitations already considered, but they are more easily understood because of their codified form. Police rights are imposed on administrative review mechanisms from without the municipal structure.

Due Process of Law

Police officers often bemoan the due process focus of the American criminal justice system. This is, in part, because they know that the system allows factually guilty criminals to go free on procedural grounds. Yet the same sorts of judicial protections that shield criminal defendants are also available to police officers when they are accused of misbehavior. Of course, there are fewer judicial restrictions on administrative investigations and disciplinary processes than there are on criminal proceedings. Nevertheless, due process requirements may hamper the thoroughness and tenacity of any review system. And these requirements are expanding to make the investigation of complaints and the administration of discipline more difficult over time (Box 1983).

Judicial decisions have historically voiced a common theme that a higher standard of discipline should be applied to police officers than to other public employees (Aitchison 1990). Yet this standard has eroded to the point that "it is seriously dimin-   57 ished today, and is limited to a very narrow set of facts. Overall, courts and arbitrators considering discipline cases involving law enforcement officers apply the same general principles which are relevant to discipline cases involving other types of employees" (Aitchison 1990: 48). This development, of course, inhibits those administrators who wish to hold their officers accountable to any sort of higher standard of behavior.

Disciplinary proceedings may be attacked on both substantive and procedural grounds. Police departmental regulations are subject to judicial attack on grounds of vagueness and overbreadth. An area of consistent litigation is that of rules that sanction "conduct unbecoming an officer" (*Bence v. Breier*). (See Table of Court Cases for case cited in this section.) These rules allow regulations to stand only where conduct is so inherently wrong and reprehensible that it would "clearly be viewed as punishable by a reasonable law enforcement officer" (*Kannisto v. City and County of San Francisco*).

Numerous court decisions also limit the tenacity with which investigations may attack corruption and malpractice. While police officers are not guaranteed the right to an attorney during disciplinary interviews, they are entitled to representation by their collective bargaining representatives. In a discharge proceeding, officers have the right to the application of the exclusionary rule with regard to evidence obtained by administrative investigators (*Rinderknecht v. Maricopa County*). Regardless of the gravity of the offense or the existence of postdisciplinary avenues, current Supreme Court decisions require that an accused officer be given some kind of hearing prior to being disciplined (*Cleveland Board of Education v. Laudermill*). While these "Laudermill" hearings need not be formal and adversarial, the evidence considered must be "relevant and credible" and must be at least "substantial" in its weight (*Kammerer v. Board of Fire and Police Commissioners*).

Finally, punishment given to officers may be judicially reviewed as to its gravity. Courts will normally allow police departmental punishments to stand. However, they will reduce discipline if its harshness shocks the "sense of fairness" of the court (*Glass v. Town Board*).

None of these procedural safeguards is out of line with the

American concept of limited government. But just as with the criminal justice system in toto, the substantive and procedural safeguards that are available to the accused officer will limit an administrative system's ability to pursue misconduct aggressively. Substantively guilty cops will not be punished for their abusive behavior because of "legal technicalities."

Criminal investigations into conduct by the police are limited by the same procedural norms as are investigations into allegations of criminal conduct by citizens. An officer's property is subject to the same search and seizure warrant requirements (*Boulware v. Battaglia*). The use of wiretaps, body transmitters, and monitoring devices is covered by the same restrictions applicable to citizens (*Allen v. Murphy*). The analogies between restrictions on criminal investigations of cops and civilians are more numerous than one might intuitively expect (or desire).

There is much to be gained by deformalizing police review processes. In order to generate a more open, healthy learning atmosphere around the process, systems should be developed that are as nonjudicialized as is legally possible. The due process rights that I have discussed here will impact directly on the ability to develop such nonadversarial systems.

Police Bills of Rights

There exist even broader limitations on investigations and disciplinary processes that have come as a result of the recent movement toward police officers' "bills of rights." Such bills of rights have been passed in California, Florida, Illinois, Maryland, Nevada, and Rhode Island. They are attempts to codify some of the judicially guaranteed rights given above and to expand the accused officer's protections in other areas. These acts specify under what circumstances a "discussion" between an officer and superiors becomes an "interrogation." Bills of rights also contain provisions related to the time and place of questioning. Each limits the number of persons who may be present during interrogations. The right to be represented by counsel is guaranteed by several acts, a right not necessarily guaranteed by the courts, as noted above.

In Maryland, the accused officer must be presented with a   59 written statement of the charges and names of all witnesses before he or she is interrogated. Furthermore, the Maryland bill allows that no force complaint against an officer shall be investigated "unless the complaint be duly sworn to before an official authorized to administer oaths" (Annotated Codes of Maryland 728). In California, the bill of rights provides that officers may not be required to submit to a polygraph examination (Government Code of California). Such polygraph examinations used to be standard procedure whenever an officer was accused of any kind of wrongdoing.

These police protections, it can be argued, discourage the citizen complainant from petitioning the government for redress of grievances. The Maryland requirement for force complaints is particularly intimidating. Furthermore, these acts, again, force the formalization of complaint investigatory procedures. Perhaps most important, taken together, they severely limit the thorough investigation of complaints.

In an early work in the field, Stephen Halpern summed up these limitations as he reflected upon the problem in Buffalo, New York, where a memorandum of understanding existed.

> The procedural safeguards won by police associations create incentives for police administrators either to resort to informal negotiations on a discipline problem or to forbear taking any action at all. In Buffalo, for example, a policeman's "Bill of Rights," more formalized internal accountability procedures, and the presence of a police association able to provide legal counsel to officers, combined to produce a situation comparable to plea bargaining. The two sides often agreed not to invoke formal adversary or arbitration proceedings, instead negotiating mutually satisfactory resolutions on an informal basis. (1974: 575)

This study also observed this kind of plea bargaining in San Francisco and elsewhere.

These advancements in the field of officer rights are not without merit, of course. Algernon Black, a former member of the short-lived New York City Civilian Review Board of the 1960s, feels that police officer rights may generate a great deal of respect among the police for the administrative process and the due process system generally (Black 1968). But, as with the criminal justice system in toto, one must remember that allowing more procedural protections to police officers limits the investigative tenacity, the substantive impact, of any kind of review process.

Discovery Law

Another set of problems comes from discovery laws already in place in California and from those expanding elsewhere. In a number of states, defendants charged with assaulting a police officer may use as a defense the argument that they were only defending themselves from a police officer's use of excessive force (*People v. Curtis*). Section 1101 of the *California Evidence Code* allows the citizen's defense to attempt to prove a propensity toward violent behavior on the part of the police officer (California Evidence Code). Under *Pitchess v. Superior Court* (1974), defendants are allowed access to police departmental files, which might indicate a police officer's history of violence. Thus internal investigations of citizen complaints can become evidence in later criminal actions.

Also, there is a new defense tactic arising in drug-related criminal cases. Criminal defense attorneys are advising their clients to make citizens' complaints about particular police officers. These complaints charge harassment. When the client is later brought to trial for drug charges, the attorney attempts to make a case that a systematic pattern of harassment exists. Internal police complaint investigations are used for this purpose. In a similar fashion to the above tactic related to use of excessive force, the harassment complaints are brought to bear on an unrelated criminal case.

Police executives maintain that opening up complaint investigations in this way will chill the ability of investigators to obtain complete and candid statements from both civilians and police officers. If statements made to investigators are later made public, it is argued, officers will never be truthful about wrongdoing on the part of brother or sister officers. Similarly, citizens will have their complaint rights discouraged if their statements are made public. They will not only fear police retribution but they will also feel annoyed at being subpoenaed into court to testify at trials unrelated to their specific complaints.

Most observers, of course, agree that police officers rarely acknowledge other officers' malpractice. Thus, on first glance, the confidentiality problem may appear to be a self-serving straw man for police organizations. As time passes, however, officers are beginning to be more candid about malpractice within the profession. Indeed, during the course of this study, numerous examples surfaced of officers officially protesting the actions of other police officers to internal affairs bureaus. In one case, two officers were fired on the strengths of a complaint of excessive force *brought initially by another officer*. Such occurrences were observed in almost every police department studied.

To the student of police behavior, police officers reporting the malpractice of other cops is certainly news. Although it has been unheard of in years gone by, this healthy trend toward self-policing must be weighed heavily by this study. If police executives find that opening up investigations might chill this growing tendency, they may discover that these practices present a very troublesome set of limitations to effective police accountability.

Civil Service Boards

One final system to analyze is that of civil service (Guyot 1991; Reiss and Bordua 1967). Civil service commissions operate in an appellate capacity, reviewing disciplinary decisions after they are determined by police organizations. In Oakland, for example, any police officer who is disciplined with more than a one-working-day suspension has a right to a hearing before the commission.

Civil service boards act in some sense as civilian review boards. They are populated by the same sorts of individuals appointed to civilian review boards; civic-minded, highly reputable members of the community. The experiences of civil service with respect to discipline are, therefore, important for this study. The dynamics that operate for civil service boards (found almost everywhere) may tell us something about how civilian review boards (found in only a few places) should operate.

In fact, civil service commissions quite often side with disciplined officers and against police administrators. During the life of this study, police officers fired for misconduct were given back their jobs in Berkeley, Oakland, San Francisco, Los Angeles, and at the Contra Costa, California, Sheriff's Department through civil service appeals. Several of the officers fired in Oakland during the Hell's Angels incident investigation got their jobs back through civil service appeals.

That the civil service boards support police is by no means unusual. As Berkley comments, "One factor which prompts American police departments to go easy on their erring members and resort to transfers is the civil service. In most states and communities, civil service regulations tend to be highly inflexible and overprotective of government employees" (1969: 141).

With civil service acting in this review capacity, its propensity to be lenient with errant police officers places tremendous limitations on the ability of review systems. The civilians of the civil service, almost always lacking any practical knowledge of police work, tend to accept the police's errant behavior as "understandable." They often take a sort of "boys-will-be-boys" approach to police abuses. Police executives, not taking this view, are often frustrated by civil service commissions' rationalizations supporting the misbehavior of unprofessional officers. This reality recurs often in this discussion.

SUMMATION

The treatment of the limits of reform herein has developed certain themes. First, the nature of police work in America and the reality of citizen's expectations create police-citizen conflict that may not be controlled by any police review mechanism. Second, extra-administrative institutions suffer from severe limitations when attempting to impact police behavior. They are limited by the strengths of the police subculture, by interdependence with the police, and by political realities. Taken together, extra-administrative review mechanisms have, at best, an indirect impact on police conduct.

Third, police accountability mechanisms are hampered by the same kinds of procedural limitations that inhibit the operations of the criminal justice system itself. With some interesting twists added, the ability of review systems to handle malpractice investigations, citizens' complaints, and discipline in general are all handcuffed by extra-administrative institutions within the

63

American legal system. Court decisions, bills of rights, discovery problems, and civil service appeals all develop their own special limitations for any system that seeks to sanction errant police behavior.

3 Criteria of Evaluation

When one compares complaint review systems, one should consider their relative effectiveness. Yet the meaning of "effective" is unclear. What indices can be developed to evaluate each of the model systems? What symbolic and pragmatic concerns must be taken into account by a complaint review mechanism? What interests must be balanced? The internal, external, and hybrid models outlined later in this chapter each have their own strengths and concomitant limitations.

This chapter develops questions about effectiveness and applies them to each review system. In the first section I consider the demands placed on police accountability structures by various interest groups. In the second section of this chapter, with an eye toward balancing these interests, I develop evaluative questions for use in analysis. Finally, I differentiate the three models conceptually. A number of authors have attempted to determine a logical typology for various operative forms of civilianized systems. I look at these schemes and fashion them into a tool that has utility for the purposes of this analysis.

INTEREST GROUP DEMANDS

Three major interest groups routinely make demands on police review mechanisms: complaining citizens, police officers, and police organizations. A fourth interest group, the community or the public, is also important. The community differs from the other three groups in that its desires are not as consistently made apparent. An effective review mechanism must concern itself with the desires, interests, and rights of each of these groups.

Complainants

Determining a profile for "people who complain about police behavior" is impossible. This is because several variables cut across the realities of who is abused by the police, who feels abused by the police, and who believes that they can have an impact on police review systems.

Individuals who believe they have been the victims of abusive behavior are outraged. Some citizens are so incensed that they overcome their fear of police retaliation in order to complain. These are the people who come into contact with review systems. But many people are also frightened; one will never know how many never come into contact with review organizations because of their fear. This discussion must take into account the openness of review systems, their proactive approach to obtaining complaints (if these systems have one), and their genuine concern that no one is intimidated from reporting malpractice.

Complainants want to be treated fairly and with deference to their plight. They want to complain without fear of retribution. Complaining citizens want to be considered honest and sincerely motivated. They do not want a review system to accept the police officer's word over theirs if that is all that the evidence presents. In fact, the opposite is the case. Complainants expect to be viewed as veracious because they have (1) been the victims of police misconduct, and (2) taken the trouble to report it.

Because of their outraged indignation, their perspective toward the police, and, in some cases, their elite socioeconomic status, complainants expect that police review systems will often find the police guilty of misconduct. Review systems seldom do this; consequently, they are rarely accepted as legitimate by those who approach them. Therefore, review systems must court complainants, in some sense, and they must attempt to consider peoples' concerns in an open, objective, legitimate manner.

It must also be understood that review systems have an illusory charge to provide citizens with an avenue to vent their anger, regardless of the substantive outcome of a complaint case. This research has found that all mechanisms find a significant number of complainants who simply relate their experiences, express their indignation, and wish to go home without formally complaining. There is no one type of complainant; and most desire to be heard without intimidation. They want a reasonably objective evaluation of their allegations. They want some action taken, not necessarily punitive, that will assure that future similar incidents will not recur. In short, they want to have their government respond to their grievances openly and effectively.

Of course, citizens will also contribute to hostile police-citizen incidents through their confusion about the law, their simplistic understandings of police work, and (at times) through their irrationality. It is important, from the perspective of the police officer, that a review system realize how many complaints, in fact, are the product of civilian ignorance, frustration, paranoia, vindictiveness, and even hysteria. Few complaints are actually the products of police malpractice (Goldsmith 1991).

Sometimes people become irate, even when police are treating them in a legal and rational manner. For example, middle- or upper-class citizens will often complain that when arrested—for drunk driving, usually—they were "searched and handcuffed, like a common criminal." Such police procedure is, of course, not only legal but also indispensable as a security precaution. But people bring this standard complaint to review systems in all seriousness. (Police officers expect a fair review system to handle this type of complaint in a manner that has no negative impact on their careers. They have every right to expect as much.)

Complainants are often mistaken about the circumstances surrounding their complaints because of their own intoxication. A significant number of complaints against the police are filed by "cranks" and "regulars." Some complainants are mentally disturbed. Some are vindictive toward the police, in general, or toward a particular officer (Kerstetter, n.d.). Some citizens are so streetwise that they understand how to use the complaint process in order to harass particular officers or get the police "off their backs." For example, the investigator for the Richmond, California, civilian review board has received a significant number of complaints from persons whom he labels as "drug dealers, attempting to avoid scrutiny by the narcs."

The police should not be given too many rationalizations with

67

which to treat complaints and complainants with contempt. It is simply important, for balancing purposes, to acknowledge that many complaints are not substantial in their content or intent. Civilian review proponents, in particular, tend to expound about police abuses without granting this reality. This causes review advocates to lose what little credibility they might already have in the eyes of the police. Again, as with the paradoxes outlined in the Introduction, this gets one nowhere. Ignoring the pragmatic realities of frivolous complaints does nothing but indicate an ignorance of the reality of all the facets of police review.

Accused Police Officers

One must remember that complaints do not normally occur because police officers are naturally abusive or authoritarian types (see Chapter 2). Occasional misconduct will manifest itself in most police officers at some time or another. In a real sense, complaints are endemic to the police experience. Of course, the police are well aware of this. As one of the officers from "Laconia" in Muir's study stated, "If you're not getting in the s—— six times a year, you're not doing the job" (Muir 1977: 26). In his study of the sociology of police work, Peter Manning tells of an internal investigator who stated, "If you don't have any complaints after fourteen years, you're in trouble! If they [a promotion board] look at a man with fourteen years and he's got no 7s [investigations of complaints against him], they wonder what he's been doing" (Manning 1977: 178).

Thus police subcultural norms support the idea that police work requires of its participants behavior that is unacceptable to many citizens, and the police are not alone in believing this.

As noted elsewhere, the police are licensed to stop and detain citizens; to arrest; to search people, houses, and vehicles; to interrogate, to handcuff; and to use force whenever the dictates of the law allow it. On the street they face the most violent, merciless, unprincipled characters that society has created. They respond to the most frightening, degrading, demeaning, and bizarre occurrences that people encounter. It would be unthinkable to expect the police to deal with this effectively without using force on occasion. A fair review system must take this all into account.

Furthermore, a fair review system must remember that the police officers with which it deals have their professional careers on the line when they are accused of malpractice. Citizens can, and sometimes do, bring complaints on a whim or in an attempt to cause consternation for individual officers. Some complaints are patently frivolous. But to the police, every complaint is substantial in the sense that its investigation and outcome determination can have an impact on the assignments, promotions, income, and professional future of accused cops. A finding of misconduct can have a direct impact on the ability of a police officer to put food on the table for his or her family. Thus a fair review system must take great care to see that its investigations, deliberations, and outcome decisions are all accomplished objectively and fairly. It must protect the officer from caprice and arbitrariness on the part of citizens.

All of the above granted, however, genuine police malpractice does exist. Police review systems must be cognizant of groundless complaints without becoming used to considering complaints petty or frivolous. While many complaints are petty, the existence of bona fide complaints cannot be questioned. The one should not be mistaken for the other. Police officers want review systems to make this balance fairly and intelligently. It is the most important concern that accused police officers bring to the equation.

A police review system must take care not to toy with the intelligence and honesty of police officers. It must not give too much credence to the truly groundless complaint. To do so would invite police officers to reject the legitimacy of the system. People operating any review system must remember that the overwhelming majority of street police officers are honest, well trained, intelligent individuals who should be treated as experts at their craft. In short, they must weigh the police officer's expertise as heavily as they weigh the citizen's indignation.

Police Departments

Removed from the emotions of individual police-citizen interaction, both the police organization and the community have their concerns about review system operations. These concerns are not mutually exclusive. An interest in the delivery of

69

police services or a generalized concern for the objectivity of citizen complaint investigations, for example, is held by both interest groups. Yet there are some differences in focus that must be considered.

Police departments are interested in maintaining control over their personnel and policies. As do all complex organizations, they seek to preserve organizational integrity and to lessen the uncertainty they face in their external environments (Thompson 1967). Police organizations seek to achieve professional status in the minds of both the public and the political elites.

These concerns cause interesting consequences for police organizational behavior. Citizens' complaints that seem to be minor are sometimes handled informally or not at all by police organizations. Dealing with complaints informally has several important consequences, which will be seen later. Essentially, the stance taken toward minor cases is a defensive one. The organization, and the individual police officer, are protected from criticism in such cases.

Paradoxically, important or "heavy" cases will often generate investigations that make even the most cynical police critic wonder at their thoroughness and rigor (witness the examples of the Detroit and Hell's Angels cases). Organizational defensiveness thus combines with political reality in some review systems to create a two-tiered approach to the problem of citizen complaints.

Police administrators tend to focus attention on individual complaint adjudication as a way of deflecting responsibility from the chief and the organization in toto. When this is successfully accomplished, the "rotten apple syndrome" allows the organization much latitude within which to operate. Cutting out an officer or two, now and then, can work effectively to span the boundaries of the organization and limit uncertainty. By appearing to act tenaciously with respect to alleged malpractice, the police organization avoids intrusions into the control of its disciplinary domain by external actors such as mayors, city councils, city managers, and civilian review boards. This action ignores the greater questions of administrative competence in selection, training, and disciplining that police supervisors would often just as soon avoid.

70 Ideally, a police organization has long-term concerns that are

separate from those of the individual complainant or police officer. Its aim is to act in a legally defensible manner relative to both complainant and accused officer, to generate long-term behavioral change in errant officers, and to develop behavioral control over all of its officers. Its goal is to learn from each incident so that the individual officer, and all police officers, can learn, grow, and change into more effective personnel.

The community also has some concerns about police review that are separate from those of any other actor. Most important is the idea that police review processes should be open to public scrutiny. This idea of openness is of particular importance to minority communities in inner cities, where police abuses are so often topical. Pressure for scrutiny has caused changes in review systems in several cities treated by this study.

Citizens' complaints about police misbehavior often involve volatile issues of racial and sexual discrimination. They concern abuses of power and the violent behavior of society's agents of law. Complaints are sometimes so highly politicized that they capture the imagination of the media. As with the Rodney King incident in Los Angeles, newspapers, television, and radio can become fixated with a single interaction between the police and citizens. All of this means that the community will be concerned with police review from time to time. But it will not concern itself with the day-to-day, ongoing operations of review mechanisms. The community will thus focus on the symbols and imagery of alleged police malpractice and police review, often to the exclusion of reality.

The financial responsibility of municipalities for police misconduct is great, in part because of the propensity of the legal profession to attack their "deep pockets." Small jurisdictions can have their entire fiscal base threatened by just one act of police malpractice. Thus both the citizenry and city administrators may become fixated on how individual complaints of police misconduct are handled. In addition, the public may be concerned about the fiscal costs of elaborate review mechanisms. Some systems expend significant amounts of tax dollars to per-

form their tasks; and today, when many municipalities are bankrupt, the expenditure of dollars on police review systems may
not be politically responsible.

EVALUATION STANDARDS

Because police review is such a volatile topic, and because there are so many concerns to be balanced, integrity, legitimacy, and learning should all be considered as separate indices
of evaluation.

A system may score high in one area and low in another. The
trade-offs necessary in this analysis are numerous. Legal concerns at times clash with organizational considerations. Short-
term individual complaint adjudication often conflicts with
long-term behavior control. Consequently, no one system answers all concerns. No one mode of operation satisfies complainants, police officers, the public in general, the municipal administration, the media, and so forth. These facts make this
discussion both fascinating and disturbing, and they confront
one with a question of balance.

Integrity

From the perspectives of the individual complainant
and the street cop who is accused of misbehavior, complaint review systems are adjudicative bodies. The first set of questions
about their effectiveness relates to this adjudicative function and
to the "integrity" of the system. Integrity is an amorphous concept to evaluate. When one questions a system's integrity, one
asks whether it is fair, thorough, and objective. The question of
integrity focuses on the way the process deals with specific complaints as cases. Is the review thorough in its investigatory processes? Are its procedures fair to both citizen-complainants and
police officers? Are decision-making conventions reasonably objective in their evaluations of facts and statements? This is all
difficult to gauge, for integrity, like beauty, is most certainly in
the eye of the beholder. To attempt a genuinely objective evaluation of the integrity of different systems is problematic.

There are numerous problems, for example, in attempting to

define hard data. The citizen's notions as to the objectivity and thoroughness of review processes may only be perceptually linked to the actual conventions of that process. In most review systems, complainants are privy to only a small part of the system's operations. Thus, while the complainants' perceptions of investigative procedure and systemic integrity are important, they may be factually inaccurate.

Also, the citizen complainant's evaluations of a system's integrity tend to be directly related to the outcome of his or her complaint. Of the complainants surveyed for this study, 89.4 percent were dissatisfied with any review system, civilian, internal, or monitor, that found the police to be correct in their actions. Put bluntly, if a complaint, on one hand, is found to be unsubstantiated, the citizen usually feels that the process was unfair or biased. On the other hand, if a citizen's grievance is upheld and an officer is disciplined for misconduct, the complainant then tends to support the integrity of the review system. Since most complaints are not substantiated by any kind of review mechanism, most complainants are not satisfied with review mechanisms, whatever their form.

Police officers, too, are so closely involved in police-citizen interactions that their analyses of review systems are colored by personal perspective. Thus one must look equally askance at police officer evaluations of review processes. Though they know much more about the law and police procedures than do citizens, often police officers are far too defensive of their own conduct and that of their fellow officers to objectively evaluate review systems.

Thus evaluations of the integrity of the three models must be based on a balanced analysis of several factors. Police officers' thoughts, complainants' evaluations, direct observations, and theoretical discussions must all be brought to bear on these assessments.

How should this question of integrity be applied to the Rodney King beating case? In this instance, it is important to ask whether King was allowed free access to the complaint process. Were all relevant statements taken? Was appropriate evidence collected? Were the rules applied to the disciplined police officers understandable, consistent, prospective, and impartially

73

considered? Were factual conclusions drawn objectively? Did the complainants obtain their "day in court?" Were the officers treated fairly and legally?

Legitimacy

Separate from the analysis of the integrity and morality of complaint review systems as adjudicative mechanisms is a consideration of the perceptions held about those systems. As the ACLU asserts:

> Only a small percentage of police misconduct cases are sustained. It is important to be able to show to the complainant and the public that all cases are fully and fairly investigated and that the evidence supports the conclusion that no misconduct occurred. . . . As for the sustained cases, secrecy about the investigation and results prevents other officers in the department from determining whether or not their fellow officer is being "scapegoated" and prevents the public from evaluating whether or not the discipline is appropriate for the offense. (Hoffman and Crew 1991)

A community must have faith in the legitimacy of its public institutions. The police, in particular, must maintain external images that foster cooperation. Without community-based support, no modern police organization could maintain order in mass society.

Nowhere are citizen-based concepts of the police more squarely focused than on police misbehavior of the type that this study considers. This means that review organizations must make every effort to deal with abuses effectively. But it means more. Police review systems must *appear* to be open rather than secretive. They must also appear to the public to be objective and thorough processes for adjudicating grievances. Particularly problematic is the distortion that external perspectives bring to such appearances. As with the individualized perceptions of complainants, community perceptions of the legitimacy of a review system may not be realistically related to the actual operations of the system.

A community's ideas about the thoroughness of police review systems can affect the politics of the budgetary process. Such

74

impressions can influence the amount of political pressure exerted on police administrators. The ideas the community holds can relate directly to the stability of the administrative hierarchy of the police organization and indirectly to the morale and productivity of street cops. This concern about perceptions, apart from more substance, may seem like mere window dressing. Yet the perceived legitimacy of police review systems can be of the utmost significance to police-community relations. It is as important as is the actual amount of malpractice that a community experiences. According to Manning, "The law serves as a mystification device or canopy to cover selectively, legitimate, and rationalize police conduct. It does not prospectively guide police action, nor does it provide the principal constraint upon police practices" (1977: 101).

Similarly with respect to police review systems, the "mystical ideal" of police accountability must be served by a review system. That system must appear to be objective, thorough, and rigorous. It must also appear to deal sternly with errant police officers when their offenses so warrant. The social solidarity that this punishment develops is important to the conceptions of limited government held by people in the general community (Durkheim 1933).

But legitimacy is another two-edged sword, for a regulatory process must be considered legitimate from the perspective of the policed population, and a police review system must also take care to exonerate those officers falsely accused of misbehavior. Without the general approbation of the majority of its local police officers, any type of review mechanism will fail. If police officers seek to circumvent a review process in order to have the support of their peers, police review can turn into a hollow exercise in futility.

How, then, does one evaluate legitimacy? Regarding the two specific events in Detroit and Los Angeles, one must ask the general community if they perceived the two cases to have been properly handled. Is there citizen faith that the victims of malpractice were dealt with fairly? Does the community believe that police officers guilty of misconduct were properly disciplined? Does the community feel that the review organization has not covered up more abuses than it admits? If the community is convinced that these cases were handled properly, is it also convinced that such prudent action is not idiosyncratic to such particularly volatile incidents?

Important, too, are the perceptions of officers not involved personally in these two incidents. Do the police, in general, believe both chiefs to be serious in their approach to misconduct? Do officers generally consider that the accused cops were treated fairly? How legitimate and measured was review system response to external criticism? Does it seem to the cops on the beat that the system supported their daily efforts when dealing with errant behavior?

Legitimacy is measured in this instance by putting together several different pieces of information. Important are complainants' attitudes, measured directly by this survey's research. Perceptions of the community in general have been gleaned from various sources. The study extensively monitored media coverage of singularly spectacular events, as well as general police practices. Dozens of interviews were conducted with local political elites, members of governing boards (such as civil service commissions, attorneys, and administrators within municipal governance structures), and members of outside interest groups. The American Civil Liberties Union, the National Association for the Advancement of Colored People (NAACP), other ethnic minority action groups, and attorneys who litigate in the area of police malpractice were contacted in every city studied. It is difficult to survey the populace regarding such issues, but there is some limited data available (Terrill 1982).

For the police officers' side, this study conducted direct observation of cops in action on the beat, in-depth interviews with randomly selected groups of officers from six jurisdictions, and a written attitudinal survey of 180 officers. Thus a montage of sources was used to develop an understanding of the rather amorphous concept of perceived legitimacy.

Learning

A third set of questions is cogent to this discussion. As one former police administrator noted, "The structures of corruption control are irrelevant compared to the 'messages' sent out about corruption control" (Sherman 1974). Therefore, the concern is whether a review system deters future malpractice. A system may be fair to both citizen and police officer and may receive good press in the community, yet it may not really have any significant impact on police behavior.

A review system may affect future police conduct in several ways. First, the complaint adjudicative mechanism may be rigorous enough to deter malpractice overall. When an individual has the time to contemplate potential sanctions, there is evidence that such sanctions do exert a deterrent effect on behavior (Chevigny 1969). Second, the system can indirectly affect police behavior. A review process that is considered fair by police officers can generate a significant amount of respect for citizen rights, administrative rules, supervisorial personnel, and the rule of law. Tangentially, a system that observes the tenets of due process might help to foster self-monitoring within the professional subculture. Third, behavior control may be related to specific learning that develops from a review process. If individual police officers learn what types of mistakes they are making, in a positive, corrective atmosphere, they will tend to change their behavioral patterns so as to conform to this newly achieved knowledge.

This part of the discussion treats the potentiality that the systems hold for dealing informally with some complaints. As noted in the Introduction, an interesting parallel can be drawn with respect to the radical school of criminology. Just as criminal behavior in teenagers tends to wane as they get older, so too do cops learn their craft and "mellow" as they mature on the street. A system that deals in a counseling and training mode with errant young officers may very well develop improved older cops.

A fourth way review systems affect future conduct is that the police organization itself may learn through the citizen complaint process. This education may, in turn, affect individual police behavior. The citizen's complaint can be viewed as feedback or data from the community (Dugan and Breda 1991; Goldsmith 1991). Though these data may be of little use in evaluating rules and policies, a review process might glean significant knowledge from analyzing trends in complaints. It may also generate policy and training implications that can influence future police behavior.

This analysis of learning also involves the costs of police review, because the realities of budgeting in modern police organizations dictate that expenses incurred by review mechanisms will mean less money spent elsewhere. Specifically, training and informal learning mechanisms may suffer from fiscal crunches brought on by expensive, formalized, adjudicative complaint-handling systems.

Another, overarching question is pertinent to this learning criterion. One must determine how well each system performs its functions without significantly impeding the other operations of the police. A review system can induce several counterproductive tendencies in police organizations (Lewis 1991). It may impede the operations of the police organization by interfering with the authority of administrators to supervise their charges. In addition, some review systems involve themselves in the development of police organizational policy. Sometimes this policy development interferes with educated, experienced, pragmatic, in-house policy development, which normally proceeds along specialized lines of expertise. A variety of secondary complications can arise when the dilettante collides with the expert pragmatist. Allowing the dilettante control over policy can be dangerous for an organization's morale, productivity, and growth. Also, police review can cost so much that it impacts police services delivered elsewhere. Operating some review mechanisms can cost thousands of dollars per complaint.

Of course, the most important counterproductive tendency that a review system may cause in a police organization is the deprecation of the services delivered by that organization. Review systems can actually generate more complaints; they can make police officers reluctant to make arrests and to deal with situations; and they can introduce policies that severely limit police responsiveness and efficiency.

A review mechanism may be so tyrannical, so aggressive in its pursuit of malpractice, that it actually "turns off" police officers. It can be considered such a vile and unprincipled enemy that it may actually create more malpractice than it cures. Under such a tyrannical system, "assertions of commonly accepted truths—

78

that the chief is a psycho or that the job sucks and that morale has never been lower and that they're all going to hell in a hand-basket—are simply not challenged. Cops accept the myths circulating around them because resistance carries a risk of ostracism" (Bouza 1991: 72). The collective wrath of self-righteously indignant police officers operating under a tyrannical review system can fall on the citizenry in a way that makes all of the efforts of the review mechanism seem wasted.

Regarding the incidents in Los Angeles and Detroit, this analysis of behavioral impact questions whether the respective systems used these cases to deter future malpractice. Were the officers involved in both cases treated with dignity so that they and others might respect the review systems in the future? Were reasonable sanctions imposed? Were supervisors held accountable for the actions of their charges? Did the chiefs indicate to the troops a "no nonsense" attitude about errant behavior? Were the review systems' expenditures reasonable?

In a less punitive vein, how did the respective training divisions view the incidents? Were the mistakes that were made turned into lessons for future officers? Did these situations generate new policies aimed at controlling such behavior and requiring stricter supervision standards? How were officers treated who were peripherally involved and only responsible to a minor extent for the misconduct that occurred? Were they handled in a manner that would be conducive to changing their future behavior?

Furthermore, consideration should be given to whether the police administrations involved went, in some sense, too far in their pursuit of misconduct. Did these particular investigations create counterproductivity in terms of further misconduct, lack of respect for the review process, or even lack of respect for the criminal justice system in toto? Finally, did the systems expend so much money that they actually interfered with other departmental functions, particularly training-related functions?

With respect to counterproductivity, did the operations of the review systems affect the rigor with which the Los Angeles and Detroit police officers pursued their charges? Did the treatment the police officers received at the hands of their departments of internal affairs create cynicism in the street officer corps about

79

their departments and the public? Basically, are the symbolic and pragmatic gains of using a given system of complaint review outweighed by the costs?

As with the integrity questions, the effects of review systems on police learning are difficult to compare. No easily quantifiable data can be generated on this point. Some available data were considered and then discarded as inappropriate in comparing the behavioral impact of various systems. Numbers of complaints or complaint-filing rates, for example, might have been tabulated to draw comparisons as to the deterrent effects of different systems. Then, too, the rates at which the complaints received were found to be valid (i.e., the police were guilty of misconduct) might have been employed in this analysis. But these figures are potentially influenced by far too many exogenous variables to be useful. It has been amply illustrated that many complaints are frivolous, minor, or procedural. If one adds to this the demographic variables (i.e., race, socioeconomic status, and, particularly, education) that differentiate the citizen populaces involved, the propensity for citizens, in general, to complain may vary greatly, irrespective of the type of system employed. As Samuel Walker and Vic Bumphus note, "A low rate of complaints may only reflect a lack of public confidence in the complaint process; a high rate of complaint [sic] may reflect public confidence in the process" (1991: 2).

For this study the direct behavioral impact of review systems was measured in two ways. Police officer attitudinal surveys were used to develop gross numbers of officer perceptions of the impact of review systems on behavior. Protracted police officer interviews were conducted to generate a specific set of responses to questions about the learning generated from the different systems, and direct observation of officers was conducted as well.

This analysis also attempted to consider the organizational learning involved. The study looked for connections made between the complaint adjudicative mechanism and police training systems. Through well-organized, thoughtful training, young officers can be taught role expectations that may affect their behavior on the street. This study then analyzed each mechanism to determine if any synoptic planning or regularized information-generating was attempted from the data that complaints and complaint patterns bring to each organization.

Part II of this volume brings three basic sets of questions to the analysis of the three model types of review systems. To review, the questions are as follows:

1. Integrity: Is the system unintimidating to the aggrieved citizen? Is it understandable to the public? Are complaint investigations thorough and competent? Is complaint adjudication done fairly? How appropriate is discipline in cases that find misconduct?
2. Legitimacy: Do the police consider the system fair? Does the public (including the media, political officials, and the bar) consider the system fair? Is it seen as fair by neighborhood leaders, especially in communities in which allegations of police brutality arise? Does the system allay the need for public protest?
3. Learning: Does the system deter malpractice? Does it teach officers how to behave acceptably? Does it work to clean out genuinely brutal cops? Is it sufficiently inexpensive that it does no significant harm to other training mechanisms in the department?

THREE MODELS OF POLICE REVIEW

In recent years the impact of the idea of civilianizing police review systems has grown greatly in American municipalities. Of the fifty largest cities, thirty now have some form of review system in which civilians are involved in handling citizens' complaints (Walker and Bumphus 1991).

These systems vary greatly in form and process. What is called a civilian review board in one jurisdiction may involve a completely civilianized system, from complaint reception to disciplinary recommendation. In another place, civilian review may refer to only the very-seldom-used option of complainants appealing their complaint outcomes to the extremely busy and normally uninterested police commission.

Because of this difference, one needs to focus on what models of review are appropriate for this analysis. According to Werner Petterson, "Two ends of a theoretical spectrum depicting citizens' complaints procedures could be: the internal complaints procedure, with no civilian involvement, on one end, and the external complaint procedure, with no police involvement, on the other end" (1991: 274). This study looks at operative systems that cover Petterson's spectrum, without including so many options that the discussion is muddled.

Wayne Kerstetter (1985), Werner Petterson (1991), and Samuel Walker and Vic Bumphus (1991) have all developed three tiers, or classes, of review, and this study retains that idea. Police-operated "internal review" is on one end of the spectrum, and completely external, "civilian review," is on the other. The middle case is the "civilian monitor" system. In the latter, the police conduct the investigatory phase of the review process, monitored by civilians who also conduct the input and output functions.

At the time of this writing, these model organizations have been studied for sixteen years. They were each part of the original six organizations chosen for this study in 1977 (see Appendix A). These mechanisms have continued to be open to research endeavors. More important, they have developed institutional structures and operational procedures that continue to identify each of them as emblematic of the best one can expect to find in their respective places on the spectrum. What follows is a brief overview of the systems studied. In Part II they are discussed in depth.

Internal Review

The Internal Affairs (IA) Section of the Oakland, California, Police Department has been one of the most-respected organizations of its kind for several decades. Its reputation for thoroughness and integrity is among the best of police-operated, internalized systems anywhere. Its input mechanism, investigatory procedure, and decision-making system are all police-operated. It answers to a chief and an administration that are genuinely motivated toward holding Oakland's police officers accountable for their actions. It provides an example of the very best of systems for the analysis of internal review and the potential effectiveness of police-operated systems. This model represents the overwhelming majority of review system types; 83.9 percent of all police review systems are exclusively internal, completely police-operated systems (West, n.d.).

Civilian Review

The Berkeley, California, Police Review Commission (PRC), founded in 1973, is the longest continuously operating civilian review system in America. During this twenty-year period, the PRC has been sufficiently institutionalized, thus it was chosen for the purposes of this analysis. All its operational phases, from complaint reception to adjudicative hearing, function completely externally to the Berkeley Police Department. The PRC, through its recommendations, works in an advisory capacity, reporting to the city manager and not to the chief of police. Furthermore, the Berkeley system engages in a policy formulation function that is advisory to the police. It is thus the most archetypical example in the country of the civilian review end of the spectrum. (Only 6.5 percent of America's systems are so organized [West, n.d.].)

Civilian Monitor

In Kansas City, Missouri, since 1969, the Office of Citizen Complaints (OCC) has operated as a monitoring body that reviews citizens' complaints. It represents the oldest, most thoroughly institutionalized system of its kind. In 1969 many hailed it as a system of "civilian review" (and still do), but the operations of Kansas City's OCC most properly can be characterized as those of a "monitor." They may also be closely analogized to the operations of classic ombudsman systems. Complaints are initiated at OCC, forwarded for investigation to the police department, then reviewed by the OCC after investigation is completed. The civilian monitor system is a growing phenomenon. Kansas City's system represents 9.7 percent of those in operation (West, n.d.).

SUMMATION

Of the three sets of questions, each is related to the others. The integrity with which a system operates obviously influences the external perceptions of its legitimacy. Police officer perceptions of legitimacy will have an impact on whether or not cops learn from a review mechanism, and so on.

Yet these questions in a sense are separate concerns. One of the three types of review systems might speak most readily to one concern at the exclusion of all others. The most obvious example is that external review will be perceived to be more legitimate by many outside of the law enforcement experience. If one applies these sets of questions, however, it may be possible to develop a rich understanding of the types of trade-offs that must be made by those who develop and maintain accountability systems.

To achieve a meaningful comparative analysis of police review systems, although difficult, is not impossible. Analysis may be fraught with some of the dichotomies and paradoxes that police officers must deal with daily. Nevertheless, it is important to attempt to determine which systems are appropriate and effective at dealing with a problem that has been debated heretofore only on intuitive grounds.

It is not an easy task to develop a system that will balance the interests of the complainant, the accused officer, the police organization, as well as the community, without alienating some group along the way. And no one model will surface that does all of this for every type of community.

Part II describes the operations of three quintessential models of review and sets up an analysis of the best system in Part III.

POLICE
REVIEW SYSTEMS

4 Internal Review

Until the last several decades police departments traditionally dealt with civilian complaints in an informal manner. The local precinct captain, lieutenant, or sergeant would attempt to pacify indignant citizens and investigate misconduct if time permitted. (When this study began [1977], the Contra Costa County Sheriff's Department in California was included in the research plan because it still possessed a noncentralized, case-by-case method of handling complaints.) In departments with no systematized complaint reception and adjudication procedure citizens were influenced, cajoled, and even threatened out of making complaints against the police. Such practices, while commonplace, did not become the subject of controversy until the 1960s.

During that decade, the growing prevalence of urban riots, mass demonstrations, and what were later described as "police riots" illustrated for many previously disinterested citizens the increasing problems of police misconduct. Academicians and politicians alike began to trace some of the unrest among blacks and reactionary violence among middle-class white students to police abuse. Several commissions were then formed, which began to scrutinize citizen complaint processes within police organizations. For example, the McCone Commission, looking into the causes of the 1965 riots in the Watts section of Los Angeles, called for internal investigative units to be set up within police organizations to handle complaints (Governor's Commission on the Los Angeles Riots 1965). Academicians echoed this appeal (Berkley 1969; Goldstein 1967, 1977). For instance, Edwin Schur called for "strong internal investigative units to insure . . . fair and effective means of handling citizen complaints" (1969: 142). As a result of these actions taken by citizens, police organizations, and state and local governments, most large and mid-sized police departments now have "internal affairs" units, which are charged with the responsibility of receiving, investigating, and adjudicating citizens' complaints. These units are usually attached to the office of the chief of police.

Of course, the problem of police misconduct was not newly outlined for police administrators during the 1960s, but the popular pressures of the era brought forth a fear within police circles that their control of police organizations would be lost to external sources. Calls for external civilian review abounded during this time period (Platte 1971; Skolnick 1969). Former U.S. Attorney General Ramsey Clark is illustrative on the subject: "Police review Boards in which citizen panels finally determine allegations of police misconduct and appropriate penalties . . . are desirable to most cities. Some civilian review of police conduct, whatever the form, is always essential. Ultimately, the police are responsible to the public, not to the Chief of Police" (1970: 143).

The formation of rigorous, tenacious, and at times even tyrannical internal investigative units was seen as one method of forestalling the formation of external review bodies (Buckner 1967). As former Chicago Chief of Police O. W. Wilson put it, "It is clearly apparent that if the police do not take a vigorous stand on the matter of internal investigation, outside groups—such as review boards consisting of laymen and other persons outside the police service—will step into the void" (Wilson and McLaren 1963: 208). Thus a conscious pressure has developed over time within police organizations to avert external review by using rigorous internal processes.

The number of civilian review organizations is growing, but there are only a total of forty civilianized systems (of any size) in the country at this time, though there are twenty-five thousand police jurisdictions of varying sizes (Bayley 1985). Thus the overwhelming majority of America's police officers and police forces are reviewed by internalized, police-operated systems.

The existence of in-house systems may not explain the lack of external civilian review mechanisms in operation today; but the police at all levels believe that it does. In their opinion, the rigorousness of their internal investigative systems stems the tide of civilianization. This belief, combined with a general fear of civilian review on the part of the police, results in an interesting dynamic: Although most cops do not like internal affairs, nevertheless, they defend its operations as necessary. They argue that civilian review is unfair because it is operated by individuals unfamiliar with police work.

Every member of the law enforcement subculture understands that police abuse exists. Even police administrators and police union representatives no longer argue that malpractice is imagined. There is a growing awareness among the police that pressure must somehow be created that will suppress abuses. Of course, because of their solidarity, the police subculture as a group tends to resist the maintenance of formal antiabuse pressure. Police officers are reluctant to question officially the behavior of fellow cops unless that behavior is grossly offensive. Understanding this, police administrators are moved toward centralized, internally controlled review systems.

But why do police departments favor the internal affairs model? The answer is simple: It is because police officer professional organizations have failed to develop standards of conduct or to monitor police behavior. As Reiss notes, "faced with either administrative [internal] or external review of police practice and lacking the protection of collegial forms of review, police officers increasingly opt for union rather than professional ways to handle complaints about police practice" (Reiss 1971: 128).

Police professional organizations are often involved in defending officers accused of misconduct. They lobby for legislation that will expand accused officers' procedural rights. It is a laudable goal to insure that police officers are not subject to capricious administrative action. The inability of employee organizations to take the lead in the area of professional ethics and standards, however, leaves police departments no other choice than to set up their own internal systems. Centralized control mechanisms are also products of self-defensive dynamics endemic to police organizations. Internal review organizations help to protect the department, in general, and the police chief, in particular, from criticism. The centralization of the internal review function is, therefore, a response to several sets of stimuli. Dynamics evidenced in most complex organizations combine with pressures uniquely applicable to police systems to require such centralization. A consideration of the specific internal review system of the Oakland Police Department will help explain how such mechanisms work.

THE INTERNAL INVESTIGATIVE PROCESS

The Oakland, California, Police Department is an organization of seven hundred sworn officers, with a Patrol Division of three hundred men and women. Oakland's population is 360,000, of whom 62 percent are minorities. The police department has a 53.3 percent minority-group membership.

The police organization in Oakland is known for its efficiency (in a military sense) and for its professionalism (in a legalistic sense). Its officers are well educated and are put through a training academy that is one of the best in the country. Instruction at the academy is not only limited to traditional police science courses but also includes ethnic studies classes and role-playing exercises of a diverse nature. In the province of law enforcement, the Oakland Police Department is considered a model department. It also enjoys the respect of local academic elites.

The Oakland internal review process provides a good model for this inquiry. It is the best that one can expect from internalized processes, and the effectiveness and tenacity of its members have been noted by a variety of scholars (Douglas and Johnson 1977, Guyot 1991; Potts 1983; Skolnick and Bayley 1986). This study found no internal process to be more thorough in its investigations, and none was populated by more concerned investigators, genuinely motivated toward objectivity.

In 1982 Oakland added a civilianized review system. It is not a particularly effective mechanism and will not serve to displace any of the analysis of Berkeley's genuinely independent civilian board. Nevertheless, it is interesting to note that all of the rigor of Oakland's internal system did not dissuade local political actors from moving toward civilian review. (This underlines the difference between integrity and legitimacy discussed in Chapter 3.)

The Internal Affairs Section of the Oakland Police Department works closely with the chief of police. It is housed within his office complex. The chief's no-nonsense approach to citizen's complaints directly influences the working style of IA investigators. The chief and the deputy chief of investigations both have daily contact with the supervisor and officers of the section. The progress of specific, problem cases is closely monitored by the top executives.

As do most police executives, the chief regularly interacts with local political elites. He attempts to monitor the feelings of the community through these leaders. Through direct contact with the complaint system and with such elites, he maintains a fix on both police and community perspectives on the problem of police abuse. The chief sees IA as a boundary-spanning device, interacting as much with the public as with the police.

As is true in most police departments, Oakland's IA Section handles both civilian complaints against the department and internally initiated complaints. It also serves as the investigative arm of the City Attorney's Office for civil matters. The staff includes one lieutenant, two sergeants, and five investigators. They handle a work load of approximately two hundred and fifty citizens' complaint cases per year, and they investigate an additional two hundred and fifty legal claims cases for the City Attorney's Office. IA finds officer wrongdoing in approximately 11.5 percent of its citizens' complaint cases. This is an average figure for large police review systems.

The investigators on the staff of IA usually seek appointment to the section in order to obtain investigative experience. It is known to the rank and file cops that both the chief and the organization favor IA experience when selecting people for advancement. The beat cop learns that assignment to IA is one way to enter the fast track toward promotion. Then too, some officers wish to get away from the rigors of uniformed patrol work. Sometimes, however, IA people are "drafted" into service; for example, a respected homicide detective was once persuaded to take the very important job of heading the section. This occurred even though he had some personal misgivings about how enjoyable it would be compared to his previous assignment.

IA investigators are required to rotate out of their positions after two years. This convention aims to ensure that IA officers do not lose touch with the reality of street work. Rotation also helps to spread knowledge about the IA process throughout the organization. The chief also rotates newly promoted sergeants through a short stay in IA as "intake officers." This is done in order to build in every sergeant on the street an understanding of the problems faced by this organ of the department. Ideally, this helps to educate sergeants as to how they can creatively influence their troops so that the officers can avoid complaints. Equally pragmatic, rotation attempts to protect investigators from becoming permanently labeled by line troops as "IA types."

IA investigators are viewed by many police officers with skepticism. They are even seen by some, as is sometimes true of quality control people, as traitors. While most cops understand the logic behind the existence of IA, it is illustrative that a handful of the officers surveyed by the attitudinal questionnaire, (8 percent), believe that there is no need whatsoever for a system to investigate citizens' complaints.

The Oakland IA Section presents an example of the optimum in internal review systems in its thoroughness and in its members' commitment to objectivity. The chief takes its operations very seriously, and so do its investigators. A number of officers within the patrol ranks who have worked in IA help to· pass to other officers the knowledge they have gained from IA about citizens' complaints. These dynamics all combine to make the IA Section respected and understood by police officers.

Input Mechanisms

Analyzing input structures involves asking critical questions about police review. These questions regard where complaints are to be filed, before whom, and under what circumstances. Is it important to have other than police-operated locations for this purpose? Or would it be a waste of money to set up storefront locations to assure that complaining citizens are afforded complete access to the complaint system?

The Internal Affairs Section at Oakland, as is true of almost all IA operations, is housed in the police departmental building. In the past, the Oakland chief tried to establish a system of intake of complaints at other-than-police sites, but the attempt proved unsuccessful. Now, complaints may be filed at the Internal Affairs Section, at the Patrol Division desk, or at the Traffic Division windows. The department's official policy, therefore, is that anyone anywhere should accept a complaint if a citizen wishes it taken.

Where complaints should be received is a separate issue from who should receive them. Even though IA intake people are almost always police officers and civilian review people are typically civilians, this is not always the case. At the Oakland Police Department, for example, the chief has experimented with the use of civilians at intake, but this experiment has gone by the boards in this age of fiscal conservatism.

While most review mechanisms request that citizens submit complaints in person, many allow for complaint-filing by telephone or mail. This is true of Oakland's system. In addition, the Oakland Police Department accepts anonymous complaints; many other police departments do not. In most systems, anonymous complaints are handled with varying levels of seriousness. Complaints of police corruption, of use of excessive force, or of racial bias are usually followed up everywhere. Latitude does exist, however, to disregard, at the discretion of the supervisor, those anonymous complaints that appear to be hoaxes, patently false, or impossible to investigate. This latitude can be abused, of course, but in virtually all of the mechanisms studied, the police used discretion at the entry level concerning anonymous complaints.

Additional flexibility exists at the IA intake level. A complaint need not be handled formally if it is of "such a minor nature that the unit or person first contacted can dispose of the incident *to the satisfaction of the complainant* [emphasis added] without the necessity of a formal investigation" (Oakland Police Department 1978). Thus a case may often be dismissed or settled sooner if the complainant is given a "satisficing" explanation. Herbert Simon coined the term "satisficing" in 1957 to refer to the propensity of administrators to offer a satisfactory explanation that will suffice as a reason for official action (Simon 1957). Within the context of this discussion, "satisficing" is the perfect word to describe the type of quick, informal explanation that those in a review system offer to complaining citizens, in a short-circuiting endeavor to avoid formal complaint investigations. If the police are thus able to generate satisfaction, they then may be able to reduce the number of official investigations.

Similarly, in the case of minor complaints, the supervisor in charge of the IA unit may refer them for disposition to the immediate supervisor of the employee involved. Seventy-eight percent of police-operated systems encourage informal complaint-handling (West, n. d.). If an officer's immediate supervisor deals with complaints at the supervisory level, that officer may learn more from the process than if the complaint were passed to someone in IA. But as with the other informal process of the police officer's superior trying to satisfy the complainant, this procedure is also potentially abusive of complainant's rights.

On hearing of a complaint, each of the three systems studied treats the initial interview in a like fashion. The civilian complainant is asked to give a statement either orally or in written form. Policy at all review organizations allows investigators to go into the community to take complaints, but investigators usually encourage complainants to come to review system offices.

During the initial interview of the complainant, the investigator ascertains the time, location, names of officers present (whenever possible), and the nature of the alleged misconduct. When a complainant cannot or does not wish to write out his or her statement, the investigator will write it. There is a pronounced tendency for investigators to do so because they believe this helps them to develop a clear understanding of the circumstances and alleged misbehavior, but it is another part of the process that might be criticized. Having investigators compose the complaint might allow them to alter its intent or specific content. Thus the Oakland IA section has begun to tape some of its interviews.

Continuing with the input procedure, the completed initial statement is read to the complainant, and he or she is then asked to sign it. If a complainant refuses to do so, this is noted, and this action completes the complaint-input process. (There are police departments at which refusal to sign a statement would be grounds for the immediate termination of the complaint process.) Following the input procedure, the actual investigation of the complaint begins.

Investigative Procedures

The complaint case is assigned to an investigator, usually someone other than the intake officer who initially briefs the complaint. The investigator gathers documentary evidence by reviewing arrest, crime, and medical reports; reviewing booking slips, property tags, and evidence receipts; examining photographs and radio and video tapes; and by analyzing physical evidence. Under certain circumstances, the investigator may take additional photographs. This is all straightforward police investigative procedure.

The person in charge of the inquiry then interviews witnesses. The police officer charged with the alleged offense is normally contacted last. He or she is required to give a truthful statement to the representatives of the IA Section. If the officer refuses to respond, he or she is then subject to disciplinary action, which may include termination for refusing a direct order of the chief.

Because of the police officers' bill of rights (see Chapter 2), an accused officer in Oakland may only be interviewed during normal waking hours, by no more than two investigators, and only with a union representative or attorney present. Again, officers who refuse to cooperate and give statements in administrative investigations can be disciplined or even fired (*Garrity v. New Jersey*).

In a few jurisdictions, police officers can be required to take polygraph examinations as a part of the internal investigation. In Oakland, the California police officers' bill of rights specifically precludes this. In most places, this practice has fallen by the wayside because of the expense of conducting such exams; in addition, most state courts have disallowed the coercive practice of requiring these exams. The logic is that polygraph results are inadmissable in criminal court and therefore they should be unacceptable for the purposes of administrative investigation (Aitchison 1990).

In Oakland, the completed complaint investigation is then forwarded to the supervisor of the IA Section. There, it is either accepted or sent back for further work. When the IA commander is satisfied with the completeness of the investigation, the case moves to the decision-making level.

Deliberations

A completed investigation is normally submitted to the immediate supervisor of the departmental employee concerned. The supervisor discusses the case with the employee and makes recommendations as to the outcome, the need for further investigation, or, in the event of a sustained finding, the disciplinary action to be taken.

There are four possible outcomes. These results tend to be similar for both internal and civilian review systems. Since all of the organizations studied use very similar categories they will only be discussed once:

1. Unfounded: The investigation conclusively proved that the act or acts complained of did not occur. (This also applies when it is determined that the employee accused was found not to be involved in the act.)
2. Exonerated: The acts that provided the basis for the complaint occurred; however, investigation revealed that they were justified, lawful, and proper.
3. Not sustained: The investigation failed to disclose sufficient evidence to clearly prove the allegations made in the complaint or to conclusively disprove the allegations.
4. Sustained: The investigation disclosed sufficient evidence to clearly prove the allegation made in the complaint.

If the investigation indicates that the police officer was not in error, the matter is filed and closed. If the investigation indicates misconduct, however, the supervisor makes a disciplinary recommendation. This convention follows the dictates of the classic police administration text by O. W. Wilson. "The first recommendation for action should come from the lowest command level, so that . . . the . . . officer . . . will not feel that he has been given a summary sentence" (Wilson and McLaren 1963: 211).

This caveat is meant to insure that line supervisors have a feeling of responsibility for the actions of their charges.

The case is then referred up the chain of command for review. Subsequently, the report and all attending comments are forwarded to the chief of police. In consultation with the IA supervisor and deputy chief of investigations, the chief decides if the charges are to be sustained. If they are, he also decides on appropriate discipline.

Quite often there is a discrepancy between the disciplinary actions recommended by the accused officer's commanders and the chief of police. The Oakland IA commander estimated that 50 percent of the time such a disparity exists. This dynamic is important because a police officer's immediate supervisor tends to identify with and protect the accused employee. The first-line supervisor is almost always a sergeant of patrol. This supervisor is on the street every day as a police officer, too. Thus a direct empathy exists between the sergeant and the employee because they are fellow cops.

The sergeant's supervisors typically tend to go along with the recommendations of their subordinate. These command officers usually feel that the line supervisor knows what is best for the errant officer. Thus the chief may find a sustained complaint coming to his desk with an unacceptably light suggestion of disciplinary action and will, in turn, often increase the gravity of the punishment.

Chiefs of police carry out their jobs removed from the street experience, and they usually have only an organizationwide perspective. Chiefs are responsible to local political elites for the performance of their departments in toto and for the image that their disciplinary mechanisms portray. In Oakland, the city's modern police chiefs have never shied from this responsibility of increasing disciplinary penalties. Oakland chiefs are often seen from below as abusive of police officers, always increasing punishments, never going along with lighter recommendations.

Oakland, however, may not be typical. In some jurisdictions, police chiefs tend to act as middle managers and follow the same path of support for lower-level recommendations. In San Francisco, for example, the chief has tended historically to accept the recommendations that flow up from line supervisors. These recommendations are usually for leniency. Consequently, disciplinary decisions appear lax from the outside. In San Francisco, during the six years from 1984 to 1990, 129 sustained complaints were sent to the chief with requests for disciplinary action. In only 47 cases was any discipline at all handed out by the chief (*San Francisco Chronicle*, 29 May 1990).

This may bring us to the most important indictment of internalized systems: that their tenacity is personalized and not systemic. Rigorousness only obtains when a highly motivated, strong-willed, impeccably honest chief is in command.

As we noted in Chapter 2, an additional review process may develop. When a police officer is penalized with more than one day's suspension, that officer has the automatic right to a hearing before the Civil Service Commission.

Two points must be made here. First, the right of appeal on serious cases is always available to police officers. This right creates access to a hearing process that is similar to those held by civilian review boards. In other words, civilian hearings are a part of all law enforcement review systems when misconduct is sustained because of case law and codified law. Second, in civil service appeals hearings the hearing officers typically either rubber-stamp the decisions of the chief (as later described in the discussion of Kansas City) or they lessen the penalties imposed by the chief (as is usually done in Oakland). In the Oakland Hell's Angels case, for example, the Civil Service Commission gave several police officers their jobs back after the chief had fired them.

Police boards or civil service boards do not usually develop a tendency to be harder on the beat cop than the administrative review system and the chief. This fact is of critical importance because civil service commissions are, to some extent, "civilian review boards." They are composed of citizens—not police officers or administrators—who review police conduct and in-house review mechanisms. As the chief of the San Jose Police Department confided in an interview in 1977, "Policemen already have 'civilian review' and they love it. It's called the Civil Service Commission." Thus these citizens from outside the police system are not subject to the protective influences of the police subculture and are not prejudiced in favor of the police. They are motivated only by civic-mindedness and, in fact, tend to go easy on cops. They do not hold the police to some higher standard of conduct than the chief does, and the same is usually the case with genuine civilian review boards, as the next chapter illustrates.

Confidentiality

Inside police organizations, access to information is limited. This is true for several reasons, one of which is personal confidentiality. Crime victims, witnesses, accused persons, and complainants all have concerns about their privacy. On occasion, complainants' names have ended up in newspapers. Some complainants consider having their names and cases made public to be a breach of privacy.

Aside from personal embarrassment, other reasons exist for limiting access to information. Some citizens wish to keep their complaints secretive because they fear police retaliation. This fear is not an irrational one. In Canada, for example, random monitoring of complaint investigations by the Royal Canadian Mounted Police Public Complaints Commission found police retaliation following the making of complaints (RCMP 1991). The Christopher Commission in Los Angeles found intimidation of complaining citizens and delays in investigations commonplace in that jurisdiction (Christopher Commission 1991). Reports such as this may lead one to believe that retaliation is not unusual.

Complaint investigations are also kept secret for very pragmatic, organizationally self-serving reasons. These complaint files can provide food for civil litigation. Of course, allowing the police to "cover their tracks" is a concern for all students of police review. But opening up police files could cost municipal administrations a great deal of money. This is not to say that the police should be allowed to forestall the development of accountability just because they fear what access might mean in court. But to understand the practicalities involved, one must consider the protective tendencies of today's cities. Municipalities, strapped by ever-increasing debts and income shortfalls,

99

necessarily take serious steps to keep themselves protected from litigation.

The propensity for police organizations to limit information dissemination is almost universal. Though 54 percent of police departments publish some sort of end-of-the-year statistics about complaints in general, none that this study examined publish information regarding particular investigations (West, n. d.). Internal affairs investigations are even held secret from other organs of the police department itself. This confidentiality, of course, implies favoritism and affects the externally perceived legitimacy of the internal review system.

But there is more to confidentiality. The policy also allows police officers themselves to come forward, without fear of retribution, and freely indicate when other cops have erred. Thus the policy is partly aimed at the blue curtain of the police subculture. Both as witnesses and as complainants, police officers are increasingly prone to find fault with their peers. Research has uncovered instances at several police organizations in which officers were found guilty of using excessive force and lost their jobs on the strength of reports filed initially by other officers. Not only have police officers begun to break the code of silence by giving corroborative statements but also they have actually initiated complaints about abusive behavior.

It may be that the breakdown of these secrecy norms is idiosyncratic to particular police officers and occasions. Nevertheless, officers interviewed during this study confirm a certain lessening of the strength of silence norms over time. As one officer confided, "Nowadays, if somebody were to really do a number on a guy, you know, I mean really beat him up, the guys on the street just wouldn't stand for it." Dorothy Guyot confirms that "although nationally there remains widespread reluctance of officers to come forward against a fellow officer, it appears that in a growing number of agencies, officers tell the truth if directly questioned [about wrongdoing]" (1991: 181).

The fact that some officers feel they are free to initiate such investigations is very interesting. It indicates that it is not at all naive to expect police officers to use self-sanctioning, socializing processes for behavior control in this arena. Police administrators point out that confidentiality is necessary to maintain the development of self-policing.

Nevertheless, the internal affairs policy of confidentiality can create numerous problems. At the end of an investigation, the citizen complainant receives a form letter called the "close-out" letter. This communication indicates the investigation's finding. It is the only information about a specific case that most of the police departments make available to the citizen. This study's complainant-attitude survey indicates that complainants are not satisfied by such limited feedback. The replies to survey questionnaires suggest a great amount of complainants' confusion about the final outcomes of their complaints. In the Oakland complainant sample, 37 percent of respondents indicated that either they did not find out the outcome of their complaint or they did not understand what they were told. Supervisors at Oakland's internal affairs related that very few complainants ever recontact the IA Section to discuss their confusion.

Adherents to the theoretical utility of the adversary system point out an additional difficulty with maintaining confidentiality. If police departments keep the internal process closed to citizens, all of the facts may not emerge in an investigation. With the addition of the ongoing input of the complainant and counsel, points made by police personnel may be refuted. If internal affairs divisions opened their case files, perhaps the credibility of citizen-complainants would be challenged or additional leads would be developed in investigations. While the process would definitely be more time-consuming and complex, the truth may be better determined without this policy of confidentiality.

Finally, in the study of the Oakland IA Section, it was found that summaries of complaint statistics are prepared monthly and circulated throughout the police department. These statistics indicate trends in complaints. A training bulletin uses examples to illustrate a procedure or discretionary decision that caused an otherwise preventable complaint. The Oakland IA Section also conducts a quarterly training session for all street officers. These feedback mechanisms are designed to provide the department with information from the potential pool of knowledge that is available in internal affairs.

One may see the efforts of the Oakland Police Department as a glass that is half full because of these attempts to generate knowledge, learning, and behavioral change from internal investigations. This police department does far more than most organizations do in this respect. Only 28 percent of police organizations utilize complaint data in this way (West, n.d.). And, though in-service training is operative in most places today, complaint mechanisms almost never have any direct participation in such endeavors.

EVALUATIONS

This discussion has covered the procedures and processes of an internal review, with specific information gleaned from the study of Oakland, California's IA Section. It now turns to the evaluations of internal review systems, based on those criteria already discussed in Chapter 3.

Integrity

An examination of Oakland's Internal Affairs Section and its process illustrates some of the best and some of the most problematic dynamics operative in police internal review systems. Through this study's observation of its investigations and the review of hundreds of cases, its procedures have been found to be thorough and competent. Its system has the confidence of most of Oakland's police officers; and it is more tenacious than are most, if not all, civilian review mechanisms. Its integrity is unsurpassed. Yet internal review systems, in general, have significant drawbacks. Because of their rigor and lack of due process restrictions, they can be tyrannical and unfair toward police officers. Because they are staffed by the police and located in police headquarters, they may stifle the complainant's ability to file grievances and to obtain an impartial hearing.

No one is sure how intimidating police buildings are to those who wish to file complaints, but as the U.S. Civil Rights Commission notes, "Receiving complaints at a variety of locations is likely to be less threatening to most complainants than requiring them to go to police headquarters" (U.S. Civil Rights Commission 1981: 51). The survey of complainants found that 26 percent of them would rather file a complaint at some kind of community center; 18 percent preferred a building other than that of the police department, and only 21 percent of respondents felt comfortable filing their complaints at the police building itself. (To 27 percent of complainants, location did not matter.)

Law enforcement personnel tend to be very cynical about the intimidating aura of police buildings, but it must be remembered that those who complain have been (or believe they have been) mistreated by the police. Their right to petition the government to redress their grievances may very well be chilled by requiring that they come face-to-face with their "oppressors." The uniforms, badges, guns, and paramilitary carriage of police officers at a station house might be too much to confront for more passive complainants. A system that receives complaints cannot be made available exclusively to those citizens having the audacity to confront the government.

The arguments made about the intimidating environment of the police department's structures can also be made about the atmosphere complainants encounter when facing police officers. The survey of complainants' opinions found that 64 percent of respondents would rather bring their complaint to a civilian investigator than to the police; only 19 percent would wish to speak to police officers.

All review systems receive calls for action and complaints of a minor nature every day. These may range from a civilian's request for an explanation of a parking ticket to a complaint from a citizen who feels a particular officer should be chastised for taking long coffee breaks. These are perfectly reasonable calls for service; however, they are not the sort of problems that one would wish to be the subjects of full-blown investigations. Clearly, such minor matters can be handled without taking statements, writing reports, and formal processing.

But handling minor cases informally is problematic. If an officer's superior attempts to satisfy a complainant without holding a formal review, the police department is open to criticism, for it is then allowed to decide summarily that a complaint is minor. There are no definitive guidelines for making this determination. The police may also unilaterally decide that a complainant is "satisfied" before an alleged incident report is officially filed. One cannot overlook this convention's potential for exploitation by police who wish to avoid the internal review process.

Most police administrators would argue that such a caveat is not abused. Although this study found no direct evidence that this informal process was being misemployed, there is no guarantee that abuses of this discretionary decision-making power do not sometimes occur. In fact, there is a rather infamous example of this kind of input-level discretion being improperly used. At the Los Angeles Police Department in 1991, the Christopher Commission performed an external audit of five years of complaints processed by the department. The commission found that hundreds of complaints, perhaps thousands, had been written off the police department's books.

The informal review policy of the Los Angeles Police Department had become one within which street supervisors covered up instances of misconduct. They would use the discretionary latitude of the policy to intimidate citizens from filing complaints. They sometimes made citizens wait for hours in solitary rooms if they wished to file a complaint. They characterized force complaints as "minor." They used all of the carriage of their office and the atmosphere of the police station to quash complaints at the intake level (Christopher Commission 1991). (When the Christopher Commission uncovered these practices, the Los Angeles Police Department had to abandon this policy.)

Perhaps the primary strength of the internalized review process is the competence and professionalism of its investigators. Investigators in internal review organizations are accustomed to doing physical evidence evaluations, balancing witness credibility, using standards of proof, developing leads, employing interviewing techniques and confidentiality requirements, handling informants, and preparing cases; all endemic to criminal investigations. They thus possess a type of expertise that laypersons lack.

But how much of this expertise will police personnel develop that civilian investigators doing the same job would not? It is obvious that *most* of the knowledge required to conduct investigations could be developed by civilians. Nonpolice investigators can learn how to collect and weigh evidence, how to interview citizens, what information is generally relevant to an investigation, and so forth. However, there may be important areas of understanding that might never be obtained by the civilian investigator.

Sworn police investigators are particularly knowledgeable about police subcultural norms, the nuances of how departmental regulations are applied over time, individual beat problems, citywide geography and demographics, crime patterns, supervisorial techniques, and the executive management styles of their particular police organizations and municipalities. These are important insights. Such information can be of great significance in understanding situations as they are presented in the form of complaints. It can also facilitate obtaining information from police officers who are reluctant to cooperate with the investigative process. Furthermore, as discussed from the outset, although the police subculture's code of silence tends to work in favor of police departmental investigators, it inhibits civilian investigators.

Besides a general feeling for subcultural norms, internal investigators have a feeling for the specific police organization under review. This insight can help in other ways. First, it facilitates the internal review officer's ability to short circuit complaints through a simple process. The internal investigator is easily able to explain to complaining citizens street cops' actions, when they are legal and proper. This process can often satisfy citizens without using time and money for formal investigations. The Oakland Police Department estimates that almost 75 percent of its walk-in contacts are handled in this fashion.

Such particularized knowledge can be beneficial, but the police subcultural and organizational membership that gives a sworn police investigator this perspective can also produce a prejudice that can be used, even inadvertently, to quash valid complaints.

This study observed a complainant assert that when he was stopped late at night for a simple traffic violation, he was confronted by six uniformed officers in four police cars. He felt that such an intimidating array of police power was well beyond what was reasonable under the circumstances. He complained that the police not only "should have better things to do" but also that they should "know better" than to attempt to frighten citizens in this way.

The experienced IA investigator looking into the matter had a "feeling" about what had probably happened. He was able to make a quick phone call to the Communications Division and then one to the Patrol Division to talk to a sergeant who had been on duty at the time of the incident. The investigator was then able to advise the complainant that the excessive "coverage" was due to the end of what was called the "swing-over" shift. This patrol shift lasted from 5 P.M. until 3 A.M. Its purpose was to add extra "cover" cars to the late evening hours and to aid in drunk-driving coverage, which was often needed just at 2 A.M. when the law requires the bars to close in California.

The police had stopped the man for rolling through a flashing red light instead of coming to a complete stop. The officer making the stop wanted to see if the driver was drunk. All of the other police cars had been in the area because they were en route to the police building after working their shifts throughout the city. They were all on a nearby major parkway when the traffic stop was made. They heard the car stop being made over their radios and "dropped by" to assure that all was "code 4" ("OK" in police parlance.)

This particular discussion at the internal review office took all of ten minutes. In that amount of time, the investigator was able to accomplish several things. First, he let a street supervisor know that some informal pressure should be brought to bear on the "young lions" of the swing-over squad to avoid such unnecessary shows of force. Second, he was able to learn about this incident himself and to convey it to the Training Division, where it could be brought in an informal, nonthreatening manner to the attention of the entire Patrol Division. Third, he had avoided spending time and money on an investigation that would have been wasteful from any reasonable perspective. Fourth, he treated the citizen-complainant to a "satisficing" explanation. The would-be complainant was quite impressed at the responsiveness of the department and (from all appearances) was completely satisfied with the investigator's actions. He thanked the investigator profusely when he left the Internal Affairs Section.

Such scenarios, involving "satisficing" explanations of police behavior, are not at all unusual. All review organizations receive significant numbers of these types of "complaints." They are not really complaints so much as they are calls for explanation. The operative question is, could a civilian investigator have accomplished all of these tasks in such a short period of time and thus avoid filing an official complaint? The answer is probably not.

A civilian investigator may or may not have been able to put the facts of the case together so quickly and conclude what had happened. It might be unreasonable to think that someone who has not worked the streets of Oakland as a cop would add together the existence of the swing-over shift, the time of night, the geographic location, and the citizen's story. In addition, experience with civilian review dynamics tells us that an informal call to the sergeant involved might not have led to the quick explanation given. Instead, a call from a person outside the department may have moved the sergeant to respond in a more formal, cautious manner. He or she might not have been responsive to a civilian investigator and might have treated the citizen's story as a "complaint" and thus as a threat to his or her officers and to him- or herself. In short, the entire interaction may have led to something other than the quick, responsive, informal learning experience that it was for the police. In addition, it might have been something other than the "satisficing," "noncomplaint" experience that it was for the citizen.

What do police officers say about all of this? The survey of one hundred and fifty police officers in Oakland and Berkeley found them to be supportive of IA investigators by a substantial majority. Eighty-eight percent of surveyed officers felt that internal investigations were either "very thorough" or "fairly thorough," and 84 percent of police officers were "satisfied" with their internal affairs systems.

This confidence in the professionalism of police investigators is echoed by Wayne Kerstetter, who has been studying in the field for more than a decade. Kerstetter points out that police investigators are "less susceptible [than civilians] to being confused by misleading statements or lack of understanding of police procedures. Further, the ability to think oneself into a situation and understand the dynamics of it is of crucial importance in ferreting out evidence" (Kerstetter 1985: 179). Because the science of investigating is one that involves "muddling through" at times, there is reason to believe that, on balance, police expertise can help in reviewing police conduct.

Patrol officers, by and large, feel that they will get a fair hearing from internal investigators. The survey indicated that 25 percent of the sample queried believed IA investigations to be "completely fair" and 67 percent believed them to be "mostly fair." Only 4 percent of respondents believed that police-handled investigations were unfair (4 percent responded "don't know"). Although dealing with internal review can make officers cynical and bitter on occasion, the study found that, in Oakland and Berkeley, at any rate, there remains a general feeling of kinship among peers.

As Kerstetter notes, there is reason to believe that the policewise investigator tends to be "snowed" or "conned" by police officers less often. "Knowing what they know" about police work and their particular organization, cops are more likely to stifle effectively any externally imposed investigation.

Critiquing the deliberations phase of the Oakland Internal Affairs system involves a consideration of two questions: (1) who should decide the finding of guilt or innocence on the part of the accused police officer, and (2) who should decide what punishment is given out when a complaint is sustained? Of course, at Oakland, the chief of police serves as both the jury, in terms of determining officer responsibility, and the judge, in terms of assigning punishment.

If one has faith in one's local police organization, especially its chief and management team, one will feel moved to place a great deal of trust in interorganizational decision making. But even if this is the case, this analysis cannot ignore certain realities. The chief may be (as he is in Oakland) an individual possessed of high ideals, integrity, and a commitment to his or her community. That does not mollify the fact that his or her police departmental and subcultural perspective make that person a "cop" in his or her own outlook. Anyone involved in the police departmental milieu cannot be expected to fairly evaluate the evidence, weigh the statements of officers and citizens alike, and objectively draw conclusions in all cases. Though an understanding of occupational standards of conduct and specific departmental pragmatics is important to the decision-making formula, they cannot completely substitute for the kind of objectivity that the jury function demands.

Officers have histories, as do chiefs. The individual complaint incident might very well be treated in an inappropriate manner due to ongoing exigencies known only to those inside the organization. The outcome of a particular investigation, then, might be slanted in one way or another, toward a finding of the cop's guilt or innocence, due to circumstances completely irrelevant to the complainant involved. Thus, having the police chief decide complaint outcomes might call into question the integrity of the system.

A separate consideration involves the determination of punishment. Again, if one has faith in the honesty, objectivity, and intelligence of one's local chief, one is moved to side with organization theorists who assert that the chief executive *must* have control of disciplinary determinations. Proclaiming that authority must accompany responsibility, accepted management principles dictate that the person who bears responsibility for the operations of the organization (in this case the chief) must be given the tools with which to accomplish this task (Brzeczek 1985; Garmire 1982; U.S. Department of Justice 1989). One of those tools is control over disciplinary sanctions.

It could be argued that one has arrived at the same perspective problem given above, but there is a different set of dynamics in operation here. There is good reason to side with the organization theorists and allow the chief this power. The job of a chief of police includes determining the kind and severity of punishments meted out to line officers. If a chief does not do so with an intelligence and competence level that generates support from the city council, mayor, or city manager, then the chief should be removed in favor of someone who can accomplish this admittedly difficult task.

If police departments remove control of such functions from organizational supervisors, management may be placed in an awkward position. Line officers may very well begin to look over the shoulders of their immediate supervisors to those who "actually" control discipline. Under such circumstances, it would be completely rational for the beat officer to ignore the directions of immediate supervisors in favor of attempting to ascertain what those elsewhere, in the disciplinary decision-making arena, want in the way of performance.

In fact, with the exception of Berkeley's civilian review system, almost all police review systems in America allow the chief of police the final say in discipline. Walker and Bumphus's 1991 nationwide study indicates that all civilianized systems (again, save Berkeley's) recommend outcomes to either the chief or the police commission.

Because of the enumerated problems with in-house review systems, it might seem that internal review is receiving a poor rating with regard to the question of integrity. This is not the case. This study has found that the Internal Affairs Section at Oakland is quite rigorous in its pursuit of malpractice. How can this be? One must consider the due process dynamics involved in internal police review. As a rule, the more open to public scrutiny a process is the more procedural protections are afforded the accused officer. In Chapter 2 there was a discussion of the limitations that administrative hearings place on municipalities when they attempt to discipline errant police officers. Traditionally, civilian review boards have allowed expansive due process protections to accused officers in the name of being fair. Because they are not so shackled and can require officers to answer questions under the threat of losing their jobs if they refuse, internal processes are prone to develop more complete complaint incident pictures. In fact, owing to the powers that reside in internal affairs departments, their investigations can go even further; they sometimes become abusive of police officer rights. No matter how comfortable the police in general may feel about IA, internal review has a dark side that can threaten an officer the way no external system could.

Also, it is critical to remember that Oakland has a strong, independent chief, who is genuinely interested in thorough IA investigations. He is committed to developing community faith in the legitimacy of the system. His personal philosophy fixes the "no nonsense" ethos of the IA system. He stays in daily contact with Internal Affairs and monitors particularly important investigations as they progress. He rewards IA investigators regularly with positive feedback and (eventually) promotion. As noted above, his disciplinary decisions are so tough that they are often overruled by the civilians of the Civil Service Commission, who consider them too harsh on police officers.

This is a crucial point, because the Oakland system may not be transferrable to other jurisdictions. Some chiefs simply do not have the kind of control over discipline and departmental ethos that the chief does in Oakland. Local politicians may protect the police from accountability of any kind, such as is the case in Boston (*Boston Globe*, 18 January 1992). Police unions may wield so much power that instead of the chief controlling the department, the police officer's association controls the chief's tenure (Hudnut 1985). Chiefs may be changed so readily that they are not able to develop a solid grip on the department for the purposes of generating professional attitudes and accountability, for example in Minneapolis during the 1970s (Fraser 1985).

The integrity of the Oakland IA system, then, is very good, when taken as a whole. Its investigations are thorough and genuinely dedicated toward objectivity. The system is usually fair toward police officers and complainants alike. If any attack can be made on the objective correctness of the system's outcomes, it is that the two-tiered approach treats some complaints differently than others, owing to their apparent gravity. Officers in Oakland take a great deal of time to satisfy complainants, short of generating formal investigations. This may be seen as abusive of citizens' rights. Yet when an officer is apparently guilty of misconduct, the system treats him or her sternly. As one street officer lamented, "You've gotta prove to IA that you're innocent, instead of the other way around."

Of course, it is not enough that the internal model receives high marks for its integrity; its legitimacy is important as well. When this analysis considers this criterion, one sees that the police-operated mechanism encounters difficulty.

Legitimacy

The crisis in legitimacy that modern police organizations face is not wholly a product of the secretive nature of internal investigations. Indeed, it may be the least important of many complex causes that form the basis for community skepticism. But dissatisfaction with internal review mechanisms is not at all irrelevant to such citizen attitudes. In a strange way, the attempt of the police to appear legitimate by "cleaning their own houses" adds to the very problems they seek to alleviate. The establishment of internal review systems by police departments, shrouded in secrecy as such systems are, has not silenced critics of modern police organizations, in fact, it seems that this has generated even more distrust and cynicism within the community.

A study in Michigan found a "widespread distrust of the internal police trial procedures by the major minority groups around the country" (Galvin and Radelet 1967). A California study found similar problems in Philadelphia and San Diego (Lohman and Misner 1966). David Bayley and Harold Mendelsohn (1968) found the same in Denver. The riots in Los Angeles following the trial of those accused of beating Rodney King, though related to a criminal trial verdict, were indicative of how little faith many have in police integrity and the objectivity of the system.

This study's survey complainants confirmed these findings when they indicated that they thought internal review processes favored the police (rather than being objective) at a rate of ten to one. The complainant attitudinal study also confirmed these findings for Oakland's internal system. Forty-four percent of complainants polled said that they felt the police-operated system was "completely unfair" to citizens. An additional 35 percent "did not know" if the system was fair or not. This second statistic is important because it reflects the secretive, interorganizational nature of the process. Thus legitimacy is problematic for the Oakland internal review system, no matter how high its marks might be for integrity.

When asked who should investigate complaints, not one surveyed complainant opted for police officer investigators: 10 percent of those questioned trusted police supervisors, 25 percent chose lawyers, and fully 52 percent wanted civilian investigators (11 percent had no preference). These findings are not particularly unexpected. They are only the quantitative confirmations of assertions that have been made for decades about the unacceptability of police-operated systems to those who complain about police misconduct.

The Commission on Civil Disorders, formed to look into the causes of the inner city riots of the mid-1960s, put the problem concisely: "We believe that an internal review board—in which the police department itself receives and acts on complaints— regardless of its efficiency and fairness, can rarely generate the necessary community confidence, or protect the police against unfounded charges" (1968: 331).

Several indices seem to confirm to the community that internal investigations are less than rigorous. Statistical reports of internal affairs organizations indicate a pro-police bias. According to the Oakland Police Department, in only 11.5 percent of its 1991 cases did Internal Affairs find officers in error. In Boston, 13.3 percent of cases were sustained by internal affairs (Boston Globe, 28 July 1991). In Los Angeles, 21.4 percent of citizens' complaint investigations were sustained (Los Angeles Police Department 1989). And in Minneapolis, 34.8 percent of complaint investigations were sustained by the police-operated system in 1990 (Minneapolis Police Department, 1990). John Dugan and Daniel Breda (1991) found that, nationally, about 25 percent of all internal investigations, from departments large and small, are sustained.

These numbers vary largely because of the different systems for assigning complaints for investigation. In Los Angeles, for example, so many complaints are handled at the division level, rather than by Internal Affairs, that sustentation rates might appear higher than in Oakland. Sustentation rates often tell more about complaint-routing systems than they do about investigations (Sparrow, Moore, and Kennedy 1990). To the eye of an external observer who possesses no confidence in internal police systems, even the rate of 34.8 percent at Minneapolis might appear low. It shows that 65.2 percent of the time the police are not found guilty of misconduct. These numbers seem to indicate that the internal investigative process is less than objective.

A second phenomenon appears to suggest less than thoroughness in internal processes. It is difficult for individual complainants to obtain feedback from police internal bodies. As noted, a large number of complainants either never find out the dispositions of their complaints or do not understand them. Most police departments do not give citizen complainants information relating specifically to the allegation charged. From the perspective of those outside the organization, the complaint has become, in a sense, the property of the police. It seems to have vanished into the "black hole" of the department.

Typically, no indication is given that any attention whatsoever has been paid to the specific complaint. This project found many complainants over the years who genuinely believe that *nothing* is done with complaints. They believe that the police department simply waits for a few weeks before it issues a form letter, a blanket statement absolving itself of culpability.

As Paul Chevigny notes, the amorphous final letter is neither specific enough to satisfy the individual complainant nor believable enough to legitimize the process in the eyes of external observers. "The report which is sent to the complainant should instead evaluate the evidence and show how the [internal police] conclusion was reached" (1969: 261).

How can the Oakland Police Department and other departments maintain internal review systems if the systems have legitimacy problems? The Internal Affairs Section in Oakland protects the organization by pacifying irate citizens. The City Council, city manager, mayor, Human Rights Commission, Public Safety Committee, ACLU, and other bodies might potentially be approached for redress of police-oriented grievances. But after contacting the police and going through their process, the overwhelming majority of complainants fail to take further action.

Surveys over the years have found that most complainants do not go further because they have lost hope in the effectiveness of the system. It is an unpleasant, but nevertheless cogent, reality that many complaining citizens have a monolithic image of "the establishment," "the man," "the powers that be," and so forth that lumps together all of these potential avenues of redress. After their internal review experience, complainants feel that they have put forth their case and have met with the system's answer. After the Internal Affairs experience many give up and go home.

The Oakland Internal Affairs Section is known by the city manager and City Council to be quite rigorous in the pursuit of its function. The fact that the Civil Service Commission often overturns the chief's disciplinary sentences in favor of more lenient punishment for police officers is not lost on these local political actors. In an interesting twist, they tend to defend the rigor of internal affairs while acknowledging the political importance of Oakland's young civilian review operation.

A lack of community-based legitimacy is perhaps the most crucial problem associated with the internal review system.

This study involved intensely observing Oakland's processes, which included conducting interviews of complainants and police officers, holding discussions with the chief, observing Civil Service Commission hearings, and gaining complete access to hundreds of complaint investigations and files. As noted in the integrity section, there is no doubt that after monitoring all of this, it can be seen that the Oakland system is a thorough, competent, tough investigatory and disciplinary system. There is also no doubt, after interacting with hundreds of complainants and conducting several surveys over the years, that none of this matters to complaining citizens. It is perhaps the Waterloo of internal police review that community-based support is so very low for these systems. The almost universally positive police officer evaluations of internal review aside, it is easily the least accepted system outside the subculture.

This study now turns to an analysis of learning. As with integrity, the results of this particular criterion in the evaluation of internal police review systems are distinctly positive.

Learning

Despite the problems outlined above, one must acknowledge the ability of the internal review model to effectively "clean house" within police organizations. The Oakland system is tenacious, even tyrannical, in its pursuit of police malpractice. It is extremely effective in influencing police behavior. In fact, its rigorous enforcement may even generate counterproductive effects. It may be that the most critical problem with internal review is that it is too tough and too unforgiving, not that it is too easy on police officers.

The internal review process is effective in controlling police behavior for several reasons. The police officers who staff the operation attack the job with the same rigor as do police investigators in other sections. In fact, many street police officers point out that IA investigators become overzealous. This may be because, as one investigator stated, "Cops are held to a higher standard of conduct. *They should be*" (emphasis added).

Some IA investigators tend to employ several of the same semilegal and illegal tactics that police officers employ in criminal investigations. In other words, they are guilty of focusing on the same substance-driven procedures of which the police have always been accused. (The growing phenomenon of the establishment of police officers' bills of rights is emblematic of how often internal investigative units have, in fact, abused police officers' due process rights.)

A second dynamic operating in favor of the criterion of learning from internal review is the increased development of police professionalism. While many authors agree that the professionalization of the police has not been achieved (Banton 1964; Geller 1985; Wilson 1978), that has not dampened the ardor of police officers and police administrators. Many authors feel that a crucial element of professionalism is the self-application of collegial codes of ethics (Comber and Blum 1964; Rueschemeyer 1964; Wilson 1972). Police officers and administrators universally voice the opinion that police officers in the internal review system have achieved this goal.

It is also important to understand how the "rotten apple" idea operates here. When a police officer appears to have botched a job, the subculture tends to react unexpectedly. Rather than exhibiting the solidarity for which the police are famous, it tends to abandon the individual who has done something truly embarrassing or heinous. As P.A.J. Waddington notes with respect to police shootings in Britain, there is no "evidence that police close ranks and protect officers involved in controversial shooting incidents; indeed, the available evidence points in the opposite direction. The behavior of some senior officers towards subordinates who have shot people in the line of duty suggests a tendency to abandon those who might cause embarrassment or controversy" (1991: 66).

Both the tenacity of IA and its perceived potential for professionalization are important to the individual street cop. Most police officers seek the social status, financial income, and political influence of the true professional. Most feel that a tenacious, unforgiving IA department will directly "clean up" the corps of street troops while it indirectly helps to achieve the much-coveted professional status. In the words of Gene Radano:

We must consider deterrence directly. The mere mention of PCCIU [Internal Affairs for New York's Police Department] is enough to get the immediate attention of all cops. No cop ignores talk about this unit. Its members are feared and despised with an intensity second only to the feeling German Jews must have had for the Gestapo. The slightest rumor that a PCCIU shoofly is around is enough to clear a coop of cops as quickly and with as much panic as a bird flies aloft at the sight of an approaching cat. (1968: 124)

These assertions are confirmed by this study's observations and by interviews with randomly selected police officers. Some officers maintain that no system will deter them from handling situations with their own common sense. But those who did sense some influence of regulatory systems refer to IA as the source of that influence. In jurisdictions possessing several review forms, cops seem to feel universally that IA systems were most effective at influencing behavior.

The attitudinal survey asked police officers directly about their perceptions of the behavioral impact of internal review departments. Of those polled, 43 percent felt that IA had a positive influence on police behavior; 28 percent indicated that they felt a "slight" impact; while 11 percent felt they had no affect. Only 12 percent of police officers felt that internal affairs departments were counterproductive. Though these responses may seem self-serving, they are ubiquitous in law-enforcement circles, both on the street and at administrative levels.

There can be no doubt that internal affairs organizations, though at times not appreciated, are never ignored, never taken lightly. As the head of the New York Police Department's Patrolmen's Benevolent Association said recently, internal affairs members "would lock up their own mothers" (Boston Globe, 19 July 1992). More than any other control system studied, internal systems force street police officers to consider prospectively the consequences of their actions. Police officers often talk about IA in the locker room and on the street; its influence is ever present.

There is another reason to believe in the efficacy of learning from the internal review process. Internal systems seem to be most effective at generating individual learning among errant police officers. For learning to develop, street cops and their supervisors must accept as "reasonable" the feedback they receive from a review mechanism. When the source of that feedback is an internal body, populated with the officer's peers, such acceptance is more likely. Indeed, the overwhelming majority of street officers believe that other cops will bring an expertise to review mechanisms that is lacking in nonpolice people.

One must acknowledge also that internal systems are less likely to "get in the way" of informal learning channels, which could limit peer-oriented learning. When a complaint of a minor nature is turned into a case by an external system, the police officers involved tend to become defensive. They seek legal counsel. No matter how apparently minor the incident may be, they tend to react in a negative, audacious manner to being held to answer by outsiders.

There is no doubt that learning is better generated by systems that allow sergeants, beat partners, and other fellow cops to become involved in teaching errant officers more acceptable behavior patterns. The creative sergeant, for example, might assign an excellent officer to a partnership with a cop who is receiving "attitude" complaints. The supervisor might ask an older, respected officer to "have a talk with" a younger cop who is learning bad habits. Or the effective sergeant might take a police officer aside and counsel the individual in a positive manner about problematic behavior. These sorts of informal, unofficious, subcultural teaching experiments go on all the time in modern departments. Oakland, for example, has a "peer review" system, *invented by patrol officers at the squad-room level*, that handles potential problems in a positive way. (This is discussed in Chapter 7.)

This kind of learning is almost impossible to generate within the framework of external review. The strength of the police subculture tends to work against opening up the minds of young officers to change.

Internal review does have its drawbacks with respect to learning. In their attempts to be rigorous and thorough, some IA systems can be guilty of overzealousness; that is, they are so much on the minds of the police that they produce counterproductive results. Several of the Oakland Police Department's officers outlined examples of IA investigative zeal that they felt was illegal, semilegal, or, at the very least, inappropriate. These practices

118

may generate poor morale among patrol officers. The administration and the system become unfair, tyrannical enemies. Productivity may drop off as a result of investigative excesses; arrests may diminish; and citations may not be issued as rigorously. Police officers can begin to lack the aggressiveness that is necessary for the civilian populace to receive the police service it requires. As one officer put it, "Why bother with people's problems if the administration is just gonna hassle with you when you do get involved."

The comments of William K. Muir, Jr., are illustrative. He discusses one chief's "reign of terror," wherein he used the internal affairs process so ruthlessly and tyrannically that it violated "every assumption of due process." This IA system was slanted *against* police officers. Consequently, Muir notes:

> The policemen came to treat Internal Affairs as an unscrupulous enemy. The lack of dispassionate neutrality entitled good men to lie to it and deceive it and try to beat it. . . . By abjuring the limits of judicial inquiry, Internal Affairs lost its moral entitlement to be treated fairly in return. Men who would not have felt right about lying in a courtroom found themselves justifying purposeful deception in defiance of the naked force of Internal Affairs. (1977: 248)

Today's police are the products of thirty years of education. They have been given a feeling for procedural safeguards that are central to the concept of limited government. When the internal investigative system ignores these safeguards, as well as normal concepts of fair play, the legitimacy of that organization suffers in the minds of the troops and the learning potential also decreases. Its ability to function, then, can be severely limited by police secrecy and solidarity.

In an example from the Contra Costa Sheriff's Department, the department fell victim to a scandal in 1975 involving several deputies who were fired for stealing. Since no internal investigatory body existed at that time, the sheriff himself had to appoint a group of officers to handle the investigations. After they had completed their work on the scandal, and before they were reassigned to their original positions, these investigatory police officers were "loosed" on the department with no particular job assignments. Almost as an experiment, the Sheriff had them carry out clandestine surveillance of officers on the street.

The results of having this type of spying going on in and around the Patrol Division were devastating. The Sheriff's Department officers were upset and disheartened. The first-line supervisors (sergeants) were outraged. They saw this "spy" group as an entity completely external to the chain of command, answering to no one to whom the supervisors could protest. "Snitch and Snatch," as the investigative officers were dubbed by the troops, popped up here and there, reporting all forms of the most "unimportant" behavior patterns (such as having coffee for longer than fifteen minutes). Morale plummeted. The sergeants joined the line officers in universally decrying the investigators.

Most important, the citizenry suffered. Police officers who had once been ambitious and hard-working became apathetic and cynical. Many of the patrol officers became "anonymous citizens in uniform." They became uninterested in the problems of everyday citizens. Policing suffered to a great extent because the integrity of the organization's management was in question.

Under such circumstances, police officers may begin to shy away from certain types of troublesome situations. They may stop experimenting with different methods of interpersonal problem-solving and instead "play it by the book." This tendency was particularly important in the rookie cops studied by Muir (1977: 251): "The reign of terror appeared to inhibit 'taking a chance,' the trial and error necessary to a young policeman's development. It made the young officer too responsible too quickly, forcing him to adhere to a proclaimed way of doing things rather than encouraging him to discover an appropriate way for himself."

Overly tenacious internal review in Muir's study of the Laconia Police Department thus tended to create rigid, rule-oriented police officers. Many arrests ensued in situations in which the interests of justice might have eschewed official intervention. Then too, laws were not enforced when common sense or compassion might dictate otherwise.

In the Contra Costa Sheriff's Department and the Laconia Police Department, as morale slipped, the status of each department's worst cynics was elevated. Their recusant explanations of internal review activities found support in the actions of investigators. Worse still, the process fed on itself over time. As the cynics gained a larger audience, they became louder and more in evidence, and they played on their own newly found status. Every action of the internal investigative team became suspect. Soon each administrative policy statement and each suggestion from a supervisor received comment from the cynics. They were tireless in indicating the potentially negative repercussions of any policy or action. Exhortations that morale would worsen owing to such-and-such a policy change became self-fulfilling prophecies. The general negativity that is a part of the police experience was magnified by such cynical dissidents.

The judicial system provided no defense to the street cops who faced an oppressive regime. Police and sheriff's officers saw that the legal system shrouded factually guilty criminals in cloaks of protective procedures while it denied the same to their "honest and hard-working" fellow officers. Though the legal analogy is not technically correct, this apparent disparity of treatment deeply offended the officers' collective sense of justice.

Thus the tendency for officers to suffer from anomie was exacerbated. Due process goals had been defined for these police officers by the institutionalized training process of the modern American police system. Yet the "reign of terror" in both Contra Costa and Laconia indicated to these cops that the means of attaining those goals were not at their disposal. What is more, such means were at the disposal of "murderers, muggers, and thieves." The counterproductive effects of crises were felt within these departments for some time afterward. The reverberations of the IA department's tyranny were manifested in residual resentment and cynicism, so easily passed from one generation of officers to the next.

In any organization, those who are responsible for quality control can be the subjects of ridicule and ostracism. This is particularly true in some police internal review mechanisms. Those who work in IA can appear to have transgressed subcultural norms of solidarity (*New York Times*, 29 July 1992).

In departments in which the chief does not promote a positive, high-status image for IA, there can be significant problems for former IA officers reassigned to regular duties. Sometimes these officers suffer social ostracism from the troops they used to monitor (though this is by no means always the case, according to officers interviewed who are so situated). On occasion, open hostility toward former IA officers makes it unwise for the organization to assign them to normal duties after their investigative time is served. Because of this, it can be argued that intra-organizational tension might actually be lessened if police review responsibilities were removed and given to civilians.

Finally, with respect to learning, one can analyze the financial costs of the system. The Oakland IA process costs the taxpayers a little under $1,000 per complaint investigation. This is about standard for police-operated systems. This figure may seem high to some, but internal review is less expensive than civilian review by a factor of three or four to one. In a succeeding chapter readers will find a comparison of the costs of each system. What follows here is a brief summary of the evaluation of internal review systems.

SUMMATION

To suggest that [Internal Affairs] units can operate as the world's greatest washing machine—everything that goes in dirty comes out clean!—is understandable. It is obvious to many people that such units fail to vigorously pursue abuses of authority, abuses of power, and arrogant bullying. (Germann 1971: 420)

A. C. Germann's statement is indicative of a legitimacy problem critical to this police review systems study. It is also indicative of a lack of practical knowledge of the operations of police internal investigative units.

As evidenced by the study of the Oakland Police Department, the classic internal review model is not at all as sinister as has been asserted by external observers. The deterrent effects of internal investigative mechanisms are significant. Police officers on the street are cognizant of the existence and effectiveness of internal control systems. They often consider the ramifications of their actions with respect to those systems. There is much to be learned from the professionalism and genuine dedication of police investigators as they seek to clean their own houses, and to further their subcultural goals. These goals are not necessarily at odds with society's interests in holding police officers accountable for their actions.

There are, however, significant problems in legitimizing such potentially self-protecting processes as internal review. The community's perceived legitimacy of police review systems is of critical significance. Despite its pluses, the IA system faces tremendous problems in developing this legitimacy. The credibility gap between the actual integrity of Oakland's system and the perceptions of those outside it speaks to the overall credibility problem of police institutions. It cannot be ignored, even in the face of the effectiveness of behavior control of IA systems.

Then too, it must be remembered that Oakland's system is exemplary. It represents the very best that can be expected of internal review. It is manned by dedicated, competent people who treat the public's problems seriously. It is supported by a chief who is unswerving in his efforts to protect (and require) its objectivity. Thus the problems that are endemic to Oakland's system are the very least that one can expect from such a process.

The next chapter considers review processes that may appear more legitimate but that are substantially less effective at deterring police malpractice than are internal review mechanisms.

5 Civilian Review

No subject has generated more controversy over the relationship between the police and the community than civilian review. Calls for this type of review have come from politicians and academicians of a variety of political persuasions. A concomitant concern over the "threat" of civilian review is almost ubiquitous in police circles. From police executives to patrol officers, the notion that civilians might review alleged police misconduct is the source of great apprehension.

Civilian review of police conduct is a growing phenomenon. Nevertheless, it is still used in a very small percentage of cities. Most of the systems that have been set up have been created during the last ten years. Thus the long-term institutionalization of civilian review processes has occurred in only a few locations. In addition, research into the field has been sparse. There has been a great deal of theorizing around the issues of civilian review, but precious little studying has actually been done that tells how it works in operation.

As noted in the Introduction, the politics accompanying the formation of civilian review boards have traditionally caused vehement reactions from police officers and police executives. The fight of the New York Patrolman's Benevolent Association to dismantle the civilian board in that city is illustrative.

> Press advertisements and T.V. commercials pictured the police with their hands tied or handcuffed while a white girl walked down a dark street in a setting which suggested that she might be assaulted at any moment. [In another advertisement] a policeman was pictured as saying, "Next time I turn my back!"—implying that the way to avoid civilian complaints was by inaction. (Black 1968: 209)

Civilian review is seldom debated in a rational and logical fashion. It is much more than just an alternative method of personnel management. Usually, calls for external review of the police occur during crisis periods in which the police have clashed with citizens in violent situations. In fact, Paul West of the Police Executive Research Forum gives credit to "a series of incidents in which particularly flagrant abuses of power and authority by officers" kept the civilianization movement alive during the 1970s (West, n.d.: 8).

Charges of racism, brutality, and corruption frequently surround discussions of civilian review. On occasion, this rhetoric spills over into the absurd, and genuinely antipolice rhetoric inflames the debate. The police response to such discussion is aggressive. Witness the statement of patrol officer John J. Cassese, a former president of the Patrolman's Benevolent Association of Philadelphia, when referring to the call for a civilian review board in that city, "I'm sick and tired of giving in to minority groups. Racial minorities will not be satisfied until you get all Negros and Puerto Ricans on the board and every policeman who goes in front of it is found guilty" (*New York Times*, 29 May 1966).

J. Edgar Hoover, former head of the FBI, stated openly and frequently that he thought Communists were behind civilian review boards. As Hoover put it, "Their altruistic mouthings are a front and a sham[,] for they have already prejudged law enforcement as an enemy to their nihilistic cause. Their real objective is to intimidate and harass police" (FBI *Law Enforcement Bulletins* 1970). There is no doubt that these rather hysterical assertions have lessened in number and impact in the recent past. However, there are circles in which such admonitions are still taken seriously (Goldsmith 1991; Manning 1977; Moore and Stephens 1991; Terrill 1990).

On one hand, the central theme of the discussions of those who favor civilian review is intuitively persuasive; some external perspective should be brought to bear on the investigation and deliberation of allegations of police misconduct, or the police will be left to police themselves. On the other hand, there have been some interesting assertions over time about the failure of civilian review (Americans for Effective Law Enforcement 1982; Christopher Commission 1991; Garmire 1982; U.S. Civil Rights Commission 1981). Without citation or analysis, it is often tersely noted that civilian review boards have simply "failed." The lack of substantiation is understandable. This study has found no evidence that civilianization can not work or has not worked. The demise of several civilian boards because of intense pressure from police officer groups aside, those who have observed civilian boards in operation generally have not come away with a negative appraisal of this model. They have not found civilian review to be abusive of police officer rights or less than responsive to citizen-complainants. In short, the opposition is supported by an intuitive logic that is perhaps based on paranoia about "what might happen" under civilian scrutiny.

This chapter evaluates a model system of civilian police review, that of the Berkeley Police Review Commission. The PRC has its own completely independent investigatory staff and procedures. It has the authority to recommend disciplinary action and policy changes to the city manager and to the City Council. This makes Berkeley's system unusual. It is one reason that the PRC is one of the most completely independent systems in America. The PRC board members report directly to the city manager, bypassing the chief of police. Occasionally, the PRC has been involved directly with the City Council during the course of that body's consideration of particularly volatile issues.

POLICE REVIEW COMMISSION PROCEDURES

The Berkeley Police Review Commission was created by a vote of the people of Berkeley on 17 April 1973, and it is the oldest continuously operated civilian review system in the United States. Its enabling referendum was passed after a tumultuous political struggle. Radical politicians, favoring the formation of the board, argued that the Berkeley police were systematically racist and brutal in their application of the law. The predictable police reaction was to decry the referendum as a political attempt to control the police department (*Berkeley Gazette*, 8 January 1973; 16 April 1973; 19 April 1973).

Initially, the members of the PRC expected little cooperation from the Berkeley Police Department, and perhaps they did not desire any. The PRC, rather than being populated by civilians interested in doing an objective job of evaluating complaints against the police, was composed of numerous board members who were outspoken critics of the police department. This analysis of the nature of the political stance of commissioners is the consensus of the commissioners who sat on the initial board, commissioners who sat on subsequent boards, individuals involved in the Ombudsman's Office in Berkeley, people working for the City Manager's Office, street police officers, and police administrators. All agree that included in the ranks of those taking office initially as commissioners were a majority of "antipolice" people.

The expected conflicts between the Berkeley Police Department and the Berkeley Review Commission were not long in developing. Lawsuits filed by the police officers' union sought to limit the board's authority or to destroy it altogether. Shows of emotional rhetoric and public venting of antipolice and antiestablishment ideas were a regular part of PRC meetings. Even complaint hearings sometimes degenerated into diatribes about what ailed the Berkeley Police Department and American policing in general.

Police officers in Berkeley already mistrusted the PRC when it was first formed. They possessed a police subcultural prejudice about the idea to begin with. They then faced personalities on the board who convinced them that their prejudgments were correct. Even after twenty years of operation, tension remains between the PRC and the members of the police department and police union. Over time, the stand of the Berkeley Police Officers' Association has been mollified. This union, which was involved on numerous occasions in litigation that questioned administrative practices, access to personal files, and the authority of both the PRC and the police department's Internal Affairs bureau, now has chosen a more rational, cooperative attitude about civilian review. Concomitantly, after almost two decades of operation, the PRC is finally beginning to have an impact on the police department.

Recently, the PRC has been much more politically moderate than it was initially, and the difficulties and animosity that it originally encountered have lessened to some extent. The new police chief, who was appointed in 1990, has been cooperative and receptive beyond what had been experienced historically.

The Berkeley PRC is composed of nine volunteer members, 127

each appointed by a separate member of the nine-member City Council. (In some jurisdictions, civilian review boards are populated by members picked by the local mayor.) The Berkeley system is designed to widen the political spectrum and the indirect accountability of the PRC. Observations of the PRC in operation over several decades confirm that this diversity rule has worked. Instead of representing a thin slice of local political perspectives, the Berkeley commission represents a broad spectrum of attitudes and philosophies.

In addition to its oversight of specific complaints, the PRC has another charge. Because the PRC is advisory to the city manager, it holds public discussions regarding police departmental policies. All nine members sit together when considering policy recommendations. Three-member tribunals sit to hear individual cases of alleged misconduct. The staff of the organization includes three investigators and several clerical support people. The 1992 PRC budget contained $320,000 of direct support, with a number of additional operating costs born elsewhere within the city's fiscal structure. According to the chair of the PRC, the overall cost of operation is approaching a half-million dollars per year.

The police department monitored by the Berkeley Police Review Commission is an unusual one. Its Patrol Division, with approximately one hundred uniformed officers, polices a city of 104,000 residents. The department is largely made up of college graduates, and at least two years of college are required for all officers. A number of street police officers have advanced degrees in criminal justice, law, or the social sciences.

The Berkeley police organization consciously avoids the militaristic trappings emblematic of so many police departments. Officers wear uniforms, but grooming standards and military-type inspections are eschewed. Some police officers sport full beards, and several men have ponytail-length hair. Because of their educational level, Berkeley officers enjoy a great deal of latitude when working on criminal investigations. Street officers followup all felonies (even homicides) with the help of a support staff of detectives. This felony follow-up responsibility is unparalleled in large police organizations.

In Berkeley, complaints per police officer and per citizen are the highest of any department studied. The members of the police department are well educated and known for their restraint under trying circumstances. Nevertheless, it seems as if the large minority populations, and the members of the intellectual or academic communities in particular, generate a great number of grievances. It is unclear why this is so. The Berkeley Police Department has traditionally been acclaimed as a pacesetter among police agencies, both by law-enforcement practitioners and by external analysts.

Two separate organizations exist in Berkeley that receive and investigate citizen complaints about the police. The Police Review Commission is completely separate from the Berkeley Police Department. It receives, investigates, deliberates, and makes decisions on citizen complaints independently. An internal affairs section also operates within the police departmental structure. (California requires police departments to have formalized processes for the reception and investigation of complaints [California Penal Code].) Berkeley's internal review mechanism is similar to Oakland's, which was outlined in Chapter 4.

Any civilian wishing to complain about police procedures or specific abusive acts in Berkeley can grieve either to the Internal Affairs organization or to the Police Review Commission. The yearly caseload for the PRC is about one hundred cases. The Internal Affairs Section caseload is about 160. The PRC investigates only those cases that citizens bring directly to it. The IA system investigates those cases filed at the police department *and* those cases filed at the PRC.

Input Structures

The Berkeley PRC is located in a city office building next to the police building. All walk-in complainants are interviewed by the PRC's civilian investigators. In 1991 the PRC handled 60 complainants' inquiries "informally" and investigated 104 cases. Its rate of sustained findings of police officer misconduct was 17 percent for 1990. In use of excessive force cases, the PRC's sustained rate is slightly higher, at 20 percent.

Of course, the literature about civilian review is replete with statements about the "tip of the iceberg." There is almost no

realistic way of determining how many unreported, yet legitimate, complaints might exist. Some studies indicate that there
are areas, particularly in inner cities, where significant numbers
of people report observing police misbehavior on a regular basis.
Law enforcement practitioners, however, often present evidence
to try to disprove the existence of an "iceberg" of complaints.
They point out that the creation of civilian review boards has
not increased complaint filing. In fact, this is true in most jurisdictions, according to comparable internal affairs and civilian review intake data obtained by this study. Actually, as is true in
Berkeley, evidence suggests that civilian-operated systems take
in fewer complaints than do parallel police-operated systems.
This may be because not all complainants desire the openness of
civilian systems. Complaints may be filed by telephone or by
mail in Berkeley. For the convenience of investigators, however,
the PRC attempts to get the complainant to file in person (as
does Internal Affairs in Oakland).

Civilian review boards have varying procedures, some of
which are subject to the same criticisms as are police investigatory processes. For example, a body calling itself a "civilian review board" in Richmond, California, requires complainants to
sign complaints and gives a stern warning about the prosecution
of false statements. Not unlike the police officers' bill of rights
in Maryland, this procedure can be criticized on the grounds that
it is intimidating to citizens. It quashes one of the arguments
put forth historically in favor of civilian review.

The Richmond situation illustrates that civilianization does
not necessarily expand externally perceived legitimacy or develop substantively different procedural effectiveness than that
of internal review. Just as internal affairs systems should not be
considered inappropriate merely because they are police-operated, so too Richmond's review mechanism shows that civilian
review boards are not necessarily more "open" or legitimate.

Irrespective of Richmond's procedure, at the Berkeley PRC (as
at most civilianized systems) complaints of all sorts are accepted; complaints filed in person, over the telephone, in the
mail, and anonymously are all considered legitimate until
proven otherwise.

130   In its early operations, the Berkeley civilian police review sys-

tem rarely short-circuited complaints with "satisficing" explanations of police procedure. Because of the chances for abuse, every complaint generated an official investigation at the PRC. This procedure was followed for ten years because those involved in the PRC policy development were particularly concerned about the externally perceived legitimacy of their system. They did not wish to appear to be apologists for the police department. This practice meant that early PRC hearings often involved complaints that would have been handled informally elsewhere. But it also made some hearings appear to be frivolous.

Civilian review boards have historically allowed a great deal of latitude for "satisficing" explanations. In Philadelphia, Pennsylvania, for example, a conciliatory process existed, which many felt was an important plus in that system (Bray 1962; Coxe 1961). This kind of short-circuiting mechanism also operated in the ill-fated New York City Civilian Review Board of the mid-1960s (Black 1967).

Over time, the Berkeley PRC has loosened up its "satisficing" procedures. It has given latitude to intake personnel to give explanations of police policy and behavior where applicable. The system in Berkeley has begun another interesting development, that of mediation, though this is still in an experimental stage.

The PRC allows mediation between citizens and police officers when complaints are of a minor nature. Thus mediation occurs only when the PRC staff are sure that the nature of the complaint does not warrant it being handled officiously and only when the complainant agrees to the informality. Also, the police officer or officers involved must agree to the process. The police officer and citizen-complainant hold mediation or "settlement" meetings with one member of the PRC. A company that provides such services to businesses and to families in need of counseling has trained the commissioners in mediation techniques. The participants in mediation attempt to generate an understanding of what occurred, to discover the actors' different perceptions, and to agree on a resolution.

This mediation process, though in its infancy, shows promise for allowing several dynamics to obtain at once. When it is coupled with communications with the Training Division of the police department, it lets individual police officers and the police organization learn from mistakes and misperceptions. It allows complainants to air their grievances and to receive an open and empathetic response from the government. Mediation also saves a great deal of time and money.

The discussion of PRC procedures now turns from input to the investigative phase.

Investigations

The PRC investigator begins the investigation process in much the same manner as would an IA investigator. As is true of the overwhelming majority of citizens' complaints, statements taken from police officers, complainants, and witnesses make up most of the investigation. Rarely is there any physical evidence to consider or any objective evidence supporting either party.

The police department and the PRC are both required to notify the other organization of complaints received. The PRC offers its services to those who have complained directly to the police by sending complainants a form letter. The police department's Internal Affairs Section investigates complaints filed at the PRC and at the police department. Thus the caseloads of the two organizations are different. The IA staff investigates about one-and-a-half times as many complaints as does the PRC staff.

The civilians who investigate complaints at the PRC have been trained in law or in mediation. They begin at the PRC with no formal training in investigation; however, some possess substantially more legal knowledge than do police IA investigators. This legal background is reflected in the language of PRC written investigations. Case citations and legal terminology are often included as part of PRC investigative summaries. Such case citations, language, and rule explanations are absent from most IA investigations. They are considered superfluous for the audience at which they are aimed, police supervisors.

As noted in Chapter 3, civilian systems meet opposition from within municipal political hierarchies because their openness can threaten the city's fiscal base. Almost all civilianized systems pride themselves on their openness. (There are exceptions, such as Richmond, California, whose review system holds no open complaint hearings or deliberations of any kind.) But because of concern over civil litigation, city attorneys and city managers usually side with police organizations and resist the opening up of access to information contained in complaint investigations.

This dynamic poses an access problem for civilian review mechanisms. Police investigators from Internal Affairs can, of course, obtain access to any police information they require. Booking slips, arrest reports, prisoner property inventories, and so forth are all at issue. The pragmatic reality is that civilian investigators sometimes must fight for access to this kind of information (even in court) and this creates delays. In some jurisdictions, it also creates "holes" in investigations. Despite lawsuits filed by the police to thwart PRC access to information, in Berkeley the civilian board is now generally able to achieve access to all information that is required for its investigations. With the backing of the city manager, and the somewhat begrudging support of police management, IA and the PRC now exchange information on a daily basis.

In the beginning, the PRC's procedures included advising police officers of their constitutional right to remain silent and to have an attorney present during questioning. The California policeman's bill of rights gives the officer the right to have an attorney or representative present during an administrative questioning session. Yet administrative law clearly does *not* allow the right to remain silent during such interrogations. This PRC convention was established in the interests of fairness to police officers. Although this was a laudable goal, as a policy it was a disaster.

Once the Berkeley police officers found that they need not talk to the PRC investigators when they were accused of wrongdoing, they did not. Under the advice of their professional association's lawyer, police officers refused to give statements to the PRC. Witness police officers were required to talk, but accused officers were not, and the statements of the accused were absent both from the written report of the investigation and from the record of the PRC hearing procedure. This made PRC processes less than thorough and well balanced. Cases were essentially

133

formed around the statements of civilians, without regard to what accused officers might offer in the way of explanation for their actions.

Thus the PRC's early efforts to protect the rights of accused officers backfired. They produced exactly the opposite impact as intended. PRC hearings had all the earmarks of the kangaroo courts that police officers throughout the nation always believed citizen review systems would have. This type of system turned out to be patently unfair to the police perspective. It offered one side of what are always two-sided debates. This one-sidedness in the Berkeley PRC confirmed the worst fears of the police, and it gave ammunition to police elsewhere fighting the battle against civilian review.

In recent years the PRC, the Berkeley chief, and the city manager have worked out a procedure for requiring the participation of accused officers in the process. When it is time to interview the accused police officer, the PRC formally requests the officer's appearance before its investigators. It sends a written memorandum to the city manager. The city manager then advises the chief of the request, and the chief, in turn, writes a memo to the individual officer, ordering attendance at the interview.

This process is long and tiresome, but it had to evolve because of the constant legal maneuverings of the participants. This case-by-case procedure does seem somewhat problematic in that there is no generalized departmental regulation that requires officer participation in all cases. No one anticipates a conscious lack of cooperation to develop. But the procedure does give the Berkeley chief the power to keep his officers out of an investigation if he sees fit to do so. This is an analytical sticking point in the system.

It takes a great deal of time for the PRC to conduct investigations. In fact, because the usual investigation time is three months, the PRC's investigative and hearing processes are not completed until well after those of the police department's internal review. Many times the chief of police has already meted out punishment for an errant officer before the PRC has even finished its hearing. This often makes the PRC's deliberations moot. It is not so much the civilian investigative staff's actions that cause such delays as it is the difficulty the civilian commissioners have in scheduling their hearings around their private and working lives. The lag time is a source of concern to the police and to the staff of the PRC alike. This study's police officer survey found that 65 percent of police officers believe that the delays of the civilian system have a negative impact on the effectiveness of that system. Only 2 percent of respondents thought the delays might have some positive payoffs; 16 percent of police officers surveyed believed the delays to be insignificant; and others "didn't know."

This presents some rather awkward situations. The city manager usually goes along with the discipline handed out by the chief. So the PRC's moot hearings have led to some additional cynicism in Berkeley police officers. A number of officers noted that the hearings are "a joke . . . because discipline has already been handed out."

After the completion of the investigation, in Berkeley the next step in the review mechanism is a public hearing. The following describes the inquiry process in general and Berkeley's Board of Inquiry in particular.

Complaint Hearings

The Berkeley PRC hearing process is much more formalized than is that of Internal Affairs. Investigations result in public hearings before three PRC commissioners. The nine commissioners rotate through these "Board of Inquiry" duties. Boards of inquiry hold semijudicialized hearings. The standard of proof is one of "clear, convincing evidence."

Evidentiary standards are rather lax, from a judicial perspective. Much evidence is accepted at hearings that would not be accepted before the bar. The Board of Inquiry uses an overall standard of "fairness" to the citizen, to allow the kind of hearsay that is not normally heard in a courtroom. This fact, of course, is not lost on the police officers of Berkeley. They are accustomed to courtroom procedures and know when hearsay is being admitted. They tend to resent this rather open-ended caveat.

Civilians may be represented by counsel before the board, but they normally are not. They may call witnesses and cross-examine all who testify. Accused officers may testify, but they often eschew this opportunity; however, witness officers must testify. After testimony has been heard and evidence accepted, the Board of Inquiry discusses the case in public. After discussion, the commissioners vote on outcomes, and formal notice of a decision is then sent from the commission to the accused police officer and to the citizen complainant.

Even though the confusion of complaint review functions with policy formulation functions has been eliminated from the Berkeley Police Review Commission's method of operation, it remains a problem for many civilian review systems. This is a critical point, because discussions of general policy have no place in specific complaint deliberations. An example is illustrative. During a hearing regarding an allegation of misconduct by the police, the members of Oakland Citizens' Complaint Board (OCCB), or civilian review board, were discussing the behavior of several police officers who were part of a drug enforcement task force. It was the job of these officers to ferret out drug activity and to make dealing and purchasing drugs difficult. A suspected drug dealer had accused the officers of harassment. In the middle of the hearing about this particular incident, the civilian members of the hearing board began to discuss the appropriateness of the police department's use of police personnel in this kind of task force. Specifically, several board members took issue with the assignment of police officers to "no particular beat" for the purposes of "harassing" citizens. The expenditure of tax dollars in a task force approach to a particularized form of crime may or may not be considered acceptable by the citizens of a city. It is perfectly reasonable for representatives of the community to debate the existence of this task force and its tactics or for them to discuss the chief's thoughts about developing such an elite corps. But it is *not* acceptable for an accountability process to mix its debate over such policies with its consideration of individual complaints. It is *not* appropriate to hold the police officer on the street accountable for the existence of such a tactical unit.

Such behavior by members of a review mechanism changes the rules by which police are held accountable—in the middle of the game. It makes the system inconsistent. It causes police officers themselves to question the mechanism's integrity. These kinds of actions by review systems amount to ex post facto rule application.

In addition, when those in review systems turn an individual complaint hearing into a policy formulation discussion, they ignore the part police executives should play in policy formulation. Civilian and police professional perspectives go hand in hand in this arena. To attempt to develop policy for a police organization without community-based input is to invite the police to become a law unto themselves. Yet to create policy without utilizing the feedback and experience of professional administrators is equally irrational. It ignores the pragmatic expertise that the career police officer develops over time. Civilians and police professionals are partners in policy development. To have one go about it without the other, as was the case during this particular hearing in Oakland, is to operate the process without benefit of all available data.

Finally, such a procedure upsets the delicate political balance that police review systems must maintain in order to function effectively. The police are neither likely to cooperate with, nor to give credence to, an accountability mechanism that does not give deference to their experience and wisdom. No professional organization or group of individuals will do so.

Unfortunately, such a mixture of policy and complaint adjudication is not the exception in the field of civilian review. Numerous civilian review structures suffer from this confusion of functions.

From the discussion of hearings to analysis now turns to the decision-making process.

Outcomes and Discipline

After the Berkeley PRC has held a hearing on a complaint, it sends copies of its finding and of the investigative report to the city manager. If a police officer's disciplinary action includes three or more days of suspension, the city manager must make that suspension himself. This is an extra accountability loop for the protection of officers. When the chief of police wishes to assign a suspension, the city manager receives two complaint investigations, one from the Berkeley Police Department Internal Affairs Section and one from the PRC. The city manager must then weigh the evidence from the two and decide the outcome.

All parties in Berkeley agree that only on extremely rare occasions do the outcomes of IA and the PRC differ, and on those occasions, the city manager invariably sides with the chief. No official statistics are kept of these infrequent occurrences, but according to the city manager they occur only once or twice each year.

For the overall pattern of cases (grave and minor combined) the Berkeley city manager believes that the police department is slightly *more* prone to finding police officers guilty of misconduct than is the Police Review Commission. This intuitive feeling of the Berkeley city manager is consistant with several studies in which patterns of outcomes have been tracked for civilian review bodies. Civilian review boards have historically been reluctant to find the police guilty of misconduct. They have found officers not guilty most of the time or even much of the time. Of the 530 cases heard by the Philadelphia board from 1958 through 1965, only 38 cases resulted in recommendations of disciplinary action (Philadelphia Police Advisory Board 1965). In New York City, of the 135 cases disposed of by its board in the 1960s only five eventuated in recommendations for discipline (*New York Times*, 4 March 1967). The Berkeley system "has assigned blame in a far lower percentage of citizen charges against the police than has the Berkeley Police Department's internal complaint mechanisms" (California Peace Officers' Association 1970).

The civilian review processes developed during the 1980s have shown similar results. The Office of Citizens' Complaints in San Francisco, California, sustains only 1 percent of its investigations against the police (*San Francisco Chronicle*, 9 May 1990); the Honolulu, Hawaii, board sustains 6 percent of its cases; and the Cleveland, Ohio, board sustains 10 percent. The board in Cincinnati, Ohio, sustains cases at a much higher rate of 23.7 percent, but that is still lower than the police internal number of 25 percent of cases sustained nationwide.

Systems in operation elsewhere sustain even fewer complaints against the police. In Minneapolis, Minnesota, a system put into place in April 1991 received 111 cases in its first ten months and sustained only two of them. In Oakland's civilianized system, public hearings were held in only thirty-eight cases in all of 1987, 1988, and 1989. In only one of those hearings was an officer found guilty of misconduct. But are such numbers, in fact, important in a substantive sense? At this point, it is only relevant that civilian boards seem to be *less* prone to find misconduct than their internalized counterparts.

It is interesting to note that only recently (1991) has the Berkeley system reported a year in which it sustained more complaints than did IA. This is the first instance of a higher rate of findings of misconduct from the civilian review process that this study has found in seventeen years of research. In other words, *not at any time in the history of civilian review had a civilian system found the police guilty more often than had an internal system* until Berkeley did so in 1991.

As with civil service boards, systems that put citizens in a position to review police behavior invariably act in a liberal way toward individual police officers. Civilian review is neither oppressive of police officers' rights nor responsive (in a "winner" and "loser" sense) to complainants' rights. Those in law enforcement who expect that civilian review will be unfair and counterproductive because of civilians' overaggressiveness are simply wrong. Concomitantly, those outside law enforcement who believe that civilian review will be a panacea that "cures" police abuses by tenaciously pursuing malpractice are also wrong.

Furthermore, where police commissions or city managers review the findings of the chief's internal review system, such as in San Francisco, Los Angeles, or Richmond, they almost never disagree with the chief. This extra line of potential accountability, then, tends to be ineffective. Great deference is shown to the police chief by administrators outside the law enforcement experience. As one city manager who is faced with parallel internal and external investigations put it, "I never argue with the chief. He knows what's best for the department."

The PRC also has its policy formulation responsibilities, of course. Sometimes the commission holds hearings and asks people from the audience to comment. This is done in the name of democracy, but it does make for some volatile, emotional, and

139

even irrational dialogue. For example, in one discussion in the early days of the PRC a citizen suggested that the police need not use force under *any* circumstances, *even to overcome violent behavior.* This comment was communicated to the rank and file police officers of Berkeley. Their predictable reaction was to smirk at the facile view of reality held by the PRC and its "followers." Generally, those few police officers who have paid attention to civilian review rhetoric, which is not many, have tended to focus on the more illogical discussions of the PRC proponents and to attack the practical naiveté of those favoring civilian review.

In its recommendations regarding policy, again advisory to the city manager, the PRC has taken the same route that the development of all relations between the police and the commission has taken; the recommendations, in the beginning, were ineffectual, but they have since moved in the direction of openness and significance. When the PRC began its early, antagonistic relationship with the Berkeley Police Department, there was so little respect between the organizations that the chief of police essentially ignored policy debates and suggestions. The chief and the police, in general, were actively involved in deprecating the PRC and its potential. And because the city manager also largely ignored the PRC, its policy formulation functions were useless exercises in pontification.

There is good reason to believe that an external observer, interested in the well-being of an organization but ignorant of the day-to-day exigencies of its operations, can at times see resolutions to problems not apparent to those within the organization. The old "cannot see the forest for the trees" metaphor is applicable here. In the case of citizens' complaints, patterns may emerge that a PRC-type of organization can see that the police chief or the administrative hierarchy cannot.

At least in some cases, the limitations of review can be alleviated by changing the emphasis of review from punishment of a particular officer to recommendations for changes in procedure and regulations. This has been a traditional function of the Scandinavian Ombudsman, and American review boards can (and sometimes do) undertake such a rule-making function. (Chevigny 1969: 271)

As the Berkeley PRC approaches two decades of operations, the current police chief has seen in it the positive possibility of obtaining community feedback concerning potential policies. As police accountability theorists have variously suggested, the use of police review commissions is becoming a viable method to develop two-way communication. Police departments explain their policies and actions to commissions, and the commissions reflect on policy and procedures as indirect representatives of the people. Thus a legislative accountability loop is being developed in the best interests of everyone concerned.

A recent example of this changed relationship is relevant. On his own impetus, the Berkeley chief brought a potential policy question to the commission for its reflection. It had to do with the formation of a special group of police officers into a riot-control squad. Knowing that the issue would be the kind that becomes highly political in Berkeley, the chief anticipated that the commission would eventually (sooner rather than later, in all probability) hold discussions about it. Instead of waiting for this, and in order to obtain feedback from citizens, the chief brought the riot-squad issue to the commission. He asked the civilian review board what it thought about the formation of such a corps. Would it support such a move? Did it think that the people of Berkeley would do so?

The reaction of the commission was measurably positive. Some of the members that had been around for some time were very surprised at what the chief was asking. The chair was most receptive and thanked the chief profusely for asking for such advice in a proactive manner. The chief was cordial and professional, and the commission perceived him to be opening a new channel of communication that might change the relationship of the PRC and the police department substantially.

The chief, of course, had more in mind than formulating a policy. He was heading off a potentially volatile political reaction. In the long run, the chief could easily defend the decision to form such a tactical squad, if it were made in a cooperative manner with the civilian review board. If political or media-centered opposition developed, the Chief had allies on the commission already lined up in his defense.

As Malcolm Sparrow, Mark Moore, and David Kennedy point

out, "Police executives can protect themselves from unreasonable political voices by making sure that broad and legitimate community concerns are publicly framed, acknowledged, and served. That means, of course, that police will have to embrace community consultation processes rather than reluctantly submit to them" (1990: 161). This understanding by Berkeley's chief of police is both revolutionary and fascinating. It breaks new ground in the world of civilian review, and it indicates the positive and creative potential that such systems hold for the police. If other chiefs learn from the Berkeley chief, a new era in mutual understanding and cooperation may dawn in the area of police policy development.

Now that this study has thoroughly examined the procedures of a civilian police review model it is time to determine how this kind of system fares with respect to the three criteria of evaluation.

EVALUATIONS

The analysis of the internal affairs processes of Oakland concluded with a very mixed set of evaluations. Its internal investigations were rigorous, but the secrecy of the system was suspect. The prospective behavioral impact of internal systems, in general, was found to be quite effective, yet the amount of faith that external sources seem to have in police-operated review was discovered to be slight. The civilian review "report card" is similarly mixed. It outlines the distinctive trade-offs that make police review both an interesting and a disturbing topic. In the following discussion of the integrity of civilian systems, this study also points out some of the strengths that those in law enforcement perhaps did not expect to find.

Integrity

When this study analyzes the answers to the questions it has posed about Berkeley PRC's operations, the results show that Berkeley's system deserves a very good rating for integrity, for somewhat different reasons than those used to rationalize giving that same rating to Oakland's internal system. The

PRC's ease of access is important. It operates with nonpolice personnel, thereby making complainants more comfortable. This study found no negative dynamics associated with civilianized locations or with civilian personnel for complaint input.

When one considers investigations intuitively, one finds every reason to believe that those investigators who are removed from the police department and who are not members of the police subculture may be more rigorous in their pursuit of police malpractice. Their operations, in theory, are not subject to the hidden assumptions productive of the police experience. But there are reasons to question this logic. As argued in Chapter 4, these assumptions and these subcultural understandings about behavioral norms and standard operational procedures might provide investigators who are police officers with important information to use during their investigations or when they are hearing a case.

Consider a specific example. During an investigation in Berkeley, the civilian board put together a case in which it seemed to find facts congruent with a citizen's false arrest complaint. The police had arrested the individual for shoplifting. The citizen protested his innocence and, from the perspective of the police, attempted to "cover" his guilt by filing a complaint. He produced a friendly witness and a believable story. He maintained that he was prematurely arrested and that he had fully intended to pay for the goods. His witness confirmed that they had entered the business specifically to *purchase* these goods. According to the PRC's investigation, it appeared that the individual had been falsely accused and arrested.

The police investigator in Internal Affairs had the same statements and original information to go on, but in his investigation he discovered some additional data. Because the PRC's investigator was not a police officer, he did not think of checking the suspect's booking slip. The IA investigator realized from his police experience that it would be critical to see the suspect's "property tag," filled out at the time of arrest. It turned out that the complainant did not have any money on his person when he was arrested. In such a case, this is an important piece of evidence, indicating an intent to steal; with no money available, the individual certainly did not intend to make a purchase.   143

When he was confronted with the IA information, the individual dropped his complaint. He was later found guilty of petty theft.

If civilian-generated investigations can suffer from lack of specific knowledge, then so too can decision-making processes that depend on civilian investigations. The PRC's lack of understanding of subcultural norms and occupational standards can lead to unfair and, at times, even silly decisions.

There is no definitive answer to the question of which type of investigator is superior. The observations of a police officer in Chicago, one with a great number of complaints on his record, are interesting in this regard. This particular cop had been investigated in his younger years by Internal Affairs and in his later years by the Office of Professional Standards (OPS), a civilian review system. He offered that "guys from Internal Affairs are chicken s____. They want to fry everybody. They never quit 'til they've got something on everybody. The OPS guys [civilians] play the game fair. If they can't get ya, they drop it!" This comment about "soldiering" by civilian reviewers might help one balance the two sides of the debate about who is better at investigating complaints.

One should consider the argument that civilian complainants are more comfortable with civilian investigators. The intuitive logic of this argument is persuasive, and the complainant survey numbers bear this idea out (see Chapter 4). But, by the same logic, police officer witnesses should then be more comfortable with police officer investigators, and this study's data from police officer surveys bear *this* out (again, see Chapter 4). Civilian investigators may have even more trouble getting critical statements from police officers than police interrogators have because of the blue code of silence, and this may tend to make civilian-generated investigations suspect with respect to their completeness.

One, therefore, faces two pieces of self-serving conventional wisdom: From the police subculture comes the idea that the police perspective is important in complaint investigations because it assures rigor and thoroughness. From the civilian review proponent's side one hears that only an outside, nonpolice perspective can assure objectivity and tenacity. Can both of these axioms be true? Do review systems *need* to involve the police perspective and at the same time *need* to include an external, civilian perspective? The answer is yes, of course they do! It is critical to consider the community's perspective when one is holding the police accountable for their actions; yet to be fair to police officers, one must be moved to understand their training, street experiences, subcultural norms, and the day-to-day pragmatics of police work. The discussion of the problem of perspective, central both to this chapter and to the discussion of internal review, continues in Chapter 6, where this study discusses some of the utility generated when a system is created with the specific purpose of putting together the two perspectives and their separate sets of strengths.

Evaluation of civilian review must take into account more than perspective, of course. The integrity of civilian review systems can be judged by an examination of their hearing processes. The openness of hearings makes a convincing argument for a system's integrity. First, openness underwrites the legitimacy of the entire disciplinary process. Existing prejudices or assumptions are subsumed into the review process and are available to public scrutiny. Second, when a review system employs an open hearing method, both sides of a complaint investigation are then able to air their grievances fairly. Civilians are allowed to cross-examine police officers and to bring witnesses. Equally important, many police officers bemoan the lack of confrontation in IA systems. Because they wish to be able to confront complaining citizens directly and refute their charges, they may prefer to have access to hearings that are open. Thus both the officers and citizens involved in a hearing may benefit from unrestricted hearings. Third, open hearings provide a variety of due process protections for the individual police officer because of their openness: Representation by counsel, not allowed in all jurisdictions for administrative investigations, *is* allowed for public hearings; evidentiary standards are stricter, in a legal sense; and police officers are allowed to call their own witnesses.

The judicialization of complaint-handling in this fashion allows positive protections for police officers and for police organizations. An offshoot of allowing these types of due process protections may be a lessening of internal departmental tensions caused by overzealousness in internal review investigations. It is this study's contention that the more open and accessible a hearing process is, the greater the integrity of its review system. But what can one learn about the integrity of a system from observations of its treatment of the police?

As noted above, the evidence suggests that civilian review boards are anything but abusive of police officers. How can this be true? Why are the intuitive fears of the police wrong about the integrity of civilian review? Civilian boards may not often find officers guilty of misconduct because of the cloak of due process just discussed. Also, because some civilian investigators lack an understanding of police subcultural norms and police practices, their investigations may not be as thorough and insightful as those of Internal Affairs investigators. They may err on the side of finding the police guilty when they should not, as in the example of the shoplifter given above, but they may also do the opposite.

In addition, there is a central reality to civilian review that has been hard for its strongest proponents to accept. It is a substantive point about police misconduct. Put bluntly, the police have acted in a legal and proper fashion in the overwhelming majority of citizens' complaints cases. No fair system will find the police guilty of misconduct very often because, in a legalistic sense, *the police are not guilty of misconduct very often.*

One must also consider a sociological reality. Most civilian review board members develop an appreciation for the police and for police work. Over time, they are less and less prone to be tough on officers, and they actually begin to find fault with complainants. Those studying the Philadelphia system reached this conclusion, and observations of the Berkeley PRC and Oakland's new system resulted in the same finding. Individual interviews with commissioners of the Oakland board, in particular, indicate a significant amount of support for the police and deference to the difficulty of their charge.

This propensity for civilians to "go easy on the police" was also illustrated by the jury's verdict in Los Angeles in 1992 in the first trial of those accused in the Rodney King beating incidence. The middle-class, suburban jury from Simi Valley acquitted the police officers of assault under color of authority even though on exhibition was the now-world-famous video tape showing ninety seconds of clubbing. Furthermore, the police department's internal disciplinary system, criticized elsewhere in this discussion for its slow-paced handling of the incident, eventually disciplined ten police officers on the scene, *apart from the four indicted in criminal court.* These ten officers received discipline involving everything from written reprimands to forty-four days suspension without pay. Even the observer in the Los Angeles Police Department helicopter that night was disciplined. (Los Angeles Police Commission 1993).

The reality that civilianized systems side with the police most of the time does not sit well with many who feel that civilian review will substantially change the efficacy of police review. They expect that more findings of police misconduct should be the result of civilianization. Absent such findings, some feel that civilian review does not live up to its potential.

This study found one additional dynamic directly responsible for civilian review boards having lower rates of complaints sustained than internal organizations: Police chiefs are almost universally fixated with the idea that police officers must be truthful when dealing with internal review systems. Most departments have general orders that make it a specific offense to tell a lie to Internal Affairs. Truthfulness with Internal Affairs is viewed as an essential part of the workings of the internal structure of the organization. In fact, truthfulness is so important to the police that their focusing on it to the exclusion of other, perhaps more important, concerns has been the subject of some criticism (Christopher Commission 1991).

Members of civilian boards, however, seem to have a sort of "boys will be boys" attitude about truthfulness. Practitioners of the criminal justice system (including the police) expect some people who are accused of crimes to lie about their culpability; so, too, civilian review board members expect some guilty police officers to lie about theirs. When a lie is discovered by civilian systems, it is considered to be a part of the "playing of the game," a natural product of a system designed to investigate misconduct. In short, civilians do not seem to take offense at the police officer who lies to avoid responsibility. Thus, while chiefs take lying very seriously, civilian review boards largely do not. Internal review mechanisms find police officers guilty of misconduct for lying on a regular basis. Civilian boards almost never even consider such charges seriously. This dynamic alone causes some discrepancy in sustained misconduct statistics.

It would seem axiomatic that opening up complaint investigations and making them public would be good for the integrity of the system. And so it may be. But while open hearings might tend to increase integrity, they might also *decrease* learning and behavioral impact. Another question of balance is thus presented for consideration.

The data begs another point not often pursued by anyone studying or practicing in the field. If civilian review systems are this lenient toward officers, then maybe they are not doing their jobs as they should. Perhaps police administrators and union leaders are correct in asserting that internal systems are more rigorous, thorough, and generally "tough" on cops than are external mechanisms. If such toughness is the goal, then civilian systems may very well be viewed as inferior to internalized systems. Of course, this study has taken great pains to point out that such toughness is *not* the only concern. Fairness to police officers is also apposite. With respect to this dimension, civilian review is more than adequate. Procedural safeguards in particular protect the accused officer more effectively than those employed by internal systems.

To continue with the evaluation of civilian review systems, this study next interprets the results of the examination of legitimacy.

Legitimacy

This study's complainant's survey indicated that people who complain about police misbehavior are impressed with the civilian system; they are comfortable talking to civilians about their grievances; and they have more faith in civilian investigators. A majority indicated that they would rather not file complaints at the police building. As representatives from the ACLU point out, "If the civilian oversight system is housed at police headquarters and if complaints may not be filed at nonpolice locations, community confidence and the perception of independence can suffer" (Hoffman and Crew 1991: 10).

The logical extension of the argument that police buildings and police personnel inhibit the filing of legitimate grievances is that civilianized structures and procedures should avail more citizens of the right to complain. As openness increases, community-based perceptions of legitimacy should increase. And such increased legitimacy should mean increased participation in review systems by complainants who used to be a part of "the iceberg below the surface." As Bayley and Mendelsohn, among others, have noted, "It seems that the creation of a civilian review board would probably result in the registering of a larger number of complaints" (1968: 134). In fact, because of the creation of *some* boards there has been increases in complaint filing.

In 1966, after the creation of the New York City civilian review board, a significant increase was seen in the number of complaints filed. In 1964 only 231 complaints had been filed using police departmental internal processes; however, the new 1966 civilian board received 440 complaints in only its first four months of operation (Black 1968). Similarly, San Francisco's Office of Citizen's Complaints has seen increases, from 1,100 complaints in 1983 to almost 1,700 by 1988 (*San Francisco Chronicle*, 29 May 1990).

In other cases, however, citizens may *not* file more complaints even though review structures have been opened up. When the San Jose, California, Police Department moved its internalized operations from the police departmental building to a storefront location, its complaint numbers actually went down. When Oakland's police department created a civilian review board parallel to its Internal Affairs organization, its caseload increased for several years, leveled off, and then decreased significantly.

The Berkeley PRC, however, did not show any statistical differences in numbers of complaints filed in its first few years. Nevertheless, in the Berkeley multipronged review process there has actually been a lessening in the number of complaints handled by the system over the past decade. The New York system has also seen a decline in the numbers of complaints in the past several years, from 7,073 complaints in 1986 to 3,379 in 1991 (*New York Times*, 25 June 1992).

Although it is not entirely clear what *increased* complaint numbers mean, they may be an indication of increased police abuse, increased citizen satisfaction with complaint-filing procedures, or, as evidenced by the fallout from the Rodney King beating incident, increased awareness of police misconduct as a "topical issue." Attempting to develop a picture of the effectiveness or legitimacy of review systems by looking at complaint statistics is an illusory endeavor at best. Determining the effects of the media's "sensationalized" coverage of specific incidents is only one problem. The difficulty in differentiating between "legitimate" and "frivolous" complaints is another. Complaint-recording procedures, which change over time in both internal and external systems, can change statistical counts overnight. Also, the propensity for citizens to complain can change because of multiple variables that have little or nothing to do with police review systems, per se.

Other review mechanisms besides New York's have seen a decline in complaints since the 1960s. At Oakland's Internal Affairs Section, for example, the number of complaints per year has decreased at a fairly steady rate. This trend may have to do with the general disenfranchisement of minority peoples that some claim has occurred over the course of the 1980s. It may just be a product of increased cynicism and a loss of hope. Or it may be a result of genuine changes in police selection, educational levels, training, and behavior. There are too many variables for anyone to know definitively, but, taken together, all of these problems make "numbers of complaints filed" a problematic measure with which to attempt an analysis of legitimacy.

Complaint numbers do not have to increase, however, for the community legitimacy inherent in a civilian review process to be apparent. "Even if the volume of complaints does not rise with the creation of an independent complaint receiving agency, one can argue that it would still serve a useful purpose by demonstrating that the police force is not a closed corporation immune from examination" (Bayley and Mendelsohn 1968: 134). In Philadelphia, for example, the civilian review board received significantly fewer complaints than did the old police departmental system (Coxe 1961); yet, the executive secretary of the local NAACP was moved to note that "the only other possible relief was little short of laughable. And that was the old Police Trial

Board. For there it was certain that the police officer, tried by police officers, would not be found guilty, no matter how strong the evidence" (*Philadelphia Inquirer*, 13 October 1960).

This rather dated assertion that minority group members distrust internal systems was confirmed in the late 1960s by Bayley and Mendelsohn's survey in Denver (1968: 134). Yet as Richard Terrill notes, "There has never been a national opinion poll that suggests that the minority of citizens are displeased with police policing themselves" (1982: 399). Indeed, no information exists to confirm that now, three decades later, such feelings still exist.

In fact, our survey of complainants' opinions indicates a different, rather unexpected dynamic. When asked to rate their overall satisfaction with how their cases were handled by local civilian review systems, 7 percent of blacks were satisfied, 79 percent were dissatisfied, and 14 percent were "not sure." At the same time, 42 percent of whites were satisfied with civilian review, 29 percent were dissatisfied, and 29 percent were not sure. Thus it is clear that blacks were less satisfied than were whites with civilian systems.

Equally interesting were the responses to the same question asked about police-operated, internal review mechanisms. The percentage of blacks who said they were satisfied with internal systems was zero: 82 percent were dissatisfied, and the remaining 18 percent were not sure. Among whites, 19 percent were satisfied, 43 percent were dissatisfied, and 38 percent were not sure. These numbers seem to confirm the Philadelphia and Denver findings mentioned above. But they are problematic for civilian review proponents because they indicate only a slim margin of support for civilian review, as well as a dissatisfaction level almost equal with that of internal systems.

One is left with two realizations: First, communities in toto and certain political and academic elites perceive self-policing to be ineffective and self-serving. They find the intuitive logic of civilian review to be more acceptable and persuasive. (For more evidence of this see Lohman and Misner 1966.) Second, citizens with practical experience in dealing with internal police review systems find them equally unsatisfactory when weighed against civilianized mechanisms.

It is interesting that the confidence of political and academic elites in internal investigative processes seems also to be lacking in other professions. As noted by the American Bar Association (1970), the public tends to conclude "that self-policing is in reality self-protection." Other occupational groups and governmental bureaucracies have been attacked because they lack realistic accountability mechanisms: Lawyers (American Bar Association 1970), the Internal Revenue Service (Burnham 1989), the National Aeronautics and Space Administration (Glazer and Glazer 1989), pharmacists (Glazer and Glazer 1989), doctors (Starr 1982), and hospitals (Bogdanich 1992) among others have been accused of burying their misdeeds within self-regulating schemes.

Unlike the secretive processes of internal police review systems, the investigations of the Berkeley PRC are done openly and by civilians "unencumbered" by police subcultural membership. This would seem to make them more legitimate. Indeed, the survey of complainants' attitudes indicates a positive vote for civilian review. These complainants had experienced both civilian investigation and police investigation of their allegations. They generally favor civilian review, but their survey responses are interesting because they yield mixed results. Complainants feel that civilian-operated investigations are more thorough and complete than are police-operated inquiries. Only 31 percent of responding complainants believed that police-operated investigations were done carefully, but 85 percent thought civilian review board investigations were. Similarly, only 44 percent thought that internal police review procedures were fair overall, while 66 percent thought that civilian review processes were fair.

But when they were asked to evaluate the objectivity of the two types of systems, complainants were guarded in their support of civilian review. Concerning respondents' opinions of internal affairs departments: 32 percent thought internal police review systems favored the police officer's story, 8 percent thought them impartial, and none thought internal review systems favored the citizen. Fifty-eight percent had no opinion about the objectivity of internal affairs. Concerning complainants' opinions of civilian review: a similar number of people, 29 percent, thought civilian systems favored the police officer's story, 26 percent thought these review mechanisms were impartial, and, again, none thought civilian-operated review boards favored the citizen. Forty-four percent did not know. While these numbers lean toward citizen support of civilian review, they indicate an interesting similarity where "favoring the police officer's story" is concerned.

Taken together, these numbers paint a very limited picture of the additional legitimacy that civilian review might obtain over internal systems. While this is not grounds to reject the idea, this study has found that civilianized systems develop only marginally better acceptance than internal ones.

Police officers, police departments, and police employee organizations often staunchly resist civilian review, but they should realize that the institutionalization of civilian review processes can have positive ramifications for the police. The civilian review system can act as a public relations mechanism and may help to provide answers to the detractors of police organizations. When civilian review systems exonerate police officers of alleged misconduct, the legitimacy of the department may increase in the eyes of the public, and the civilian-operated mechanism can then be seen as a legitimizing, boundary spanning device, just as are internal affairs systems.

Despite these arguments in favor of civilian review mechanisms and despite their surprising leniency toward police officers, the police consistently fear civilian review. Police officers from the departments studied who did *not* have experience with civilian review were almost universally opposed to the idea. As Arthur Niederhoffer (1969: 189) points out in his study of the New York police, there was a "conviction that if a civilian review board were to sit in judgment it would automatically side against the police officer." In its successful campaign to fight that board, the New York Patrolman's Benevolent Association asserted flatly that "civilians were likely to be biased against the police. Only the police are in position [sic] to understand the police problem and review civilian complaints" (Black 1968: 209). Police fear of civilian review ran so high in Philadelphia before the institution of that city's board that the president of the Fraternal Order of Police stated, "There'll be a revolt in the Department if this new board idea goes through" (Gellhorn, 1969: 181). Police opinion does not seem to have changed very much; in fact, this study's officer attitudinal survey found that some of the police officers' attitudes are exactly what one should expect, given this history of prejudice against civilian review boards. Yet this study found some surprises that support the utility of the civilian-operated police review idea.

When they were asked to compare internal and external systems, the police officers found internal investigations to be far superior: 73 percent believed that internal police investigations were more competent than civilian investigations; only 8 percent believed both systems to be competent. One police officer out of one hundred and fifty thought civilian review investigations were superior. When they were asked to rate overall fairness: 64 percent thought internal review was more fair than civilian review, 11 percent thought both were fair, and 2 percent thought civilian review was more fair (22 percent did not know).

While this may seem axiomatic and more than a little self-serving, other responses indicate that these modern, educated cops have a perspective that many might find surprising. For example, the survey asked police officers to reflect what they thought were the *community's* perceptions of the legitimacy of internal versus civilian systems. Twenty-three percent felt that the community perceived both systems to be legitimate, 4 percent said that the community saw both systems as illegitimate, and 32 percent felt that the citizens did not understand the difference between the systems. (The latter is not an incorrect assertion. The complainants' survey found that citizens were frequently confused about the difference between the PRC and IA Section.)

Most interesting were the results that 28 percent of officers felt that the community probably perceived civilian review as more legitimate than internal control systems. These police officers' views were opposed by only 3 percent of surveyed officers; they felt that the community trusted IA more. While the overwhelming majority of police officers supported the professional competence of IA investigators and the fairness of that system to police, only five out of 150 officers felt that the citizens of the community would feel the same. The police officers sampled are therefore well aware of the credibility gap that the internal police review system suffers in the minds of the citizenry.

An additional potential strength of the Berkeley PRC system that may reflect on its legitimacy in particular is its mediation experiments. The practice of short-circuiting complaints through civilianized processes can be similar to that operative in Oakland's Internal Affairs Section. And, in theory, such short-circuiting can be perceived as more legitimate when it is done by a civilianized structure rather than when it is done by the police. This study found that a significant number of citizens can be satisfied by a quick and concise response to their griev-ances. Many would be more receptive to this than to an open hearing operated in a judicialized, antagonistic fashion, held months after the fact.

However, for all its apparent effectiveness in developing com-munity legitimacy, civilian review is not an elixir that can solve all police-community problems. Lohman and Misner's 1966 study of the operation of the Philadelphia citizen review board concluded that, in its seven years of operation, it did not dispel the resentment of those in the ghetto toward the police, nor did it restore confidence in complaint procedures. Walter Gellhorn asserts that "even a sympathizer may doubt . . . whether creat-ing a review board will achieve the desired results. It seems likely to soothe, but not to give lasting relief" (1969: 181).

One reason that civilian review boards may fall short of their potential is that participants may be "captured" by those whom they ostensibly regulate (Jaffee 1973). By spending time with po-lice officers, learning their problems and perspectives, the citi-zens who populate civilian review boards may begin to take the police officer's part in the same way that IA investigators sup-posedly do. Indeed, the experiences that many police organiza-tions have had with civil service commissions indicates that ci-vilians on police review boards may be too lenient with erring police officers. Some critics have suggested that this is why complaint numbers have gone down in some civilian systems. After time, this arguments asserts, people lose faith in the legit-imacy of the captured system and cease to view it as an avenue toward legitimate accountability (NYCLU 1990).

A review agency may also be captured by vociferous, radical elements of the community. Indeed, some individuals in Berke-ley have used complaint hearings and policy hearings as platforms to espouse political rhetoric aimed at the police department, at police in America, and even at "the establishment" generally. It is apparent from monitoring complaint hearings that only a very small, vocal segment of Berkeley citizens is interested and involved in the processes of the commission. Most PRC meetings usually include only one representative of the police department and the commissioners themselves. This is true also in Oakland, Richmond, and New York City. The danger that the PRC—as committed as it is to openness and free dialogue—may be captured by vociferous minorities is a potentiality that must be balanced against the side effects of the secrecy of closed, internal systems.

This lack of concern from regular citizens, of course, tends to disappoint police review interest groups. They have historically argued that "the community" is deeply troubled by not having access to police review information. When this same community ignores open review processes, one of the long-standing rationalizations for civilian review is challenged.

In this study's sample of complainants, the results indicated that, because they "lose their cases" often, they are not particularly supportive of the PRC's "pro-police" outcomes. Fully 40 percent of complainants were not satisfied with their treatment at the hands of civilian review mechanisms. They have, nevertheless, indicated a great deal of support for the PRC's location away from the main police building, for civilian investigators, and for civilian-operated hearing procedures. Irrespective of the drawbacks of this information, these views should lead even civilian review detractors to consider the legitimization potential present in civilian systems.

Police officers in Berkeley, however, seem to have finally allowed a begrudging acceptance of the PRC after its nineteen years of operation. They do support the police professionals of IA more staunchly than they do the civilian investigators of the PRC, but they also understand the legitimacy problems that may develop in internal review systems. Perhaps most important, police officers who have experienced civilian review hold no particular objections to its operations.

To continue with the evaluation of civilian review of police misconduct, the discussion now turns to the results this study obtained in its examination of the criterion of learning.

Learning

In theory, the operation of a civilian review mechanism tends to expose police officers to the uneducated, unconditioned outlook that the average citizen has toward police work. Concomitantly, civilians are educated as to police problems, regulations, policies, and standards. Especially if the review board is representative of minority communities, positive police-community relations should be generated.

In practice, these dynamics have worked only to a limited extent. The civilians on the Berkeley PRC have learned a great deal about police practices. Commission members have attended many police training sessions. They have interacted enough with the hierarchy of the department to have developed an educated perspective on police problems.

But civilian review has a very limited educational potential with respect to the citizenry in general. The complainants' attitudinal survey indicates that many are confused about PRC operations, the outcomes of their complaints, and even the difference between internal affairs and the PRC.

The dynamics are similar for police. Although the hierarchy of the police department has learned from the PRC, the average street cop hears little or nothing about its operations. Training division and internal affairs operations are much closer to the cop (physically, subculturally, and in an administrative hierarchical sense) than is the PRC. Everyday police work in Berkeley seems to be carried on independently of what goes on with the PRC.

Here again, PRC and police distrust of each other may be a controlling factor. If police departments cooperate with civilian review systems, however, they may be able to fill several voids in the learning structure of police organizations. First of all, civilianization of review systems could open up avenues for more feedback to reach the police in the form of complaints. More complaints means a greater pool of information is available to the police organization.

More important than learning from specific grievances is learning from the PRC policy formulation function. The PRC reviews complaint trends with an eye toward formulating or changing police policy. The development of policies tempered by the external perspectives of intelligent dilettantes may help the police deliver services and professionalize their operations.

This policy formulation function may also backfire, however, and create counterproductive dynamics. For example, in 1991 the Berkeley PRC discussed publishing a list of "officers who had received complaints" as a "public service" to the community. The PRC's leadership was able to deflect this idea, but it indicates the type of problem a civilianized system might develop. Publishing a list that included unsubstantiated allegations would be unfair to accused police officers. And even if the list were limited to those officers found guilty of misconduct, if published, its impact on future police behavior would undoubtedly be negative. Not only for errant police but also for those other officers who work with them each day, the long-term rejection of officers by the PRC would make that body's impact on police behavior even less effective.

Civilian review boards hold more potential for positive change in police behavior through the process of attitude modification. As noted above, the formalized hearing processes of the PRC may generate a sense of respect for due process norms. But in a police review system, due process protections mean that some abusive police officers may go unpunished. Given the expanded due process rights afforded police officers in an external system, if Berkeley's IA system were dismantled and the PRC were the only organization systematically monitoring police abuses, the police officers of Berkeley might actually be *freer* to engage in malpractice.

The police attitudinal survey attempted to obtain some feedback about the behavioral impact of both types of systems. Police officers believe that internal affairs is effectively "on the minds" of cops as they operate on the street. However, when asked about civilian review, the officers felt different. In fact, some of the acceptance of the PRC has developed over time specifically because officers feel it is ineffective. As one beat cop put it, "The PRC's not much of a problem . . . they don't really bother us. So I don't see their operations being really negative." When asked about the behavioral impact of the PRC on police officers, 12 percent responded that they felt the PRC's operations had a positive effect on behavior on the street; 37 percent of the group felt that the PRC had no impact; and 38 percent believed it to be counterproductive (12 percent did not know about its impact).

As with all of the police officer survey responses, one must guard against accepting self-serving data. Nevertheless, hundreds of hours of observation and hundreds of interviews seem to confirm that civilian review has a less immediate behavioral impact on police officers than does internal review. Police officers around the country consistently indicate that they are concerned about internal affairs. In those jurisdictions where civilians are part of the investigatory operation, cops usually appear unworried about review systems. The fact that this formula might change if civilian review were the "only game in town" only serves to underline the greater impact that internal police review systems have.

Berkeley police officers, by and large, indicated a respect for the "concept" of civilian review. They do not reject the PRC in a blindly irrational manner, as police officers elsewhere reject the idea of civilian review. It would seem, then, that their evaluations of the Berkeley review board's impact should be considered an important fact that is a part of a larger puzzle.

When one focuses on the regulation of police behavior, one may conclude that the citizenry loses something in the long run because of the inability of civilian review processes to be as rigorous as internal ones. Whatever the reasons for this failure, whether owing to a lack of understanding of subcultural norms or the expansion of due process rights, the employment of civilian review systems may expand the ability of the street cop to "get away" with abusive behavior.

Formalized systems may generate internalized subcultural and organizational pressures that mollify patterns of misconduct. The analysis of internal review systems concludes that police-operated systems do so. But formal systems may fail to generate such pressures. It can be argued that the imposition of civilian review structures, in particular, lessens the potential for the development of legitimate peer review. As Albert J. Reiss, Jr., sums up, "Apart from the question of how external review effects administrative authority, any such procedure makes problematic the professional control of professional practice. . . . Any external review board imposes a barrier to professional control by attenuating the latitude an occupation or an organization based on an occupation has to police itself" (1971: 127).

Thus, civilian review can affect the behavior of police supervisors in an interesting way. External processes, if operated without parallel internalized ones, take away a certain amount of the responsibility for police behavior that usually rests squarely on the shoulders of supervisors. If complaint processes were formalized, removed from the police, and put into the hands of others, immediate supervisors might then be able to use the civilian review process as a shield to hide from responsibility and criticism. Transferring responsibility in this way is not at all an unusual dynamic in administrative circles.

Administrative theory speaks to this dynamic directly. From the chief executive's perspective, it is crucial to organizational efficiency that the disciplinary process remain within the control of managerial personnel. To confer authority without responsibility is antithetical to accepted principles of public administration. As Edward M. Davis, chief of police for Los Angeles for many years, stated:

> The right to discipline carries with it the power to control the conduct, action, and attitudes of the employee of an organization. When the right to discipline is vested with management, management has the essential tool with which to attain the desired behavior from employees. . . . When employees are subject to disciplinary action from outside the organization, a fundamental rule of organization has been breached and the employee becomes confused, diffident, and inefficient. (Berkley 1969: 146)

Informal socialization processes, which are very effective at controlling behavior, must be encouraged, not discouraged, by review systems. Civilian review systems do not tend to foster the development of internalized behavioral control. Internalized behavioral norms, created, developed, molded, and controlled largely by peer pressure, are absolutely critical to the cop on the beat. These norms are more effective in controlling police behavior than are American values, codified law, case law, PRC operations, and internal affairs operations combined.

If subcultural norms can be influenced to sustain more acceptable behavior patterns and less "curbside justice," they can be most effective tools. But these dynamics are not likely to develop under a completely civilianized review structure because externalizing and formalizing complaint processes in the way that civilian structures do tends to make police officers act officiously and defensively. When a complaint becomes public information, a police officer has every reason to treat review systems as if they were antagonistic. After all, the system's decisions can affect an officer's career.

Civilian review, then, can inhibit genuine learning and attitudinal change. It can make all complaints, no matter how minor, turn into judicialized "cases" for consideration by sources outside the police subculture. It can limit an officer's propensity to "own up" to a mistake, to learn from it, and to go on to be a better cop.

Perhaps the most important criticism of civilian review processes is that they are too removed from the day-to-day existence of the street officer. They give little deference to the intelligence, experience, and integrity of the police, and they deny the ability of police subcultural norms to deal effectively with malpractice. Civilian police review mechanisms can take away some of the immediate supervisor's reasons for being creative, for problem solving, and for attempting to generate genuine humility and acceptance of error on the part of young, developing police officers.

Police officers and police administrators often argue that civilian review boards will destroy the morale of police officers on the street. Because civilian review is naturally abusive toward police professionals, it will create the worst of all counterproductive situations. Cops will not want to pursue their functions aggressively and will shirk their duties in the face of the power of external review systems.

In seeking to confirm such tendencies, one might point to the early years of the Berkeley PRC and to some of its genuinely antipolice rhetoric. One might be reminded of the rather inane policy discussions that occurred on occasion or of the sort of kangaroo courts into which some of its early hearings degenerated. But this would be an exercise in futility, for there is not one shred of evidence to indicate that the Berkeley system, in 161 even its darkest, most "political" hour, showed anything but expansive due process rights to individual Berkeley officers.

There is no evidence gleaned from civilian review studies that would suggest that this piece of subcultural wisdom is anything but folly. In personal interviews and on written questionnaires, Berkeley cops tended to downplay the counterproductivity of civilian review. As noted above, the statistics indicate, furthermore, that such systems tend to be "easy" on the police. This study has found that the only police review systems that have generated any significant amount of counterproductivity have been internal systems. According to the most recent survey undertaken by this study, the police of both Berkeley and Oakland are not opposed to accepting the limited participation of civilians in an ideally constructed review process. (I expand this very important discussion in Chapter 6.) This hardly confirms that morale is failing under civilian review. This information reflects findings from earlier studies. For example, Lohman and Misner concluded that although rank and file patrol officers generally opposed the civilian review board of Philadelphia, morale had not been significantly impaired (Lohman and Misner 1966).

On balance, then, this analysis is extremely critical of civilian review for exactly the opposite reasons than police subcultural ideas might suggest. Civilian review systems are *not* abusive of the police; quite the contrary, they have *too little impact* on police work on the street. Learning does not develop for essentially defensive reasons because review systems are too lenient. Learning is also limited because civilian systems are seen to be run of, by, and for people who know nothing about police work and therefore need not be listened to. And finally, because they are formalized and removed from the individual police officer's street experience, civilian systems may limit and even inhibit informal learning channels from changing police behavior patterns.

SUMMATION

The idea of civilian review of police misconduct has great potential for receiving and maintaining legitimacy from the community at large. Its openness and "control" of police discipline (and policy), however limited and theoretical it may be, may perhaps have a quieting effect on police-community relations. However, the overformalization that has obtained within the Berkeley PRC system can be seen as problematic for a variety of reasons. The process wastes time and money because of judicialization and duplication of functions. It may also have significant drawbacks because of its inability to develop legitimacy in the eyes of police officers.

The impact of civilian review on police behavior is indirect, at best. One must remember, of course, that a conscious lack of cooperation by the police has limited the effectiveness of this system. But as cooperation increases over time, the police in Berkeley, at least, are finding that the PRC is anything but abusive of their interests. The due process protections it affords police officers are considerable compared with those allowed by internal police systems.

On balance, the civilian review idea has potential. If populated by thoughtful, responsible members of the community, civilian systems can act both as monitoring devices and as protection mechanisms. They can assure the community that genuinely abusive behavior is being dealt with openly. Concomitantly, they can, in the vast majority of cases, exonerate police officers and the police departments of wrongdoing in ways that no internal mechanism can. The Berkeley Police Review Commission's political and functional problems aside, civilian review can be a workable, legitimate alternative to more traditional systems.

The following chapter describes and evaluates the third model studied, the civilian monitor.

The Civilian Monitor

It is apparent that no system will speak to all of the interest groups involved in police review. It is equally obvious that no system can receive a perfect evaluation on this study's scale, using the three criteria of integrity, legitimacy, and learning. Internal review is effective at impacting police officer behavior precisely because of the dynamics that make it unacceptable to external perspectives. External review is less effective at influencing police officers largely because of its procedural fairness and objectivity; two of its greatest assets. This may be intellectually fascinating, but it is frustrating to practitioners. Happily, there are an increasing number of hybrid review systems that attempt to put together the best dynamics from each of the two sides.

One such system, the Office of Citizen Complaints (OCC) in Kansas City, Missouri, has been in operation for almost twenty years. It seeks to produce rigorous investigations, generate community support, and influence police behavior in a positive way. It uses the investigatory and subcultural strengths of police-operated review, yet it tempers these dynamics with an openness and objectivity that answers many, though not all, concerns of external interest groups. It does not make everyone happy, but it presents a relatively conservative, balanced approach to the multiple problems of police review.

Kansas City's system is essentially a compromise. It developed from attempts of various groups to impose civilian review on the police and from police efforts to maintain control over their organization. It most cogently illustrates the compromises between police and community interests that are the baseline of this discussion. Underwriting the intuitive utility of this sort of system, Robert Reiner notes that "effective regulation of police powers and accountability requires that the rules . . . should be broadly acceptable to and respected by the police. Internal disciplinary procedures must mesh with the external structure. . . . If external controls are forced on a hostile police, they are likely to prove empty or even counterproductive gestures" (1985: 178).

Because the OCC's processes speak to this balance, analyzing its successes and failures is critical to this endeavor. At the time of its inception, the Office of Citizen Complaints had the guarded support of the administration of the police department, the backing of the police board (commission), and the acceptance of local community groups. This is not to say that the organization had grass-roots support everywhere in the community or within the ranks of police officers. Such support took some time to develop. Nevertheless, unlike almost all civilianized systems, this mechanism was put together through negotiations that included many groups interested in police review and the police department itself. This gave it a head start rarely enjoyed by civilianized systems. In the words of David Bayley, "The art of achieving accountability, especially when there is clamor for reform, is to enlist the support of the police in disciplinary activities. If they become alienated, a crisis will emerge that is not to the benefit of discipline, public confidence, or law enforcement" (1988: 61). The trouble Kansas City took to enlist the support and participation of the police in formulating the OCC system is worthy of consideration by those who would create civilianized systems elsewhere.

The Office of Citizen Complaints is entrusted with an input and output responsibility relative to the internal affairs organization. It does not do investigations itself. The OCC may take action, however, on those rare occasions when it feels that the police department's internal affairs organization has fallen down on its responsibilities. It can use the power of persuasion and political ties elsewhere in the city administration to move the police, but it leaves alone the relationship of confidentiality that internal affairs systems traditionally enjoy. It is a hybrid system that attempts to use the strengths of both internal and civilian review.

There is a wealth of information available about ombudsman

systems. Because it is analogous to civilian monitor systems, this study defines the ombudsman office and includes it in this discussion.

THE OMBUDSMAN AS A CIVILIAN MONITOR

The term "ombudsman" has been loosely translated from German to mean "referee" and from Swedish to mean "representative" (Anderson 1969). Ombudsmen offices function as generalized complaint bureaus, available to the public for little or no expense. Citizens may complain about the actions of all sorts of governmental agents

Ombudsman-type offices have been set up in some places to handle police-directed citizen complaints. This study's research examined ombudsmen offices in operation in Berkeley and San Jose. Ombudsmen typically mediate between aggrieved citizens and governmental officials and act as advocates for citizens. Many systems in place today that call themselves "civilian review boards" are, in fact, closer to ombudsmen offices in their daily operations. These systems monitor investigations done by police internal review structures. Similar U.S. systems operate in New York, Houston, San Diego, Dallas, Indianapolis, Baltimore, Portland, Atlanta, Albuquerque, Pittsburgh, Miami, Fresno, and Toledo. New South Wales, Western Australia, and South Australia also use ombudsmen review mechanisms.

In order to pursue their function, most ombudsmen are allowed almost unlimited access to governmental agents and official documents. They are encouraged to express "an ex officio expert's opinion about almost anything that governors do and that the governed do not like" (Gellhorn 1966: 10). They not only look into specific grievances but also consider policy implications. In some jurisdictions, ombudsmen conduct independent investigations (Pickl 1983); in others, such as at the Kansas City OCC, they monitor investigations done by internal systems.

Ombudsmen generally do not have the power to order any administrator to act. The weight of the ombudsman's findings lies only in his or her personal and professional logic. These representatives use personal persuasion to generate compliance with their policy recommendations or acceptance of specific investigative findings. When administrators are uncooperative, ombudsmen sometimes attempt to obtain support from elsewhere in the governmental milieu. Kansas City's OCC director operates in this fashion. His influence stems from ties developed within the police substructure and the entire subculture of the city's administration.

Only the power of exhortation is at the ombudsman's command, and, effectively, this power, developed through publicity, argument, coercion, and persuasion is great. In Sweden, the ombudsman's office has existed for over 150 years. Its ability to have an effect on policies throughout the government's administration is tremendous. (Similarly, in Kansas City, after more than two decades of operation, the OCC exercises significant influence in police investigations and on policies, without possessing control.)

In terms of police review, the ombudsman's office may act as an input point, monitor complaint investigations, and request further information or investigation, if necessary. If the ombudsman strongly disagrees with the chief of police, he or she may send a case to a higher authority, that of the City Council, the mayor, or the city manager. The ombudsman also reflects an external perspective on police policy and training. If the ombudsman exercises his or her powers prudently and empathetically, he or she may have a great impact on the police and may effectively represent the citizen and the citizenry. What follows is the study of a civilian-monitored police review system that is very similar to the office of an ombudsman.

OFFICE OF CITIZEN COMPLAINTS OPERATIONS

The Kansas City Police Department runs its own modern police academy. It has state-of-the-art substations and equipment, and its training and educational system is among the finest in the country. The number of complaints of police malpractice received in Kansas City is neither inordinately high nor low for its population (420,000) and Patrol Division size (700).

Kansas City's police department, like Oakland's, has been cited as a leader in the field of police review. The department was praised in 1973 by the National Advisory Commission on

Criminal Justice Standards and Goals for its exemplary treatment of complainants. Its chief was lauded by the ACLU in 1991 for his actions with respect to a particularly volatile incident of police misbehavior (Hoffman and Crew 1991). Kansas City's OCC thus presents another "model" system worthy of this study's evaluation. This examination begins with a look at OCC's mechanisms for receiving complaints.

INPUT STRUCTURES

In Kansas City, a citizen may make a complaint at any one of the five police substations or at the downtown police administration building. The central clearing house for citizens' grievances, however, is the civilian-manned Office of Citizen Complaints. Citizens may file complaints directly with the OCC at its offices, located several blocks from police headquarters. Regardless of where complaints are originally filed, all are forwarded to the OCC for numerical control and routing.

The OCC is staffed with civilians, none of whom have any experience in law enforcement. They are appointed by the civil service and must take competitive exams to obtain their positions. Thus, the civilian involvement in Kansas City's OCC is similar to that of the PRC in Berkeley. Because they possess investigative and legal backgrounds of various sorts, OCC analysts are essentially professional administrators.

The OCC first reviews a complaint and then forwards it to the internal affairs office at the police department. The initial outlining of a complainant's grievance is done by an analyst from the OCC. This outline serves as a directive to IA investigators and to OCC personnel. The analysts working at the Office of Citizen Complaints require citizens to make statements about their complaints in person. This is done to screen out a significant number of "frivolous" complaints. The OCC staff feels that anyone with a bona fide complaint will be willing to take the time and effort to contact the complaint system in person. Much like police-operated systems, then, the OCC assumes that the openness of its operations are self-evident and legitimate; those who do not contact the civilian-operated system in person bear the potential burden of not being paid attention to by the office.

Kansas City's OCC does a significant amount of "satisficing." The civilian input people sometimes take great pains to explain departmental policy to complaining citizens. While they do not do so for use of excessive force or discrimination complaints, they will sometimes go so far as to contact the police department and arrange a meeting with an appropriate supervisor to explain policy. Resolving complaints in this way, "to the satisfaction of the complainant," is considered an important part of the function of the organization. A file of conciliated complaints is kept in the OCC office, and the OCC director uses this information for communications with the police chief, internal affairs, and others. The director takes great pains to discuss patterns of minor complaints that occur with significant frequency.

There are several disturbing rules affecting the input function of the OCC that have been forced through compromises with the police. First is the requirement of filing a complaint in person. Second, as is the case in Maryland, complainants "shall be required to swear under oath as to the truth of the allegations" (Kansas City Police Department 1990). Third, a complainant's statement must be notarized. Finally, the complaint reception person is required to make notes with reference to the sobriety, mental capacities, and apparent credibility of complainants.

These procedures sound very much like the practice of putting complainants through records and warrants checks, which used to be followed in many police jurisdictions. This was an overt attempt to "find something on the complainant" and thus squelch the complaint at the outset.

After OCC analysts outline the complaint, they label it a "category I" or "category II" complaint. Category I includes all complaints of use of unnecessary or excessive force, the abuse of authority, discourtesy or use of abusive language, and ethnic slurs. All other complaints are category II types. Complaints are then sent to internal affairs for investigation.

INVESTIGATIONS

The Internal Affairs Division of the Kansas City Police Department is required to investigate all category I complaints received from the OCC. There is latitude within the system to allow the delegation of category II complaint investigations to local precinct commanders. Thus an officer's immediate superior may handle complaints about excessively long coffee breaks, delayed response times, or improper report-writing. This option is quite often exercised and opens up a less formal investigatory process. The investigation of category II complaints by police departmental supervisors is accompanied by a significant emphasis on complaint conciliation.

The investigative processes of Kansas City's Internal Affairs are similar to those of the Oakland and Berkeley IA departments. Investigators are all sworn police officers. The process of compiling statements and physical evidence is similar to that operating in any investigative organization. Internal Affairs officers spend a tremendous amount of time in creating investigative files that are complete and thorough. They prepare transcripts of every recorded witness statement. Thus Kansas City's investigative files are normally more voluminous and complete than those of other internal affairs departments.

Internal Affairs in Kansas City does not recommend possible investigation outcomes or disciplinary actions, as is done in many other police organizations. Investigations from IA include only evidence, statements, and investigatory summaries. After its completion, an IA investigation is forwarded directly to the OCC without comment.

In Missouri it is still legal for an internal investigator to require that an officer take a polygraph exam. (The police officers' bill of rights specifically prohibits California internal affairs departments from exercising this option.) Kansas City internal investigators state that they prefer not to use lie detector tests, and seldom do. Street police officers, however, reported that in a significant number of complaint investigations accused and witness police officers are given polygraph examinations.

Missouri administrative law allows a police department to use polygraph examinations if it is not specifically prohibited from doing so by local employee-employer agreements. Courts throughout the United States are divided on this issue. A few courts allow police officers to be fired if they refuse to take polygraph exams when they are ordered to do so. As long as the questions considered are "specifically and narrowly tailored to the performance of the officer's duties," these courts allow the requirement of an exam to stand (Aitchison 1990). But most courts in America now disallow such practices, because the "same unreliability which prevents the polygraph's admissibility in court should preclude the dismissal of a police officer for failure to take a test" (*Farmer v. City of Fort Lauderdale*).

After IA has investigated a citizen complaint, the Training Division of the Kansas City Police Department receives a copy of each complaint investigation. This type of systematic feedback from the complaint adjudicative mechanism to the police department's teaching arm is absent in most systems.

Outcomes and Discipline

Each completed case referred to the OCC from the Internal Affairs investigative staff is assigned to one of the OCC analysts, who reviews the investigation for thoroughness, clarity, and objectivity. This review is similar to that exercised by supervisors in most internal affairs departments. It is also analogous to reviews done by ombudsmen. OCC analysts may require that additional witnesses be contacted, that additional evidence be gathered, or that specific questions be asked of witnesses previously contacted. Although the OCC does not have the power to require a lie detector test, it may direct IA to ask specific questions of police officers taking a test. (In practice the OCC seldom contacts the Division of Internal Affairs to initiate further work on complaints.)

After the assigned analyst approves a complaint investigation, he or she formulates a suggested outcome. The suggested finding is reviewed by another analyst and the director of the OCC. When agreement is reached, the OCC process is complete, and the investigation is referred to the chief of police.

At this point, the policy of the Office of Citizen Complaints allows all complainants and their attorneys access to the investigative file. There are some circumstances under which the chief of police has the right to withhold specific statements or pieces of evidence when a file is being reviewed. Generally, however, complainants are allowed to view the entire file. This review must be done in the OCC offices. Copies may not be made. This openness is everywhere absent in internal affairs processes (Potts

1983). Allowing citizens open access to their files can be an important procedure because it can help to generate a complete investigation in a way that secretive investigations may not. It allows the complainant to bring up additional information, reflections, or suggestions that can help the organizations involved with their police review tasks.

The chief makes the final complaint finding. The consensus of a variety of actors in Kansas City is that the chief almost always agrees with the recommendations of the OCC. If the chief of police disagrees with OCC recommendations, he meets with the OCC director. (These meetings have been infrequent.) Both the chief and the director indicate that on the rare occasion that such a meeting occurs, agreement is reached after a brief discussion.

This propensity to agree about outcomes is not unusual in parallel police review systems. In New York, the police and civilian-monitored systems agreed on all outcomes in 1988 and disagreed on one (out of 169) in 1989 (NYCCIB 1989). In Toronto in 1989, of the 671 complaints received, the civilian commissioner of the monitor organization called for formal hearings (disagreed with the chief) three times (.4 percent) (Toronto Public Complaints Commissioner 1989). And the Royal Canadian Mounted Police (1990–1991) monitor process found disagreement between the police and the civilian commission in 34 out of 2,465 cases (1.4 percent) in 1990. This information emphasizes the statement of the Berkeley city manager that the police and the PRC are in agreement almost universally.

It bears repeating that this agreement between police departments and civilian-monitored review systems is doubly significant. First, it shows that the police are doing a reasonable and judicially defensible job of operating their own mechanisms, and second, that civilianization does not result in any substantial abuse of police officers or police organizations.

At this point, after an investigation has been conducted, those involved in the Kansas City process may still attempt a conciliation meeting. The OCC director conducts these meetings in a noninvestigatory atmosphere and only under certain circumstances. A conciliation meeting may occur if it has become clear from the investigation that the citizen-complainant has misunderstood the actions of the police officer because of the citizen's ignorance about the law, policy, or practice. At this conference, the director provides the complainant with a particularized explanation of the case. This caveat is unusual in the law enforcement field and is an interesting legitimizing process.

Cases may also move toward conciliation if (1) a case appears "minor," (2) an officer was wrong, but is willing to apologize, or, (3) a simple one-on-one disagreement can be ironed out.

Official policies of conciliation have been operable throughout the brief history of civilianized review (Coxe 1965). When police departments use conciliation, they allow informality to develop in situations that all too often are "reduced" to formal complexity and legalization. "One-on-one exchanges are preferable in resolving disputes, as such an arena respects confidentiality and offers the opportunity to mutually determine what took place. These exchanges will help assess the contradictions between the ends and means of policing and provide pieces to the 'moral consensus' puzzle" (Petterson 1991: 278).

In Kansas City, as in Oakland, the chief requests that line supervisors make recommendations as to what disciplinary action to take against a police officer. The chief also makes the final determination of disciplinary action.

If a complaint is sustained and a police officer is suspended for fourteen days or more, Kansas statutes allow an appeal to the Board of Police Commissioners. A public hearing then ensues, in a semijudicialized process similar to that of the Civil Service Commission in Oakland. These hearings are extremely rare, partly because the board invariably sustains the findings of the chief and the OCC.

From the citizen's perspective, no realistic potential for appeal exists within the Kansas City system. This, of course, is not at all unique in police review systems. The citizen whose complaint is unfounded by the OCC and then by the chief may seek reconsideration by the Board of Police Commissioners, but such a request is rarely successful.

The uniqueness of the Kansas City civilian monitor system lies in the indirect influence that a few civilians have on the review structure. As an input-screening mechanism and, concomitantly, as an output review mechanism, the OCC can have a significant impact on the internal affairs process. The OCC also has input into the policy formulation processes of IA and the rest of the police department. The director of the OCC, in particular, as do ombudsmen in Berkeley and San Jose, has an ongoing, positive, influential relationship with the chief and other high-ranking officers. This kind of close relationship may serve to make civilian monitor review systems more effective in their determinations of discipline.

This discussion now turns from the operations of civilian-monitored systems to the results of this study's evaluations of this type of model.

EVALUATIONS

The influences that police-operated and civilian-operated systems have on each other are often subtle, but they produce dynamics important for this discussion. This evaluation of the standards that effective police review mechanisms must meet shows that, in civilian-monitored systems, not all of these dynamics are positive. The police influence on the Kansas City OCC input mechanism, in particular, has been deleterious in several ways, and this surely effects its integrity.

Integrity

The input procedures of the Office of Citizen Complaints are particularly problematic. Although they are not necessary to a monitor system, they allow one to consider input questions that relate to many police-operated systems. They challenge the openness of the entire process. The influence of the police on OCC input scheme is evident when one examines the very intimidating practices that have been put into place in the past several years.

The requirement that a complainant must make his or her statement at the downtown office of the OCC is much more limiting than most might believe, for Kansas City is the largest city in America in terms of square area. Complainants who reside to the north of the downtown area, in particular, may be living 10 or 15 miles from the OCC office. Of course, these individuals may file their complaints at the North End police station, but this ignores the arguments about the intimidating atmosphere of police buildings, which prompted the storefront site in the first place. The requirement that a complainant file in person most certainly dissuades some individuals from filing legitimate complaints; how many is difficult to ascertain.

Furthermore, it is hard to understand why the OCC imposed the requirement that a complainant must sign a complaint and have it witnessed by a notary public. In fact, to accommodate this practice there is an "on-duty notary" available round-the-clock. There can be no doubt that facing this officious procedure is threatening to some. The would-be complainant might ask, What is the police department trying to imply with this procedure?

There is more that speaks to the integrity of this civilian-monitored system. First, the only action taken on mail-in complaints is to advise the complainant of the requirement to file in person and to have the complaint notarized. If a complainant has written in with a grievance and, after notification, does not follow it up with a personal trip to the OCC, the complaint is dropped.

Second, the OCC will not investigate anonymous complaints. They are forwarded to OCC on an "FYI" ("for your information") basis. This study noted, however, that all systems seem to allow some latitude with respect to anonymity. Nevertheless, a blanket refusal to accept anonymous complaints effectively means that access is limited to those who have not been strongly abused and to those not afraid of the entire system; the presumption of such a regulation is that no one is ever brutalized or intimidated. The unfortunate reality of police malpractice is that such a presumption cannot be made by any review system.

Finally, complainants may balk at signing their complaints when given the admonition about truthfulness by the notary public. If they refuse, their cases are terminated at that point. With little in the way of legal training, most complainants may be uncertain as to the meaning of the truthfulness admonition. Does it mean that the complainant will be arrested if his or her side of the story is not proven to be correct? Will the complainant have to face criminal charges if witnesses refuse to make statements on his or her behalf? Or does it mean that the complainant can be prosecuted only if he or she actually "lies" to the OCC or police? The average complainant does not know the answers to these questions. The truthfulness admonition may be the most deleterious restriction observed in any of the systems studied.

Taken together, these processes create more than a little difficulty for the would-be complainant. In fact, they imply that *the complainant, and not the police officer, is to be investigated.* To the citizen possessing no knowledge of the legal system, the complaint input rules at Kansas City appear to begin the process with the assumption that citizen veracity is the central question to be adjudicated. This type of input mechanism, atypical of civilianized processes, can be found in police-operated systems elsewhere. It is a throwback, in some sense, to the days when the police were not at all serious about hearing complaints.

It is possible to look at the complaint statistics for the OCC and attempt to discern artificially the impact of these regulations. During the months in 1990 following the enactment of these rather stern input measures, complaint filing numbers fell 21 percent; yet, complaint-filing at Kansas City fell an overall 22.3 percent during the decade of the 1980s. With no definitive data on which to base a conclusion, this study cannot determine the substantive impact of this. It *is* clear that the OCC (along with Richmond's civilian system) operates the most restrictive, intimidating system surveyed by this study, and this says much concerning this particular system's lack of integrity.

Illustrating the problems of the OCC system is the fact that the operational procedures described above are contained in the police departmental manual. Even though the civilian monitor system shows great promise for amalgamating the strengths of the two polar models, because the Kansas City Police Department holds direct control over the OCC's input procedures, one can see that this system lacks independence. The input operations of the Kansas City Office of Citizen Complaints must, then, receive low marks for openness and availability.

The complainants surveyed that *have* gotten through to OCC said that the location and filing procedures are not a problem: 27 percent of Kansas City complainants found filing a complaint easy, 15 percent found it hard, and 58 percent found the process irrelevant to their experience. When asked about ideal filing locations, only 10 percent indicated that locations were not important. Forty-four percent wanted to go to a civilian-operated facility, like Berkeley complainants, but 46 percent wanted to contact the police directly. Two-thirds of this number wanted to go directly to police headquarters. These numbers imply that those who make it through the Kansas City process are indeed not threatened by it. But that tells us nothing about those who do not make it through. This study was not able to determine, for example, how many complainants made it to the notarizing stage and refused to sign.

This analysis found that the Kansas City system is similar, at its investigatory stage, to that used by Oakland's Internal Affairs Section. OCC investigations are done in a like manner. The complaint form used in Kansas City, however, is much more comprehensive. Because the OCC uses completely typed statements, with nothing paraphrased for brevity's sake, the reports of its investigations are longer and in some sense more thorough than any compiled by police-operated systems elsewhere. The caveat that opens up these investigations to the scrutiny of complainants and their attorneys probably helps to make OCC investigations more complete. Given the completeness of Kansas City's investigative files and the openness of its process, it would seem that the assertions by internal affairs personnel elsewhere that their investigations are "as thorough as is possible" might be self-serving. While the Oakland IA Section's investigations appear complete, for example, perhaps they would be done with a bit more tenacity and thoroughness if they had to be viewed by civilians outside the police milieu.

Thus, the civilian-monitor function helps to generate an investigative integrity that is better than the sum of its parts. Its processes appear to produce investigations that are more thorough than that done by internal affairs offices. Yet Kansas City's IA Divison's investigations are also more insightful than those produced by civilians without access to the secrets of the police subculture.

Regarding OCC's requisite that its analysts must make outcome determinations on the basis of written records, it can be argued that without seeing the testimony being taken, one cannot develop the feeling for the truthfulness of a witness that one can develop in person. This, of course, is a criticism that American jurists levy against the European civil law system (Merryman 1969). Common law scholars might assert that the type of confrontation used in the Berkeley hearing process develops more substantively correct decisions.

Finally, the evaluation of the potentiality of civilian monitor systems cannot be complete without a consideration of the role of the monitors. This job is extremely specialized, personalized, and idiosyncratic. The monitor must be the kind of person who can understand police work without having been a police officer and understand administrative norms without being a part of the police or municipal organizational hierarchy. He or she must remain in touch with the perspectives of citizens while empathizing with the difficult job of the police officer. An ombudsman or civilian monitor must be able to relate to ethnic minorities of a variety of backgrounds and to deal with potentially volatile political issues. The effective operator of such an office should therefore be a combination politician, creative writer, analyst, and confidant. Because these traits are all required is not to say that the idea of such a monitor is not a feasible one. Although the civilian monitor system is potentially the most effective review system considered here, its dictates do not necessarily create an effective monitor. A monitor's role is so complex and sensitive that the person makes the job, not the reverse.

Clearly, the results of this analysis of Kansas City's Office of Citizen Complaints are troublesome. For as much as the OCC offers great potential for tapping both the strengths of internal and external review, it loses a great deal of its potential because of the lack of credibility and openness of its input procedures.

This study continues with its evaluation of this model by examining the legitimacy of civilian-monitored police review systems.

Legitimacy

Whether civilians are involved in the investigatory process or only in the input and output functions, inclusion of civilians in disciplinary systems can demonstrate to the public an important openness. This openness, of course, may be only perceptual. (An example of this type of mechanism is the Richmond, California, "civilian review" system, which has neither public hearings on specific complaints nor public discussion of complaints being reviewed.) This kind of system, nevertheless, may be perceived as more open to the public; thus, it may generate more legitimacy than an internal system operating on its own.

The involvement of civilians in the police malpractice review process may be viewed as a check on the police perspective. Of course, police officers consider the inclusion of this perspective as necessary to insure fairness in review procedures, and this study has noted that officers at all of the departments examined believe this. But the involvement of civilians may also assure citizens that abuses by police officers are not being rationalized as "standard police procedure."

Other researchers have studied the legitimacy and effectiveness of civilian monitor systems that employ ombudsmen. According to Gellhorn, "By finding no fault in 90 percent of the cases about which complaint has been made, he [the ombudsman] sets at rest what might otherwise be continuing rumors of wrong doing. He may even be an insulator against the heat a hostile press has engendered" (Gellhorn (1969: 150). Serving in this legitimizing position, an ombudsman or a civilian-monitored system can buy a significant amount of political legitimacy for the police organization, and this can be done without sacrificing the integrity of internal review.

Berkley's views echo Gellhorn's. "The very prestige of the ombudsman, while it makes him a more effective critic of the police, also makes him a more effective protector. When he has investigated and found nothing to criticize, public confidence in the police is often strengthened" (1969: 150). Of course, a monitoring agency cannot generate positive publicity for the police organization unless the agency itself is perceived as being objective and removed from the police.

In Kansas City, for example, although complainants may feel more comfortable interacting with civilians, the outcomes of their complaints still directly control their evaluations of the OCC. Only 6 percent of this study's respondents' cases resulted in sustained findings of police misconduct; thus, it is not surprising to find that only 16 percent of those polled thought the system was fair. Seventy-five percent thought Kansas City's system was unfair (9 percent did not know). Furthermore, only 22 percent thought investigations were done thoroughly, while 59 percent thought they were not (19 percent did not know). Only 18 percent thought outcomes were decided objectively, but 75 percent thought outcomes favored the police. (The rest were undecided as to objectivity.) As with Berkeley's PCC, none thought the system favored the citizen's perspective.

When asked to evaluate their overall satisfaction with Kansas City's civilian monitor system, 7 percent of complainants responded that they were satisfied (almost the same number of people in whose cases the police were found guilty of misconduct), while 3 percent were not sure. Ninety percent of the sample were dissatisfied with the system. Similarly, in a recent San Diego study, only 12 percent of those who complain to that civilian monitor mechanism are satisfied with the system. (*San Diego Union*, 16 August 1991)

These findings tell a great deal about how fragile citizens' perceptions of satisfaction are. Since the correlation between outcome and satisfaction is so close (see Chapter 3), one must understand that significant levels of citizen satisfaction cannot be achieved by *any* system unless it finds the police guilty of misconduct most of the time. Since the police are *not* found guilty of misconduct most of the time, no fairly engineered system will develop much in the way of acceptance from those who directly complain to it.

From the police officer's perspective, the Kansas City OCC has generated the same high level of acceptance among police officers as has the IA Section at Oakland because the police in Kansas City do not interact with the OCC. They interact, as do cops in most organizations, with IA investigators only. Thus, the day-to-day civilianized processes of the OCC are largely hidden from the street officer.

This study must make an important point about Kansas City's input operations. The system is successful in handling a number of complaints informally. By thus "satisficing" citizens, the civilians of the OCC perform a function that might be evaluated positively by complainants. It is the Kansas City police officers' opinion that the avoidance of frivolous or minor complaints in this way is a plus for the OCC system. A short-circuiting mechanism cannot do away with a vindictive or vicious complaint aimed at a particular officer, but it can do away with the time that is often wasted in dealing with a complaint that has only been created out of confusion and ignorance. The OCC is a godsend to a police officer if its "satisficing" explanation sends the irate citizen home with a modicum of understanding about police procedure and with some sense of satisfaction with the police.

As this study's surveys of police officers in Berkeley's system during its early years and in Chicago's civilian-run system (the OPS) illustrate, police officers in those jurisdictions feel that civilianized systems are "jokes." As one Chicago cop put it, "They investigate everything . . . no matter how stupid or trivial. . . . The whole system is a waste of time." To some it might seem hard to believe that significant numbers of complaints are minor or procedural. There is evidence, however, that confirms this. In those systems where no short-circuiting is allowed by civilian investigators, for instance, in Chicago's Office of Professional Standards and in San Francisco's Office of Citizen's Complaints, the rates for findings being sustained are extremely low.

It was noted that San Francisco sustains less than 2 percent of its complaints. In Chicago, the rate of sustained complaints was 7.2 percent in 1990. If a review system lacks this ability to short-circuit and thus remove a few complaints from the system, minor or procedural complaints may become full-blown investigations, and in the latter, police officers are usually exonerated. Paul West also found a weak negative relationship between input latitude of this sort and the overall percentage of complaints that were sustained by internal affairs organizations (n. d.). Thus the low sustentation rates in San Francisco and Chicago may really be equivalent to the sustentation rates of 15 percent to 20 percent found at most internal review operations. Therefore, one can see that police officers' concerns about the handling of trivial complaints are well founded. These concerns impact a police officer's perceptions of systemic legitimacy in a significant way.

According to the Kansas City police officers interviewed, short-circuiting can cause respect to develop among the rank and file street officers.

Although external legitimacy *can* be improved through the use of a civilianized monitoring procedure, there are several problems with this type of system. First, civilian elements of review systems can find themselves co-opted into the structure of the police culture and organization (Selznick 1966). The more these monitoring civilians become inculcated into the police subculture, the more they may understand the police perspective, interact with and accept police officers as people and professionals, and the more they may begin to operate as part of a boundary-spanning device for the police. Insuring that the uncertainty faced by police organizations and police officials is modified, civilian monitor systems might be "captured," as are members of civilian review boards in some places (see Chapter 5). For example, at Chicago's OPS the investigators are housed in a portion of the police department's building. They wear identification cards on their outer garments, as do plainclothes police investigators. Their closeness to the police over time has caused them to be identified with the police, both in their own minds and in the minds of complainants (Brown 1991).

In Kansas City, OCC personnel take seriously the job of distancing themselves from the police. It is nevertheless apparent that the members of the OCC also normalize certain sets of behavioral patterns and attitudes endemic to the police subculture. The police co-optation of the civilians in the OCC is a subject for debate among politicians and academicians in the city. It is important for this analysis to note, however, that the influence of civilianization on police officers may diminish over time.

The police subculture exerts an absorbing, powerful influence. Even in our supposedly sophisticated age, the uniforms, demeanor, and subcultural humor of police officers can be alluring to some, if not most, people drawn toward the OCC job. People who deal with complaints, whether as OCC intake personnel or as PRC investigators, may very well be attracted by the job that police do—dealing with crime instead of complaints, with victims instead of complainants, and with controlling society rather than controlling the police. Their daily interactions with the police force allow them plenty of opportunities to develop empathy and subliminal ties with those involved in "real law enforcement."

The survey of Kansas City complainants suggests that they are not any more prone to accept OCC's legitimacy than they are to accept that of an internal police review system. The responses given by Kansas City complainants to questions about the fairness and objectivity of OCC operations parallel those given by complainants in Oakland with regard to that city's internal system.

A second problem with the civilian-monitored OCC system is that it depends on police departmental investigations for its evaluations of police misconduct. The Office of Citizen Complaints has no direct contact with accused officers, witness officers, or witness citizens. The OCC has only a written record of testimony and statements. Because of this lack of contact, the possibility of police cover-ups in Kansas City is increased.

The respondents in the Kansas City complainants' survey were disturbed about the outcomes of their complaints; nevertheless, they exhibited the same sort of faith in civilianized systems as was shown in other cities. While only 22 percent wished to be interviewed by the police, 71 percent agreed that the OCC's civilians were appropriate for the intake function (7 percent had no preference). Although 15 percent thought the police should investigate complaints and 12 percent favored a combination of police and civilians, the majority, 64 percent, wanted civilian investigators (9 percent had no opinion). These findings are not unusual, but what is particularly striking about them and about all of the complainants' attitudinal responses is that they show universal support for civilianization.

The monitor mechanism may potentially reach populations that have usually been disenfranchised by administrative systems. In his study, Alan Wyner has found that some executive ombudsmen "attract a significant percentage of their clientele from lower income residents" (1973: 13). According to the chief of the Honolulu Police Department with regard to its ombudsman, "I would say there has been an increase in the number of complaints. I think people have felt at ease. Probably they were a little apprehensive to come to the Police Department directly,

183

but with the Ombudsman's Office . . . I think they feel a little freer [to complain]" (Anderson and Moore 1971: 212).

The civilian monitor thus possesses the capability to generate great legitimacy without negatively impacting systemic integrity.

The discussion now turns to the potential for learning generated within the monitor model.

Learning

In Kansas City, the OCC allows the internal investigative organization of the police department to maintain its operations unfettered by outside encumbrances. The potential deterrent effects of rigorous internal police review are therefore still operative under the system, and as seen in Chapter 4, these effects can be significant.

However, the civilian monitor system tends to go several steps further toward producing police review that impacts police officers on the street. The Kansas City internal affairs organization, for example, develops investigative reports that are more thorough than those constructed by internal systems elsewhere. From the perspective of the civilian's at the OCC, this thoroughness is necessary to rationalize that, in their outcome determinations, they have considered the totality of facts and statements. The indirect behavioral impact on the street cop because of this can be great.

To illustrate further, in Finland the police are constantly aware of the ombudsman's presence and potential review powers. In the words of a Finnish police official, "Don't let anyone tell you that police officers don't care about those fellows in Helsinki [ombudsman's investigators]. . . . We know they can and do concern themselves with us and that makes us careful" (Gellhorn 1969: 74). The knowledge that every complaint handled formally by internal affairs divisions will be monitored by civilians can have a positive effect on the behavior of police officers as well as on the rigor of investigations.

The system can thus add even more fuel to the fire under internal affairs investigators who see errant cops as bad representatives of police in general. The image of "clean" law enforcement pursued by internal investigators in the best internal affairs systems, such as Oakland's, may be made more public under a monitor-style mechanism. Furthermore, this system also helps internal affairs investigators obtain positive feedback for the difficult and thankless job they do. When the director of the Kansas City OCC commends the "integrity and impartiality" of the internal review process, he gives positive strokes to sworn police investigators, who obtain few such accolades in most police departments (Office of Citizen Complaints 1990). The extra effort that Kansas City's IA investigators take toward proving culpability in cases of genuine misbehavior may be well worth the costs of operating the OCC system.

The Kansas City system has also shown police officers that civilians can evaluate citizens' complaints in a thoughtful and reasonable manner, but the consequences of this in lessening police-citizen tensions are unclear. It can be argued, however, that the operations of the OCC might lessen the distance between police officer and citizen.

An offshoot of this strength is that the monitor system lacks the adversarial tone that can develop when an entirely external system is in place. Though confrontation may be important when errant behavior involves a major breach of ethics or abuse of power, it is a drawback when dealing with complaints that are not of this gravity (which includes most complaints). Police officers can learn to grow through a review process that is nonadversarial and positive in its application.

Civilian monitor systems, such as Kansas City's OCC, may develop the confidence of police officers better than do civilian review boards. While the civilian monitor system has an impact on the cop on the street, it is advisory to the chief and thus does not control disciplinary decisions. The OCC and other such systems are not so much concerned with individual police officers as they are with specific complaints. Discerning behavioral patterns is left to the chiefs. Therefore, unlike the Berkeley system, Kansas City's process does not develop the enmity that "publishing cop's records" can engender. Over time the OCC is concerned with patterns of complaints. It attempts to generate information for the department. This external monitoring function parallels that of the Berkeley system.

Nevertheless, the ability of the OCC's professional analysts to extrapolate policy implications in an intelligent manner may be greater than that of a civilian board made up of volunteer community members. As George Berkley points out,

> The Ombudsman is more likely than the civilian board to have the depth of knowledge and experience to sort out the frivolous from the well-founded complaint, to probe beyond mustard-plaster remedies in order to suggest possible panaceas. . . . He is also in a position to relate any police dereliction to larger problems, including police relationships with other governmental departments. (1969: 149)

An illustration of this potential, the "can't see the forest for the trees" metaphor (Zagoria 1988), can be found in the Honolulu Chief of Police's speech to an ombudsman's workshop in that city.

> I can recall one complaint on the towing situation. We'd all go down to the Ombudsman's office and they would have laid out on the blackboard exactly what our procedures were, and then would recommend ways in which we could improve these procedures. It seems that we would be confronted with these things every day, that we would be able to resolve them. But, you know, when you are so close to the thing you can't see it. They were able to do this more objectively, and they really helped us. (Anderson and Moore 1971: 211)

When one separates from the civilian monitor model and focuses only on the classic ombudsman, one can see that there is an additional strength of that system that is missing in all of the police review models studied. The ombudsman does not discriminate against the police or the police organization. That is, ombudsmen serve as generalized complaint-handlers for all of the organs of government.

Police officers and police administrators are very much concerned that they see a propensity for the police to be "singled out" as governmental actors worthy of external review. They point out that civilian review bodies are not constructed to monitor the activities of the Fire Department, the Health Department, the Sanitation Department, and so forth. Of course, it can be argued that none of these other organs exercises the same *kind* of influence over the lives of citizens as do the police. But there can be no doubt that each of these systems are capable on occasion of abusing their powers and of impacting the quality of life of the citizenry. The natural feeling of isolation that police officers feel relative to the citizenry and municipal power structures can be lessened through the institution of ombudsman-type review systems, which do not single out the police for "special treatment" (Berkley 1969; Black 1968; Gellhorn 1969).

This study's analysis suggests that the civilian monitor system holds great potential because it can create the best of both worlds; it can allow the positive behavioral control of the police subculture to impact police behavior and it can infuse an external perspective into both policy formulation and complaint-handling functions. But if this is true, it is equally possible for such a system to engineer a situation in which the worst of both worlds is operative. The counterproductive tendencies of both internal and external review might develop in a civilian monitor situation.

The Kansas City system may inhibit police productivity, as does internal review on occasion. The review of OCC civilians would probably not inhibit internal review from embarking on a "reign of terror." Then too, Kansas City's open access policy may produce an end to officer cooperation with investigations because of the fear of civil suits. Attorneys might use openness as a tool to produce evidence that they, in turn, can use in civil court.

This dynamic was suggested by one officer at Berkeley, with respect to the PRC's operations. The Berkeley officer pointed out in the survey's "comments" section that a prominent attorney on the Berkeley Police Review Commission also made money by bringing lawsuits against the Berkeley Police Department. The police officer asserted that this attorney was using the PRC's openness and the access that being a commissioner gave him to put together cases against the police. In other words, this commissioner had a conflict of interest with respect to the information he uncovered while on the commission.

The example cogently illustrates why law enforcement circles are so concerned about complaint investigations access. It also 187 explains why municipal administrators are protective of police-operated, in-house systems. If such systems become so open that information can be used against the city in the civil law sphere, administrators perceive that they will be "cutting their own throats."

This begs another question: How does Kansas City get away with this practice? The answer is that Missouri state law allows a municipal administration significant immunity from civil suits. Although this immunity is not complete, it has shielded the Police Department and the city enough from losses that the open-access policy has been followed for more than fifteen years now without serious consequences for the local government. (Of course, this sort of immunity is not available to most municipalities.)

A second set of problems may develop from use of the monitor system. The system may not buy more political legitimacy for the police department. At the same time, use of a civilian monitor mechanism may loosen internal control over discipline. Suspicion, poor morale, secretive behavior, and an end to learning and behavior modification might all develop out of a system that oversees police internal investigations by using outsiders. Furthermore, one might criticize this operation by saying that the cops of Kansas City do not have to worry about civilian review and thus are freer to misbehave. This study, however, has uncovered no evidence whatsoever that civilian review is "tougher" on cops than are internal mechanisms. That being the case, one must consider whether the police officers of Kansas City are more prone to worry about Internal Affairs than cops are elsewhere because Internal Affairs has to worry about civilians who review *their* work.

None of these negative potentials have as yet developed in the Kansas City system. The OCC seems to have done the opposite; it has created a good balance that employs the strengths of both internal and civilian review.

The fiscal impact of the Kansas City system is equivalent to that of internal review elsewhere. There are some additional costs incurred in operating the OCC above those of running Internal Affairs because of the separate location of the OCC operation, but it costs more to populate internal mechanisms with sworn police officers than it does to hire civilians as OCC analysts. And since the civilian monitor system does neither parallel investigating nor parallel inputting, as is done in Berkeley, the budgetary burden on the city is about the same ($1,000 per complaint) as that born by Oakland's IA Section. Thus expenditures, for training in particular, are not limited by the system. As noted in Chapter 3, this sort of cost to any police organization can have an indirect impact on expenditures for training, counseling, and so forth and must be considered in the study's analysis.

The Kansas City system seems to have been kind to police administrators, allowing them enough leeway within which to operate their organizations with creativity and fairness. Noting this dynamic, Stanley Anderson clearly states the ombudsman's potential for behavioral influences:

His independence and impartiality are buttressed through experience. His judgments carry increasing weight as his impartiality, independence, and expertise are recognized. Finally, and most importantly, his judgment alters the standards of morality. Over time, increment by increment, the decisions of the Ombudsman can clarify, refine, and humanize the ethos in which he operates. (1969: 7)

SUMMATION

The civilian monitor system can, in theory, offer a most effective police review mechanism. The types of balanced concerns that this study has focused on may all be satisfied through such a hybrid form. A civilian monitor process can be fair in adjudicating specific complaints of police abuse, effective in generally deterring police malpractice, and may be perceived as more open and legitimate to political elites and electorates alike.

Kansas City's OCC system is not perfect. Police-initiated procedures that tend to intimidate complainants into not filing grievances have been accepted by the OCC. Because of the legitimacy that must be lost as a product of these procedures, the civilian monitor system might begin to appear a sham. This, in

189

turn, may impact the ability of the system to handle specific complaints and deter malpractice.

But this analysis must not be too hard on the civilian monitor or ombudsman-style system; for, in practice, the Kansas City mechanism's only major problems have to do with its input structure, and that structure is not a necessary component of the monitor system. If Kansas City's process were combined with either Berkeley's or Oakland's input mechanism, it would represent the "best of both worlds." On balance, the internal review process, as monitored by civilians in Kansas City, shows great promise.

The system operates effectively to promote informal conflict resolution. It has been noted that the more adversarial a system is, the more it generates secrecy, police isolation, adjudicative behavior, and counterproductivity in the form of missed educational opportunities. The monitor system looks hopeful in this area because of its efforts at affording "satisficing" explanations for significant numbers of would-be complainants. And finally, the ombudsman–civilian monitor approach can aid in the formulation of police policy, tempered by both the expertise of the professional and the removed perspective of the intelligent dilettante.

The civilian monitor or ombudsman mechanism will not serve as a cure-all elixir. It will not necessarily bring together the perspectives of the various actors herein considered. This system, although effective, is not magical. The monitor mechanism will not resolve what, in some cases, are irreconcilable differences of perception and belief. Again, the words of Anderson are apposite:

> Unrealistic expectations must be avoided. It would be grossly overoptimistic, for example, to expect Ombudsmen to cure urban crises. Ombudsmen cannot cool the long hot summers of ghetto violence. They cannot create jobs, provide transportation, or build homes. But while basic social issues are more urgent and more important than the Ombudsman, the establishment of Ombudsman offices need not await the resolution of these larger issues. (1969: 72)

Having discussed the three model systems, the analysis now examines the implications of their individual strengths and

190

weaknesses. Part III addresses the potential of agents outside the administrative milieu to impact police accountability. A direct comparison of the three models using each criterion follows. And finally, discussion turns to treat the "ideal" police review system.

IMPLICATIONS

7
Agents of Change

Aside from what administrative review systems can accomplish by themselves, there are numerous avenues open to other actors for impacting police behavior and police review. This study's research found that police unions, chiefs, the media, political elites, and local bar members all have important, causal relationships to police misbehavior and influences on police review. All of these actors bear some responsibility for police misconduct. It is appropriate to consider how they might share in solving the problems discussed herein. These interested parties do more than make police review difficult; they are in some ways directly responsible for the problems of police review, and each may be a part of the polycentric solution.

Citizen-complainants make up the interest group that is most directly concerned with the problem of police misconduct. This group is distinctly *not* a part of solution-building. One would be hard-pressed to argue that complainants should in some way help develop remedies for police malpractice. Citizen complainants (for the most part) are not on-going participants in any review system. They are not organized, nor are they likely to be. And citizen-complainants cannot be expected to be more understanding about the difficult tasks to be accomplished by either street cops or review systems. Their very grievances are proof positive that they cannot or will not take the officer's part in the drama of police misconduct; therefore, they will be omitted from the incident discussion. This chapter reviews other agents of change, beginning with an elucidation of the importance of police unions.

POLICE PROFESSIONAL ORGANIZATIONS

Although police officer groups have sought to couch themselves as professional organizations, they have operated instead as unions. In doing so, police officer organizations have developed numerous unfortunate operational dynamics that tend to inhibit the movement of law enforcement toward professionalization, limit progress in reducing police misconduct, and curtail severely the effectiveness of police review mechanisms.

There was, at one time, good reason for these groups to take this union-type perspective. One must remember the abuse to which police officers were subjected historically. It is not so long ago that the police were pawns in political chess games in most municipalities (McLaughlin and Bing 1989). There were corruptions of all sorts stemming from this police–partisan politics link. In response, progressive era reforms attempted to "divorce politics from the police" (Lindberg 1991).

But these reforms had their own side effects. They created some problems that inhibit the development of police professionalism today. "When the police were separated from politics, police leaders were not made independent. They simply became more dependent on the last remaining group that was interested in and capable of influencing police operations, namely, the police officers themselves. Without external accountability, the leverage police executives have over their own organizations is limited" (Moore and Stephens 1991: 64).

Thus police officer organizations stepped into the void caused by the removal of the police from the political sphere. At first subjected to the type of union-busting that characterized the era (Bouza 1985), police officer organizations gained strength and stature over the course of the 1940s and 1950s. By the 1970s police unions had developed power and influence over their own work environments, which remains the envy of other unions (Andrews 1985).

Such power in operation has been problematic for police review systems and for attempts at control of police behavior in general. Calls for police unions to change their focus and promote accountability, innovation, and progress have come from academicians, police management practitioners, and elected leaders. Yet little has been done to change. In fact, eschewing interprofessional quality control, unions have fought against police review systems of all kinds. This study has already alluded to the legal battles between the Police Officer's Association and the Berkeley PRC, and, similarly, to the demise at the hands of local unions of New York's and Philadelphia's civilian review boards.

But these are examples only of civilian review being curtailed after it has been put in place. There are any number of additional illustrations of civilianization being thwarted in the first instance, before institutionalization, by police union efforts. A potential civilian review board in Sacramento, California, in 1991 was defeated by some nimble political footwork by the local police officers' union. The union's president asserted that "the track record where (boards) have been in place for years has shown that they're in disarray" (*Sacramento Bee*, 18 September 1991). This completely groundless assertion was taken as gospel by police officers, the police department, and local "pro–law enforcement" groups.

In Boston, Massachusetts, the police union successfully fought off the threat of the establishment of a civilian board for years before the announcement of the creation of a limited oversight system in January 1992. When the new monitor system was announced, the union president promised a court fight. He then declared in all seriousness that the board meant "the ruination [of] the Boston Police Department. I'm very disheartened. It's a sad day. And I feel I've been raped and sodomized" (*Boston Globe*, 18 January 1992).

But police union opposition to police review extends well beyond the occasional fight over civilianization. Unions also regularly challenge internal disciplinary processes in court. Former police chief Anthony Bouza writes, "The police unions, eager to protect their members, often work to thwart the disciplinary process used to curb the excesses of police wrongdoers" (1990: 71). Thus, "unions frequently become the greatest obstacles to reform and battle the disciplinary process even when it is aimed at obvious miscreants in uniform" (Bouza 1990: 267).

Of course, it is argued that unions must necessarily defend their members. Police union representatives ask, Who else will speak for the individual officer (particularly when subjected to the kind of 'reign of terror' outlined in Chapter 5)? There is something to this logic. If police chiefs and municipalities had always treated police officers with respect and fairness, perhaps unions would not have been so driven to develop the power they now possess.

Police unions could better seek to defend the greater part of their members in the long run, however, by choosing to take a more collegial, professional stand on disciplinary issues. Why have police officer organizations eschewed the idea that operates in the traditional professions that professionals themselves should take a role in discipline? Why not form citizen-complaint committees made up of representatives from police officers' unions? Why not take advantage of what the legal, medical, academic, engineering, and other professions have done for so long, and "police your own?"

This suggestion sounds farfetched in today's context. Police unions regularly act in order to protect even the most heinous offenders (Guyot 1991). But many authors have noted that the attitude of the police chief is critical to an organization (this is explored in depth below). So, too, is it critical to the formulation of rookie police officer attitudes that their unions consider moves to investigate abuses as unreasonable threats.

When the young officer sees that the union will support any kind of "cowboy" behavior and will oppose any sort of review effort, no matter how fair and impartial, the cop will tend to fall into the cynical spiral that creates the blue curtain in the first place. This dynamic not only helps to create abuse but it also limits the impact of the police chief, the sergeant, the command structure, those officers who practice restraint and work with high standards of integrity, and all external influences.

Some limited change is on the way in this area. In Berkeley, the local police officers' association has voted to limit the amount of money its officers can use out of its general fund for the purposes of defending themselves against disciplinary actions. In the words of one sergeant, "Everybody's getting tired of a few guys, there's about seven or eight of 'em, spending all of our dues money on endless lawyer bills. So we voted to pay only so much and then a guy's on his own." This is a very small step, but it indicates that Berkeley police officers resent the financial problems caused by genuinely abusive police officers.

The police have long traded on the purity of their support for tough anticrime legislation. In some places police unions spend a great deal of money supporting pro-prosecution "victim's rights bills." The inconsistency between these efforts and those of defending police officers accused of misbehavior is not lost on those who pay attention to such activities. As one columnist recently noted with respect to a Los Angeles scandal, police lobbying "against laws protecting the rights of the accused . . . is only half the story. Cops have also shaped the law to *protect* the rights of the accused—if they happen to be police officers accused of brutality, theft, drug abuse, insubordination or other offenses" (*Los Angeles Times*, 17 July 1991). Such cynicism may undercut the effectiveness of well-intentioned efforts aimed at criminal justice reform.

The impact of police officer organizational attempts to limit accountability may go even further. The excuse-making that has often taken place with regard to police review can be counterproductive for the citizenry in terms of the delivery of police services. After the indictment of four Los Angeles Police Department police officers for the beating of Rodney King, the Police Protective League of Los Angeles advised officers to be less aggressive in the performance of their duties in order to "protect their careers" (*Los Angeles Times*, 26 June 1991). These arguments help create, in the young officer in particular, the excuse that the police cannot do their jobs within the constitutional framework of American institutions. Liberal politicians, permissive courts, insensitive attorneys, ungrateful students, uncontrollable members of "the dangerous classes," and an indifferent public are all seen as being to blame for the police officer's lot. With the union behind them, the police can rationalize that the very foundation of the American system of limited government itself makes their jobs impossible. With such built-in excuses it is easy to explain failure, and it is equally necessary for the individual police officer to cleave to all sorts of explanations that justify "noble cause" corruption.

In short, police unions have failed to take police accountability seriously. They must work together with municipal administrations and review groups, internal and civilian, to pursue police malpractice aggressively. This cooperation, over time, will help police unions become "police professional organizations" who are better aware of the strength that they can generate by taking an active part in professional discipline. They may see the positive potential in informal review mechanisms and cease their heretofore universal propensities to require officiousness and adversariness in complaint-handling procedures. They may begin to see that there is nothing wrong with mediation or even apology on the part of errant officers if this can produce citizen satisfaction *and* protect the police officer's career from permanent damage. Police unions have opposed these ideas in the past out of shortsightedness.

If police unions begin to act in more open-minded and prospective ways, in the long run, they will generate for the average cop a better lot, more status, and even greater income. And, of course, this would all be good for the community, for the citizen, for the police.

Other special interest groups are also directly concerned with review of police misconduct. One of the most important groups is the nation's chiefs of police, considered next.

CHIEFS OF POLICE

The job of policing is a difficult one, replete with paradox and uncertainty. Leading the police is more involved and complex than police work alone, and there are all sorts of organizational and political dynamics that enter into the police chief's formula for decision making. As Mark Moore and Darrel Stephens point out, chiefs

> feel both vulnerable and corruptible: vulnerable because their jobs, reputations and careers are to some degree hostage to the views [mayors, City Council members, Civil Service Commissions, and the media] have of their performance, and corruptible not only because they might be asked to do something that goes against their own best professional judgment, but also because they might be tempted by the allure of celebrity status to spend more time in the limelight than they [or their organizations] think they should. (1991: 64)

Being a good chief of police is trying, and it calls for a multifaceted individual with an iron will and great personal integrity, but it is not impossible. There are many honest, competent, hard-working individuals who occupy the chief's chair and who do so without falling prey to corrupting influences or excuse-making. This study's consideration of the police chief's role in influencing officer behavior suggests numerous avenues that a creative chief may pursue when engineering police accountability.

Early warning systems, positive discipline schemes, research orientations, and middle-management approaches are all important to police chiefs' roles, but circumscribing all of these is the one indispensable role of the chief, that of leader. Although the diversity of America's twenty-five thousand police jurisdictions requires many types of organization, many styles of management, and many philosophies of policing, the requirement that the chief lead by example is universal. There is one thing that definitively separates the successful police chief from the pretender. It is not the specific programs, rules, or operational guidelines employed by a jurisdiction; it is the articulated general principles of morality that the successful chief clearly establishes for the street cop (Cohen and Feldberg 1991). Without providing positive models of behavior by his or her own actions, and within the organizational culture itself, police chiefs run the risk of having all other behavioral control approaches become ineffective.

The chief may attempt to influence police behavior before civilians even become police officers through rigorous selection standards. Police administration texts discuss the background checks, physical exams, psychological profiles, and substantive examinations that should be applied to selection (Garmire 1982; International City Management Association 1971). But, unfortunately, most police chiefs' options are limited in terms of selection strategies. The state of understanding in this science of selection arena is in its infancy.

Students of the police have called for increased educational requirements, in the name of developing more intelligent, trainable, restraint-oriented officers. One recent study found a "positive correlation between higher education, fewer disciplinary actions, and fewer citizen's [sic] complaints" (Tyre and Braunstein 1992). Other studies, however, suggest the opposite correlation. In fact, attempts to trace performance after hiring are inconclusive (Malouff and Schutte 1986).

Similarly, IQ tests have been determined to be of little value in predicting later police officer behavior (Speilberger, Spaulding, Jolley, and Ward 1979). Some have suggested hiring older, more mature people, but studies have found both positive and negative relationships between age and performance (Bartol 1982; Daley 1980). A recent study of police selection by Joseph Talley and Lisa Hinz concludes that while progress can be made, "no feasible screening index can sift through applicants in a manner allowing the accurate identification of all applicants who will later perform well and all applicants who will perform poorly with no erroneous predictions" (1990: 68).

Police chiefs do have choices in this area, however. First, they can direct their police officer selection systems to perform background checks that are exhaustive in their pursuit of previous abusive behavior. (One might guess that these background investigations have not always been rigorous. This study uncovered numerous examples of police officers involved in the use of excessive force who were hired even though they had previous histories of abusive behavior [*Boston Globe*, 2 August 1991].) There is reason to believe that it is valuable to police departments to take histories into account when selecting recruits. Positive correlations have been made between police officer misbehavior that resulted in terminations and prior histories of vehicle code violations, short stays at previous jobs, convictions for more serious offenses, dismissals from prior employment, disciplinary actions received previously, and disciplinary actions received while in the military (Malouff and Schutte 1986).

Second, there is some limited information that suggests that hiring more women and ethnic minority group members may help to influence police behavior in a positive way. With respect to women in policing, for example, statistics gathered in New York indicate that female cops receive half the number of complaints that males cops do (New York Civilian Complaint Investigative Bureau 1989). In Oakland, a similar pattern occurs, though the numbers are not as dramatic. These numbers cannot be explained in terms of female officers' lack of experience in the field. Women have only recently made up a significant percentage of street officers in most jurisdictions. Their lack of seniority would tend to make them *more* prone to be complained against than are male police officers. (Remember that officers generate the greatest majority of their complaints in their first few years on the job.)

No systematic analysis of these data and the complaint-generating propensities of women officers has been done, and it is a subject overdue for consideration. One scholar, however, has some ideas on the subject. Susan White has observed that male officers raised with less experience in dealing with adversarial situations in physical ways are less prone to solve police problems using physical methods. That is, officers with middle-class and white-collar backgrounds are less prone to use violence than are officers from lower-class and blue-collar upbringings. (White 1973: 26) Perhaps female police officers are also less likely to seek a physical, adversarial solution to problems and are, therefore, less likely to receive complaints.

Susan Ehrlich Martin points out that female officers appear to be generating fewer verbal abuse complaints because of dynamics operative on both sides of the officer-citizen formula. On one hand, female officers may be perceived to be acting in a threatening manner less often because "women's body language 'naturally' is likely to ease situations" (Martin 1980: 175). On the other hand, but equally important, people who are *expecting* a woman police officer to be "less threatening than a male officer . . . display respect . . . and offer the policewoman greater opportunity than a male officer to make polite requests rather than issue commands" (Martin 1980: 175).

In terms of minority officers, complaint-generating propensities are congruent between white and nonwhite male police, that is, minority officers receive their share of complaints. But there is some evidence that in some locations black participation in policing, especially in managerial positions, has lessened community tensions and has led to "a general decline in allegations of police brutality . . . [and] lower crime all around" (Cashmore and McLaughlin 1991: 101). Somewhat lower crime rates and more effective delivery of police services may be due to "their [black officers] greater ability to cultivate and use informants in their community" (Leinen 1984: 215).

Black police officers and their associations have a tradition of supporting the civilianization of review (*San Francisco Progress,*

27 April 1977). This study's officer attitudinal survey found this propensity to be operating in Oakland and Berkeley. When they were asked the two critical questions about civilianizing review mechanisms, black officers were more willing to support civilian involvement than were whites. While only 26.3 percent of the white officers supported combined civilian and police investigations, 45.1 percent of blacks in the sample supported the idea. And although 64.2 percent of the white officers favored combined civilian-police hearing boards, 72.4 percent of the black officers favored them. These attitudes might signify that there is less of a gap between black officers and citizen perceptions of review system legitimacy than at first believed. They might also imply a closer link, generally, between black officers and people in the inner city.

In their 1975 study of seventeen cities, Peter Rossi, Richard Berk, and Bettye Eidson found a strong link between the attitudes of chiefs of police toward blacks and the amount of aggressiveness exhibited by police officers in black areas. Presumably, a police chief's positive attitude toward departmental integration may translate, over time, into an understanding among street troops of his or her charge to developing police responsiveness to inner city peoples. A commitment to affirmative action might thus be an indirect commitment to police accountability. Observing this and understanding its potential significance for police accountability, the chief must be expected to be on the cutting edge of calls for integrated, ethnically representative police systems. This has been the case in several of the systems this study examined.

Police forces in Oakland and Berkeley, in particular, have come to closely represent the demographic profiles of their respective populations. There is no definitive proof that such changes have made a positive difference, but the inclusion in these police departments of women and minority cops certainly has not generated *more* problems or hostility, given that complaint numbers have gone down.

In order to facilitate this kind of progress, however, chiefs of police have to go further than simply to support the inclusion of women and minority peoples in the police subculture. They have a positive duty to insure that police departments' promotional, operational, and disciplinary systems do not mirror the kind of discriminatory practices that generally plague American society. This will be no mean feat in some police organizations.

Several studies indicate that minority police officers suffer from ostracism and racist attitudes within their police organizations, in addition to the problems of isolation they experience as officers on the street. The Christopher Commission survey, for example, found that "45 percent of African-American officers, 31 percent of the Latino officers, and 25 percent of the Asian officers answered affirmatively that they had encountered discrimination on the basis of race" within the Los Angeles Police Department (1991: 81). Discrimination has also been documented elsewhere (*Boston Globe*, 5 August 1991, Deal 1986, Leinen 1984).

Chiefs of police should take the lead in encouraging their police departments to require academy training that is relevant to today's policing; training that will help to control police behavior prospectively. Police academy education should include much more than the training that has been included under the traditional focus of law and patrol procedures, and some police departments are already moving in other directions. Ethnic sensitivity classes, local history studies, demographic profiles of the city policed, "verbal judo" classes, and so forth must be integrated into curricula. Police academies that emphasize militarism, such as in Los Angeles, should be made less formal and more collegial so that their environments will not only be conducive to learning but will also help to generate a department-wide problem-solving ethos. Furthermore, some part of academy training should be directly focused on the nature of complaints and how to avoid unnecessarily upsetting citizens.

But police academies make up a small portion of the cop's learning experience. Critical to the individual officer's growth and ongoing development is the first-line supervisor, the sergeant. Sergeants should be teachers and role models (Muir 1977) as well as disciplinarians and supervisors (IACP, n.d.). Unlike in the traditional paramilitary system, the sergeant should be encouraged to be innovative and flexible.

> In theory, the supervision function involves a wide array of responsibilities. These include shaping the attitudes of subordinates in terms of the goals of the agency, teaching them how to apply those goals in their own work, assessing the adequacy of subordinates'

performance, using available incentives and training to correct deficiencies in performance, and monitoring subordinates' actions to control various types of misbehavior. (Weisburd, McElroy, and Hardyman; 1989: 190)

It is unfortunate that many police sergeants and police departments do not see the sergeant's role in this light.

While sergeants dislike being disciplinarians (Trojanowicz 1980), that is how their charges view them (Goldstein 1990) and how they view themselves. This focus on discipline and tough supervision is not very helpful when crises occur. Calls to "tighten things up" and be stricter with sergeants (Christopher Commission 1991) so they, in turn, will be stricter with their subordinates only help to limit the teaching abilities of the critical actors in the police officer's life in the organization.

This is not to say that the sergeant should not be held accountable for what his or her subordinates do; it is to say that the indices used for measuring that accountability should be diverse, not only related to arrest and citation numbers. Performance evaluations should also consider whether a police officer is creative, thoughtful, and able to obtain citizen cooperation without the use of physical force. David Weisburd, Jerome McElroy, and Patricia Hardyman tell of a particularly insightful sergeant who "shifted his supervisory strategy away from a preponderant concern with controlling misbehavior to focus upon the officers' knowledge of and involvements in the community and the adequacy of their problem-solving activities. Thus, the sergeant shifted emphasis from the criteria of legality to those of workmanship" (1989: 199).

It is part of the police chief's difficult function to lead middle-management personnel to create an environment within which this sort of first-line leadership is expected and rewarded. Sergeants need to be held accountable for police officer development, behavioral change, learning, and integrity, not just for crime statistics.

With particular reference to police abusive behavior, police sergeants, together with middle managers and chiefs, must be encouraged to develop "early warning information systems [that] may assist the department in identifying violence-prone officers" (U.S. Civil Rights Commission 1981: 81). Various authors have attempted to develop schematics for this purpose (Christopher Commission 1991; IACP, n.d.; U.S. Civil Rights Commission 1981).

Oakland's police chief employs a particularly useful system. An offshoot of the studies done by Hans Toch, J. Douglas Grant, and Raymond Galvin in the early 1970's at the Oakland Police Department, it is called the "Critical Indicators Program" (Toch, Grant and Galvin 1975). The police chief has a computer tabulation put together on a regular basis that tracks indicators that "might" have a tendency to show behavior problems in the making. Every police officer who contacts the public is monitored on a quarterly basis. The chief collects statistics on citizens' complaints, use-of-force reports, firearms discharge reports, resisting arrest reports, vehicular accidents, absenteeism, and evaluations of officers' written reports, conducted both in-house and by deputy district attorneys. When an officer shows up in too many categories over a three-month period, his or her immediate supervisor is advised.

The Oakland police chief sometimes finds, to his delight, that police sergeants have already dealt with such problems. Concerning one case in 1991 the chief related that he called the Patrol Division to advise a sergeant that a "potential problem was brewing" with a particular officer. "The sergeant told me that he knew about it and had already taken steps. The officer had been through 'peer review' just a couple of days before. It was a surprise to me, because I don't even know what sort of 'peer review' they're doing down there!"

This scenario says several things about the Oakland system and Oakland's chief. First, he has encouraged innovative thinking. He was obviously delighted at the prospect that a peer review system had been developed by the troops themselves. Second, he was not egocentric about this development. It was apparent that he did not feel that every departmental experiment had to be channeled through his office. Third, the police sergeant was doing his job as a teacher and a monitor. He was ahead of the chief in this particular case and was probably elated at being able to tell the chief so. Finally, the early warning system was operating in a positive, proactive fashion. It attempted

207

to use subcultural socialization to further goals that were in the best interests of the individual officer, the sergeant, the chief, the department, and the community. This example is the quintessence of creative management and illustrates the kind of farsighted leadership that successful police executives require.

Positive behavioral modification can also happen after the fact when police officers have misbehaved. Through peer review panels, corrective counseling, additional training, informal problem resolution, citizens' complaint mediation, and person-to-person teaching from the sergeant, police officers can be motivated to change their behavior patterns (U.S. Civil Rights Commission 1981). Particularly important for the young, developing officer, positive efforts to change behavior may make a productive, effective police officer out of an individual who has developed bad working habits in his or her first few years of policing.

"Radical school" criminologists have found criminal behavior to be transient, and most errant police officer behavior seems to be transient, too. Some cops have trouble adjusting to their roles. They receive a few complaints, learn from their mistakes, and eventually grow out of their erratic conduct. If they are treated in a positive rather than a punitive fashion, most erring young police officers will respond.

These behavioral modification experiments require the police chief to possess a farsightedness that focuses on organization-wide goals and long-term implications. It requires patience. It takes some intestinal fortitude to send an entire department through violence-reduction training, as has been done for Florida's 2,400-officer Metro–Dade County force (Time, 1 April 1991), or through classes in "verbal judo," as is being done in Los Angeles (CBS 1991). Subcultural cynicism about such processes must be expected and ignored by the enlightened chief of police.

Positive, counseling- and training-oriented disciplinary systems are not just wishful thinking. California's Contra Costa Sheriff's Department has such a system in place, and it has been successfully operational for almost seventeen years. That department had experienced problems with its disciplinary processes in the form of employee grievances, civil service hearings, and court litigation. Management felt that the existing, traditional, punitive disciplinary system was ineffective. Beside the organization's problems there was the individual police officer to consider. Under the conventional system

> there appeared to be no real attempt to improve the employee's performance. There was nothing to indicate to the employee that the organization wanted him to stay with the department and to improve his performance. . . . Suspensions and demotions did not appear to have the desired effect on the employee. The employee after a disciplinary action was generally very negative in his attitude towards the department. (Contra Costa County Sheriff's Department 1975)

The new plan was based on a process developed by John Huberman, an industrial psychologist in a British Columbia, Canada, plywood mill (1964). A preliminary attitudinal survey conducted throughout the Contra Costa County Sheriff's Department indicated that morale and performance were suffering because of existing disciplinary processes (Rainey and Quartolo 1978).

The new disciplinary system attempts to take advantage of the strengths of self-controlling behavioral patterns by means of a "counseling and training" approach to discipline. The process consists of three different "phases" that allow the errant officer opportunities to correct performance deficiencies. Solutions include "friendly" interviews with immediate supervisors and "corrective agreements" between supervisor and officer. An officer can also receive specific retraining. A deputy involved in a vehicular accident, for example, might be sent to a defensive-driving class. Under some circumstances, the employee is confronted by higher commanders and is sent home for a day (with pay) to "think about" the severity of a problem. If multiple problems occur, the employee can enter the county's punitive disciplinary system and may be terminated.

Contra Costa County's "Corrective Counseling System" is a two-edged sword in terms of its utility. It seeks "to improve the employee's future behavior through . . . constructive interviews and positive training" (Rainey and Quartolo 1978: 41). In order to be a genuinely positive mechanism, the plan includes purging rules, which allow for the expurgation of written records of interviews, and "phasing" actions if officers are not involved in misbehavior for proscribed periods of time. Thus, on one hand, the misbehaving deputy who makes a genuine effort to improve his or her job performance can erase records of disciplinary actions of a minor nature. In more traditional systems, such incidents might follow an officer long after behavior has been modified (Garmire 1982).

If, on the other hand, an officer does not improve and is terminated under this plan, the department will have a well-documented record of positive efforts taken to help the errant deputy. The system aids the organization in putting together a defensible case for termination; thus, it can help the organization on both sides of disciplinary problems.

An officer attitudinal survey done at Contra Costa as a part of the research found line-officer acceptance to be substantial. Forty-nine percent of the 218 officers surveyed believed the system to be more fair to officers than traditional, punitive systems (35 percent did not know). Only 12 percent considered the system to be less effective at influencing officer behavior than traditional schemes, and only 18 percent would change back to a punitive model if given the option. Officers of higher rank, in particular, pointed out the new disciplinary system's utility in dealing with problems in a positive manner.

But perhaps the mechanism's most important selling point is its acceptance by the local Deputy Sheriff's Association. Carl Carey, president of that association, stated that he "wished there was some way of letting the younger guys know how things are done elsewhere. They are fairly supportive. But they don't really know what they've got, how positive it [the Corrective Counseling System] is, unless they know something about Internal Affairs in other places" (1991).

Lee Potts points out that "when negative sanctions are the primary focus of internal behavior control, officers will concentrate on avoiding doing bad rather than on doing good" (1983: 83). The Contra Costa "no-fault" system speaks to the discussion of supervisorial teaching and leadership mentioned above. It is a creative attempt to harness internal socialization processes in a systematic way. Of course, it is neither as precise nor as legally defensible as are strict codified rules. But it is another example of executive innovation in a field where, unfortunately, far too little in the way of such experimentation takes place (Mayo 1985; St. Clair 1992).

Egon Bittner asserts that changing existing management structures is critical to the reform of disciplinary mechanisms. It "requires the creation of collegial relations among officers. This involves the displacement of the present command structure, which, in any case, functions only as an internal disciplinary mechanism and has no functional significance for the way in which police work is done by members of the line personnel" (1990: 14).

Such an idea is the logical extension of this study's criticisms of paramilitarism and organizational dysfunction. But to take the first step and attack existing structures requires quite a leap of faith on the part of the police chief. An interesting suggestion in this area comes from Norm Stamper, chief of police in Seattle (Stamper 1991). Formerly with the San Diego Police Department, Stamper did a study of that department, which called for revamping existing structures and doing away with many middle-level command positions, specifically the positions of deputy chief, commander, and captain. Following the lines of business management, the plan eschews traditional military labels. Although not yet in place anywhere, this plan bears watching by students and practitioners alike when it is implemented.

Some police chiefs, held to both legal and legislative standards of accountability and operating an administrative hierarchy in which the lowest-level agent possesses the optimum amount of discretion, tend to be even more defensive of their police departments than are police officers. They can develop a siege mentality, which is counterproductive for their organizations. As George Cole concludes, citing Guyot, Johnson, and Walker, "Police administrators expressed a fundamental unwillingness to confront and to implement changes necessary to deal with the problems of conduct, corruption, and/or productivity. . . . Police continue to be unique in their resistance to change and are an anachronism in the modern world of public administration" (1988: 141).

Aside from the pragmatics, the police chief's primary role is that of setting an organizational tone with respect to ethical and restrained behavior, and observers from a variety of perspectives

have universally noted the importance of this (Bouza 1990; Delattre 1989; Douglas and Johnson 1977; IACP, n.d.). As Paul
Hoffman and John Crew of the ACLU put it:

> When incidents of brutality, misconduct or racism occur, the chief's
> immediate reaction to these incidents will have a great impact on
> whether the incident will be repeated in the future. A chief that
> seems more concerned with protecting the department's image than
> with identifying and disciplining the wrongdoer can send the mes-
> sage that getting caught is a worse sin than the underlying miscon-
> duct. In contrast, a willingness to publicly and thoroughly examine
> even the most embarrassing and damaging incident will demon-
> strate to both the public and the officers a serious commitment to
> avoiding the same mistakes in the future. (1991: 6)

Hoffman and Crew were alluding specifically to the Rodney
King beating incident in Los Angeles. Elsewhere in their report
they chastise Los Angeles Police Chief Daryl Gates, who "initially downplayed the King incident" (Hoffman and Crew 1991).
In fact, Chief Gates did seem to support the actions of the errant
officers. Before suspending the guilty officers he waited for outside agencies to force his hand. It was two months before he
suspended (with pay) the police sergeant in charge of the incident. Perhaps more important is the attitude Gates displayed
concerning the personal worth of Rodney King, the victim of
police abuse. *Time* magazine noted that his "apology" to King
"began with two absurd irrelevancies: 'In spite of the fact that
he's on parole and a convicted robber, I'd be glad to apologize'"
(1 April 1991). This sort of tone can imply to line officers that
the administration condones making such moral judgments
about individual citizens.

Gates's approach to the King incident can be directly con-
trasted to Police Chief Kelly's handling of the Detroit incident.
In Detroit, the chief acted immediately to place the accused police officers on suspension *without pay*. After only one month
and an extensive internal investigation, he fired four officers and
disciplined others. The chief chose to place the burden of proof
on the officers. As a political tactic it meant that they could
come back to the force only if those external to the department
(the Civil Service Commission or the courts) forced the chief to

take them back. Thus Chief Kelly built himself a framework from within which he could successfully place critics on the defensive. Furthermore, Kelly sent a message to the troops of the Detroit Police Department. "Abusive behavior will not be tolerated. People who cannot control themselves and police the streets with restraint cannot work for me or for this department." That this message had been sent out consistently over time and that it had a definitive impact on police officer behavior is shown by the cooperation that numerous officers gave to the internal investigation. Breaking the blue code of silence, several patrol officers gave statements that indicted the conduct of their peers. These statements were at least partially responsible for Detroit police officers losing their jobs.

This experience may be compared to that of the New York City Police Department. "In approximately 8,000 complaints investigated in 1987 and 1988, there was not a single instance of an officer coming forward with incriminating information about another officer" (NYCLU 1992: 22).

In Los Angeles, when the King incident developed into a media sensation and an external commission investigation, it was discovered that Chief Gates had exhibited a general pattern of light discipline in response to use of excessive force complaints. Assistant Chief David Dotson told the *Los Angeles Daily News* that "in a lot of cases . . . an officer will appeal to the chief, and the chief will (lessen) whatever the decision may have been—whether it be discipline, administrative transfer, an appointment or an upgrade or whatever" (10 July 1991). In response to Dotson's quote and his cooperation with the Christopher Commission, Gates had him removed from command of the Internal Affairs Division (*Los Angeles Times*, 12 July 1991). This action sent another message to the men and women of the Los Angeles Police Department about what was perceived to be misbehavior and what was not. Further revelations showed that the chief's perceived lax attitude toward the use of force had permeated the thinking of officers throughout the department. Command-level officers interviewed said that "the organization is light on excessive force. Light in punishment. . . . if you lie, cheat and steal, we'll fire you; if you use drugs, we'll fire you. But if you use excessive force, we won't" (*Los Angeles Daily News*, 10 July 1991).

Los Angeles's police officers thus received a different message than did Detroit's, and, over time, it had an impact. How much personal responsibility a police chief bears for an incident such as Rodney King's beating is a matter for somber reflection, but there can be no doubt that the perceptions of Chief Kelly and Chief Gates contributed directly to the ethos of their troops. No police chief can stop excessive use of force, corruption, or abuse of authority completely, but there is a point at which the chief's style of management and collective signals become responsible for the actions of cops on the street.

Although the chief's influence cannot be overestimated, other actors have an impact on police behavior and accountability in a direct way. Analysis turns to consider their roles as agents of change.

MUNICIPAL OFFICIALS

There are a number of things that mayors, city managers, or city councils can do to facilitate progress in the area of police accountability. None of them is as important, however, as is the action of sending signals to the community and the police regarding the delivery of police services.

It is a paradox of the criminal justice system that those politicians who espouse support for the police are sometimes guilty of erecting roadblocks that limit progress in law enforcement. In particular, "political rhetoric about a 'war' on drugs and a 'war' on crime has helped turn the police into soldiers— not civil servants or guardians of community order—making them sometimes more aggressive and forceful than they have a right to be in the pursuit of criminals and suspects" (Hoffman and Crew, 1991). Of course, it is politically "sellable" to pontificate in this war mode. Certain politicians have successfully made this metaphor the centerpiece of their careers. Ever-spiraling discussions of "getting tough" are joined in order to guarantee that participants are not perceived as a part of the "soft on crime" crowd. Drug war fever builds, multiplies, and feeds on itself, just as does support for military action.

The police themselves are not innocent in this regard. First, police departments suffer the same limitations on their budgets that impact elsewhere in governmental systems. Police chiefs and police unions, in particular, have fed into this hysterical rhetoric because it is in their best interests fiscally (Cashmore and McLaughlin 1991). Second, focusing attention on this sort of threat strengthens the grip the police have on their organizations. As is true with respect to the military, external security threats can result in increased military power against which it becomes difficult to reassert civilian power. (Again, the military analogy serves this discussion well.)

There are important roles for local-level officials to play in helping to control errant behavior. In particular, politicians must show the courage of their convictions and support law enforcement with tax dollars. Much police training is done in a slipshod fashion, in antiquated facilities (St. Clair 1992). In such an atmosphere, a genuine professional commitment to the career of policing is difficult to generate. As fashionable as it has become to avoid any discussion of new taxes, law enforcement professionals in many areas are paid such paltry salaries that careers are cut short, often because of financial necessity.

Aside from excessive turnover, a lack of financial support can directly produce police misbehavior. Although this practice has now largely been eradicated in some areas, the police historically extorted people on the street as a method of augmenting their meager wages. As one street officer confided to a reporter, "Corruption [will] never . . . be reduced in New York because 'City Hall' view[s] the bribes that police officers . . . [are] regularly extorting from the public as a secret part of their official pay and benefits" (Burnham 1989: 349). Today, the regular shakedown of citizens is a thing of the past in most jurisdictions, but when police interact with drug users and dealers, in particular, it remains a part of the seedy side of police work. As in the past, police officers (some of whom make less money than unskilled workers) are prone to consider members of the drug subculture as deserving targets for extortion. Professionalizing police salaries may change this reality.

In addition to their increasing fiscal support for police departments, local administrations must allow the police great latitude within which to exercise their expertise. Mayors, city managers, and city councils rarely argue with police chiefs on matters of police policy, but this deference to police expertise can go even further. The inclusion of police chiefs as municipal policy-makers might help to develop citywide policies that are more responsive to both police and citizen needs.

Reiss argues that it is important for the police to have "a strong voice in denying a zoning permit, in identifying the public order requirements for a planned public facility, in assessing the traffic and security control essential for a privately developed shopping center, or in developing and enforcing all municipal codes. . . . The police chief must share the role of policy-maker with the community that is to be policed" (1985: 66). These practices can develop a cross-pollination of ideas and democratic responsiveness that can be productive for all elements of the police-community accountability formula.

There was once a critical need to create independent, politically autonomous police organizations and chief executive positions. (This discussion has already pointed out political problems that led to progressive-era changes.) Even in recent times, however, in some municipalities chiefs have been changed almost yearly because of local political struggles (Hudnut 1985). Yet the consequent *unrestricted* tenure that chiefs now have in some places has made the development of any sort of accountability problematic.

In Los Angeles, for example, until the Rodney King beating incident the police chief had almost attained "chief for life" status. According to the Christopher Commission, the Los Angeles chief has a "'substantial property right' in his job . . . [and] cannot be suspended or removed except for 'good and sufficient cause' based upon an act or omission occurring within the prior year . . . [the cause established] in a 'full, fair and impartial hearing' before the Board of Civil Service Commissioners" (1991: 185). In practice, these requirements translate into an immunity from accountability, which has extended from 1937 to 1992 (Christopher Commission 1991; Donner 1989).

Over the years, the immunity of Los Angeles police chiefs has, in turn, produced what some consider an insularity from the local values and aspirations of populations policed (Moss 1977). Local politicians, fearing the labels "soft on crime" and "anti-police," for decades have been reluctant to step forward and suggest limiting police chief tenure.

This propensity for political elites to be reluctant to exercise authority over the chief is by no means limited to Los Angeles; it is a problem throughout the country (U.S. Civil Rights Commission 1981). Summed up succinctly by the Christopher Commission:

> The Chief of Police must be more responsive to the Police Commission and the City's elected leadership, but also must be protected against improper political influences. To achieve this balance, the Chief should serve a five-year term, renewable at the discretion of the Police Commission for one additional five-year term. The selection, tenure, discipline, and removal of the Chief should be exempted from existing civil service provisions. (1991: xxii)

Agreeing with the limited, renewable contract idea are scholars, police chiefs, and mayors of a variety of political persuasions (Andrews 1985; Bouza 1990; Fraser 1985).

Controlling the chief's tenure, however, is only a part of what these actors must do to help develop police accountability in a contemporary context. Particular circumstances may require even stricter measures. The civilian executive may have to make a particularly strong stand against a chief who has apparently become uncontrollable. In the aftermath of the Rodney King beating in Los Angeles, for example, the mayor requested the Police Commission to adopt a policy measure that would "require the police chief to describe in writing his reasons for altering any recommended disciplinary action against an officer" (*Los Angeles Times*, 17 July 1991). This is quite an unusual step, but, on occasion, local officials must stand up to the power of the chief if accountability is to be maintained.

The paradox of the Los Angeles situation is that local civilian officials shared responsibility for the police department's behavioral problems in the first place. For the previous few years, the chief and the department had every reason to believe that they were free to act as they pleased. Several specific incidents left the police with the impression that they were operating in a political vacuum.

In 1978 the chief attempted to protect intelligence operations from the scrutiny of the Los Angeles City Council. The police chief declined to answer questions about clandestine operations and asserted that divulging such information might endanger the lives of undercover officers. If an officer were to be killed, he told the council and the press, "each council member would naturally become suspect" (Donner 1989: 278). This direct threat to the members of the city's political leadership generated no censure from the council.

Equally important, and much closer chronologically to the King occurrence, was the Dalton Avenue drug raid in 1988. In this incident, more than eighty officers "rampaged through four apartments and beat their occupants while seizing an ounce of cocaine and six ounces of marijuana. None of the residents was charged with a crime" (*San Diego Union*, 14 August 1991). Internal investigators cataloged 127 separate acts of police vandalism. The city paid out over $3.4 million in damages to fifty-two people. The internal investigation found poor supervision and management to be the cause of the incident. But few officers were brought up on charges and only one was found guilty (Christopher Commission 1991). Even in the face of a stern-sounding investigative report and this scandalous, sensational, media event, no action was taken to hold the police chief or the department responsible for police behavior. No commission was formed, no changes were undertaken, and no reason was given to the chief or to the command structure of the police department to lead people to believe that those in power in the city required any other style of policing. When one considers these examples, it is difficult to hold the police command structure singularly responsible for mismanagement in King's beating.

If any sort of accountability is to develop in holding the police responsible to civilian authorities, those authorities must send out consistent signals regarding their expectations of the police. They must have the political courage to speak out and to act when necessary against police abuses. Just as with chiefs themselves, local officials must deliver messages to the police that express their views that such behavior is unacceptable. To do anything less is to invite the sort of problems that the Los Angeles Police Department had developed by 1991 and to bear some of the responsibility for them.

There is no "how-to-do-it" checklist for local officials. Balancing the various interests involved in police accountability is a complex, delicate task. Just as with the chief's difficult role in this effort, one must take care not to allow officials too much latitude because of this difficulty. If local officials are not up to holding the chief accountable for the administration of the police department and for the behavior of the police, then the people of the community need to replace them with people who are capable of making these balances.

This discussion continues with an analysis of the influence of several groups of community actors on police behavior and accountability.

THE COMMUNITY

This chapter's "wish list" for students of police accountability is replete with "what if" suggestions about the positive potentials that various interest groups and actors have for helping to produce acceptable police conduct. This section considers the potential to influence change that other, unofficial, interest groups hold. The first nonofficial group discussed is the press.

The Press

This chapter's suggestions may perhaps be least realistically applied to the press, because, in terms of accountability, the press is easily the most unaccountable political entity in America. Through its virtue of being a mechanism by which all others are held accountable, the press itself remains completely aloof from review. When it acts irresponsibly, is abusive, treats citizens, police officers, or administrators with contempt or dishonesty, there is no other institution operating to hold its transgressions up for analysis. And because the press is not used to being held accountable, it, more than any of the other entities, tends effectively to ignore prescriptions for its own change.

It is important to consider the press's responsibility when discussing the kinds of scandals it infrequently reports about the police. If local officials in Los Angeles were partly responsible for the creation of the police department's problems in 1991, then the local press, too, bears some of the blame. In its tendency to focus only on the spectacular and ignore the mundane, the press may inadvertently encourage daily police corruptions to fester and compound. The executive administrators of Los Angeles waited to see if public interest in the Dalton Avenue raid would go away over time; so did the Los Angeles press corps.

The press eschewed reporting about police abuses when they were routine and unspectacular. After reporting the Dalton Avenue raid, the press turned away from police misconduct because people seemed to have lost interest. When the Los Angeles Police Department began to develop its problem with police officers beating citizens after high speed chases (see Chapter 4), the press looked the other way. It is difficult to believe that the local press did not know about this problem, because by March 1991 it had become common knowledge among those in California law enforcement and among the citizens of Los Angeles. The press simply chose not to antagonize the police by reporting the growing number of such incidents.

Local police coverage is usually done through police "press information" offices, which makes covering the "police beat" a relatively easy endeavor. Nevertheless, because of the symbiotic relationship that normally develops between the local police and reporters, stories about patterns of abuse or of growing or potential problems are almost unheard of. There is every reason to believe, however, that occurrences of genuinely scandalous events could be avoided if daily pressure were brought to bear on police departments that seem to have been developing such problems.

As Jerome Skolnick and Candace McCoy point out, "Only a part of the police 'product' involves sensational news, but by and large, the media's focus on that aspect of a police department's productivity vastly overshadows coverage of its complex governmental side. Thus inquiry into one of our most fundamental public institutions is less varied, thoughtful, and searching than is desirable" (1985: 103). Consequently, the potential for the press to hold the police accountable for their actions is lost. Only when a Rodney King, Hell's Angels, or Dalton Avenue type of incident occurs does the press roll into action, and by then it is too late for the casualties of police abuse. They have already become victims.

Other facets of the community concerned with police accountability are the various elements of the bar.

Civil Law Attorneys

A second community group that can have an indirect influence on police accountability is composed of attorneys who bring civil suits against the police. This may seem axiomatic, because lawyers' actions can cost individual police officers and the municipality a lot of time and money.

There is an additional area of concern to police administrators that calls for restraint and a commitment to the community on the part of the civil suit attorney. This study has noted that some jurisdictions have attempted to develop early-warning systems that may detect future behavioral problems in police officers. Similarly, communities are experimenting with mediational programs and conciliatory procedures. All of these developments are good, but such programs develop data that may be used outside the police organization as evidence of police officers' propensity toward errant behavior. The same critical indicator statistics that the Oakland chief compiles to find problems may also be used in court to prove an officer's propensity to use excessive force. As noted in Chapter 2, citizens may also use such evidence to defend a charge of resisting arrest. Additionally, information about mediation or conciliation of cases may be used to show that an officer frequently gets into trouble.

When local attorneys find that experimental mediation programs exist, they are placed in a quandary. In the interests of one client's case does one subpoena these data and thus motivate the police to destroy the early-warning system or mediation program, and with it a method of prospective behavior control? Or does one keep this knowledge to him- or herself? Does one allow the chief to continue to operate an experimental system that, in the long run, will be good for everyone?

These questions are not hypothetical. Chief George Hart in Oakland related that a local attorney, who could have used the information in a case, refused to do so and thus left the chief's experimental early-warning system intact. For an attorney to make this kind of decision, in the best interests of both the community and the police, requires integrity. It indicates a commitment to the community, to the police, and to positive change and should be emulated in other circles. It is unfortunate that under such circumstances the attorney involved must remain anonymous; he or she can only receive the thanks and approbation of the police chief for his or her courageous stand.

Another unofficial interest group relevant to this discussion is the ACLU.

The American Civil Liberties Union

The American Civil Liberties Union has been involved in the development of civilian review for many years. This study has referred to several reports prepared by that body. Samuel Walker (1990), in his history of the ACLU, proudly assigns it credit for having created the first civilian review board. The civilianization of police review systems continues to be a priority item on the agenda of the organization (ACLU 1991).

This study offers some observations to consider with respect to the ACLU. One cannot fail to note what is consistently pointed out by police officers and executives throughout the country: The ACLU fights an ongoing battle for civilian review of the police but, at the same time, operates no similar system to monitor its own actions. The director of the Los Angeles Police Misconduct Lawyer Referral Service, run by the ACLU, has acknowledged that there are enough citizens who complain about the ACLU's operations to make complaints a problem. She suggested a solution to this problem: "[to create] a central referral agency for complainants that we [ACLU lawyers] have control over so we can check to see that they [attorneys] are treating victims fairly" (ACLU 1991). The paradox of this statement is not one that would be lost on many in law enforcement, because the system this attorney suggests for the purposes of monitoring errant attorney behavior is analogous to police-operated internal review processes. It would be a review system operated by attorneys to monitor other attorneys, in an effort to hold them accountable to standards determined by their peers.

Another problem the ACLU should recognize was the source of a significant number of comments in the police officers' attitudinal survey. There are several conflicts of interest involving attorneys and police review. An ACLU attorney who becomes involved in civilian review, for example, might use information gathered through the open access policies of review boards to

222

develop civil cases against the police. (This problem was mentioned briefly in Chapter 5.) Several of the boards observed by this study included ACLU attorneys, who did, in fact, involve themselves in litigation against the local police department. This direct conflict of interest is never lost on members of local law enforcement agencies. Also, ACLU attorneys often lobby for the institution of civilian review. They are perceived by the police to be concerned with, as one cop put it, "their own full-employment program." It is axiomatic that attorneys will be engaged in civilian review processes; they are hired as staff administrators, as investigators, and by clients for hearing representation.

Attorneys must be absolutely diligent in their avoidance of conflict of interest. Any attorney involved in the political fight over civilianization of police review systems must remove him- or herself from any situation later on in which he or she might obtain financial remuneration from that effort. It should be a standing policy of the ACLU that any of its attorneys participating in civilianized review structures should be considered guilty of legal misconduct if they involve themselves in civil litigation against the police organization they are monitoring.

Aside from these problems, the ACLU suffers from several tactical errors in its quest for increased police accountability. The first is that members of the organization are often guilty of engaging in inflammatory rhetoric. The antipolice tone of some of their discussions is enough to turn the police deaf to the more valid, rational parts of their message. Language about the "vicious nature," the "stupidity," and the "sadism" of police officers is insulting to the educated, honest, genuinely professional people in the field. This study can only point out that if this kind of rhetoric were applied by police officers to any group of individuals as a class, those carrying the flag of "police accountability" would be the first to label such language as "verbal abuse" and "discrimination."

Tangential to this point is an observation made by Anthony Bouza about the ACLU's tactics. The former chief notes:

In a nation of marketers, the A.C.L.U. has forgotten the importance of packaging its product. Instead of encompassing its stands in what is broadly taken to be anticop rhetoric, it should be championing tough law-and-order postures, while insisting that aggressive tactics be pursued with strict regard for the law. The A.C.L.U.'s failure to enfold itself in the mantle of the language of the law-and-order set has cost it any possible support from law enforcers and has thereby lost it the assistance of the people who love their cops as well. This has proved to be a classical case of attending to the substance while ignoring the form. (1991: 174)

An example of what Bouza would call a "lost opportunity" for the ACLU is its successful defense of the members of the New York Sergeants' Benevolent Association against unreasonable searches and seizures of their lockers (Walker 1990). Carefully advertising efforts like this to the police could serve to sell the ACLU's cause in two ways: First, it indicates the ACLU's willingness to stand by cops when their rights are threatened, and, second, it could help to create a healthy appreciation for the limitations of the Fourth Amendment and for procedural law in general. Taken together, these arguments suggest that the American Civil Liberties Union could be doing a much more effective job of conveying to the police its views about the civilianization of review, due process rights, and limited government. If the substance of these ideas is important, then taking the time to work on making them more acceptable to the police should be well worth the effort.

The final interest group for analysis is the political elite outside of the governmental subculture.

Political Elites

"Local political elites" is of course an amorphous rubric to apply to those who collectively influence politics and decision making from outside the government. The words and actions of the power elite can be critical in influencing police accountability. Local elites share the same responsibility for scandal that was noted with respect to the press and municipal officials. For example, the members of the ruling elite in Los Angeles ignored systematic police abuses for years (such as the abuse perpetrated by police in the Dalton Avenue raid in Los Angeles). To then lay the responsibility for all that ails the police on the doorstep of one person—Chief Gates—is neither reasonable nor responsible. It smacks of avoidance and excuse-making of the highest order, and it produces significant animosity within the police subculture and organizational hierarchy. This can only hurt efforts to implement change of any meaningful sort.

Equally insulting to the majority of people in law enforcement are the intellectual assumptions of elite commissions. The implicit understanding of many of these commissions is that lawyers, backed by "token academics" and business people, in a few weeks of hearings and interviews, can develop an understanding of police work, the police subculture, and police organizational dynamics. It is further assumed that this understanding will be superior to that possessed by police professionals. In some cases, this presumption produces findings that to the police are absurd. Witness, for example, the mutually exclusive suggestions of the Christopher Commission in Los Angeles. This group called for the institution of "community-based policing" and for the centralization of decision making in areas such as complaint-handling and the selection of field training officers. To police professionals, educated in the field about the grass-roots, decentralized decision-making tenets of community-based policing, such a suggestion is absurd. Nuclear control is completely incompatible with such problem-oriented policing. Yet this fact was lost on a commission composed of three academicians, one businessperson, and six lawyers, not one with experience in police work. The Christopher Commission was backed by a staff of fifteen accountants, one professor (in charge of "press information"), one police departmental adviser, and 101 attorneys; it seems that the commission's ignorance about law enforcement theory and practice was preordained.

One might assert that these commissions must be composed of persons from outside the particular agency investigated, otherwise an objective evaluation of organizational problems is not possible. Investigatory, blue-ribbon commissions are typically made up of members of the ruling elite, usually "downtown law firm" attorneys, who bear at least some responsibility for the problems of the local police. Those who argue that the police cannot be entrusted to analyze the problems of their own organization in an objective manner must also accept that these commissions will not be prone to criticize themselves and their culpability in creating corrupt police environments. This assertion holds true when one considers the specific recommendations of the commissions that have recently concluded their work and that have been analyzed by this study. In both Boston and Los Angeles, investigatory commissions issued not one word of criticism aimed at the participation of sociopolitical elites in the creation of police problems.

These commissions, however, can go outside their jurisdictions to obtain police managerial expertise. Two commissions this study examined made minimal attempts to do so. In Los Angeles, the commission heard testimony from 153 individuals; nine were from outside Los Angeles and four had practical experience in police work. In Boston, the commission heard from "hundreds" of people; four had experience in police work outside of Boston. The implication is that it is not necessary to consult life-long workers in law enforcement to discern everything there is to know about it.

The implementation of commission findings is always difficult, at best. An animosity exists between police officers and lawyers. Anyone who has ever been around the police for any length of time knows this. To have a group of "highly paid" (from the cop's perspective), nonpolice-oriented attorneys analyze police problems and present solutions is to invite all sorts of disclaimers from the police as to the authenticity of commission findings.

When such commissions are formed, as they invariably will be, great care must be taken to include more than a token police professional perspective. Depending on the problems investigated, it is preferable to have as much direct input from the local police department as can be reasonably utilized. This does not involve interviewing local cops, though that is an important endeavor. It involves having police executives and police union representatives on the commission itself. Sometimes this caveat is not realistic owing to the nature of the commission's charge, investigating large-scale organizational corruption, for example. Under such circumstances, care must be taken to consult with outside law enforcement sources. This, again, does not mean that interviews should be conducted wherein attorneys talk to police officers. It means that commissions should include police professionals who hold stature within the field and who have experience in police organizational management and problem-solving.

Reform can only be expected in the field of police account-ability when blue-ribbon commissions understand the above. Progress will come from a combination of respect for police pro-fessionals and an understanding of the pragmatic realities to be faced when implementation rolls around. Commissions operated "of, by, and for" the legal profession are destined to make little difference in the long-term behavioral patterns of police officers on the street. The control of the police over their own milieu is too great to expect anything else.

The community in general, press, attorneys, and commissions, can effectively impact the problems of malpractice only if they share both a sense of responsibility for their police and a respect for the competence of the professionals in the "new blue line."

SUMMATION

All of these agents are limited in how they can influ-ence police behavior. All, even chiefs of police, have at best an indirect impact on the strong, cohesive police subculture. Only by working with some sort of cohesion themselves can they in-fluence such a powerful group of individuals as the police.

Two Final Limits of Reform

Two realities are central to understanding how these agents and the police interact symbiotically.

First, the abuse of power by police officers, the use of exces-sive force, the development of police-community tensions, and the paradoxes of police review mechanisms will always be a re-ality unless fundamental changes occur in American society. This is a society gripped by violence, crime, racism, and class divisions that run deep and wide. Its social institutions of behav-ioral control are failing. As long as things remain this way, the police will be asked to pursue unattainable goals with imprecise

227

tools under impossible conditions. All interest groups must, to some extent, understand this or they will misunderstand the reality of police work and thus will be useless as potential agents of change.

But these groups must do more than simply understand this reality. They must bear a positive responsibility to attempt change. As Robert Reiner points out with respect to British policing in the mid-1980s:

> The worst enemies of the current police bid for relegitimation are arguably not their overt critics but their apparent benefactors—a "law and order" government which is unconcerned about destroying the social preconditions of consensus policing and the virtues of British police tradition. The present government has pursued social and economic policies which have generated rapidly increasing inequality, long-term unemployment and political polarization, leading many to re-invoke the Disraelian metaphor of the "two nations." . . . Present government policies are deincorporating sections of society, notably the young, "never-employed," especially concentrated among ethnic minorities, and swelling the ranks of those groups who have always been the hard core of non-acceptance of the police. (1985: 209)

Reiner's statement was prophetic of the America of the 1990s. Without a commitment from those both within and without government to attack the root causes of crime and violence, the police will be left alone to clean up after society. Without any meaningful support, the police out of necessity will employ whatever pragmatic measures they can find to do the job. They will do this while attempting to ensure for themselves as reasonable a zone of safety, both personally and collectively, as they can create. To expect anything else of this group of people is to live in an "Alice in Wonderland" world.

A second symbiotic relationship between the police officer on the street and external agents has been duly noted by numerous authors from different disciplines: *People get the police they desire.* Whether the focus is on municipal administrations, sociopolitical elites, or the broad spectrum of public opinion, in the long term a police force mirrors the concerns of its community. Even the most high-handed, abusive actions of the police are

228

acceptable to some Americans. In fact, several of this study's examples, most notably the Hell's Angels case, indicate that such behavior is more than acceptable; it is sometimes even demanded. It is perceived by many as the very reason for having an organized police force.

While arguing for reform and for increased accountability, Lea and Young point out, again with respect to Britain, "One of our constant nightmares is that if there was a completely democratic control of police in areas such as Hackney, the resulting police force would look exactly the same as the present" (Lea and Young 1984: 276). The troubling duality of administrative accountability is that the police officer understands this. Although the rule of law is somewhat divorced from the realities of the street, cops on the beat know that "getting tough on crime" and administering a little "curbside justice" is perfectly acceptable to many of their constituents. Too much time need not be spent in explaining to the police that they must ignore this reality, because they know better. Theirs is a most democratic occupation. These curbside administrators must always balance the pragmatics of the street against the niceties of the law. They cannot avoid this because it is the nature of their charge. Society must not be surprised when police tend to support what apparently works and eschew what apparently does not. To misunderstand this reality is to misunderstand the central problem of police accountability all together.

In the next chapter, this study pulls together all the information from the examination of the three types of police malpractice review systems, and, using the evaluation criteria, it analyses these mechanisms comparatively.

8 Review Systems Compared

Review systems are not interchangeable from one political milieu to another. The system in Chicago may not work in Oakland or in Los Angeles. Size of organization, type of population policed, police malpractice history, and local political structures are only several factors that may influence the ability of a given review system to remain effective and legitimate.

On one hand, this study has considered civilianized review systems, in Richmond, for example, that spend a great deal of money and generate little in the way of openness and legitimacy for the review process. On the other hand, it has discussed internal systems, such as Oakland's, that operate with an integrity and tenacity that is unsurpassed by civilian mechanisms. Determining whether Oakland's internal review system could be transferred to Boston, or whether employing a system such as Berkeley's PRC could improve Richmond's mechanism is problematic. Too much depends not only on these variables but also on the people—the police officers, police administrators, civilian monitors, city managers, and mayors—who operate review systems. Their individual and collective commitments to organizational integrity and to police professionalism usually determine what works for them.

Until this point, this study has concerned itself only briefly with one particularly thorny issue. In America, where many municipal administrations are bankrupt and running on credit and the momentum of their own histories, the fiscal impact of police review must be considered central to any discussion of these systems. Review systems must be operated in a manner that protects cities from financial ruin. To do so, review systems must (1) avoid spending exorbitant amounts of money on their own operations, (2) influence police misbehavior in a way that will lessen the gravity and impact of this influence over time, and (3) keep themselves as judgment-proof as possible. Everyone agrees with the first two goals, but it sounds quite Machiavellian to discuss the third, that systems must also work to protect themselves from attack even when malpractice has occurred. To those outside police and municipal administrations, this suggestion indicates a lack of concern for the plight of citizens who are on the receiving end of police abuse.

Be that as it may, it would be a serious dereliction of duty for a municipality's administrators to allow it to fall into bankruptcy and thus cease to be able to provide services to the people. One must necessarily keep in mind this long-term cost analysis in the comparison of police review systems. Some forms of police review spend tremendous amounts of resources—sometimes to little or no avail—in attempting to create external legitimacy, in particular. One must look with a jaundiced eye toward systems that are only marginally effective at impacting police behavior but expend significant amounts of the people's resources.

This comparative analysis, avoiding generalizations, discusses some cautious parallels using the three main criteria of evaluation.

INTEGRITY

In its comparison of police review systems, the results of this study with respect to the criterion of integrity suggest that all three models do a similarly effective job of fairly, competently, and objectively handling individual complaints. At the intake level, there is not much to debate. Put simply, other-than-police locations are always preferable. This examination found that no counterproductive tendencies developed and that citizen-complainants seemed to be more at ease when using such structures. Furthermore, a police review mechanism that uses intake personnel who are not sworn police officers seems also to have only positive effects on review system integrity. Because they were properly taught as to what to look for in an initial complaint interview, the analysts at Kansas City's OCC and the investigators at Berkeley's PRC, for example, were found to be professional and competent in the performance of their charges. And at Kansas City, nonpolice personnel cost the internal review operation nothing in terms of wasted time or effort (Skolnick and Bayley 1986).

Input regulations at Kansas City, in particular, have been treated at length. Suffice it to say that to increase perceptions of integrity as regards input procedures review mechanisms must take great care to operate in an open manner. They must be particularly cognizant of any tendencies to inhibit would-be complainants from filing complaints. Whether civilian- or police-operated, input mechanisms need to be receptive of any and all complaints, no matter what their apparent gravity at first glance. Anonymous complaints must be accepted and treated with an appropriate level of seriousness. Anonymous complaints about long coffee breaks need not be given importance, but charges of corruption and brutality must be treated as bona fide until proven otherwise.

Similarly, police review mechanisms must eschew citizens' requirements to notarize statements, and their employees must stop admonishing complainants as if they were somehow "suspects." Such procedures may suggest that review systems are not serious about pursuing police malpractice. Though everyone knowledgeable about citizens' complaints understands that some complaints are filed vindictively, it does no one any good to operate a system that accepts this as universally true. Richmond's system is illustrative. This small municipality receives and investigates an average of sixty-three complaints per year at the police-operated internal affairs organ. It receives only eleven complaints per year at the civilian system, and this, at least in part, may be because of the admonition the civilian investigator gives to prospective complainants about "truthful statements" (noted earlier).

From an observer's perspective, most of the systems examined appear to do a thorough job of investigating alleged police misconduct. Oakland and Kansas City's internal procedures are surprisingly good for their thoroughness and tenacity; they are far more rigorous than external observers believe them to be. In Oakland, this reflects the personal style of the chief of police, who is determined to pursue abusive behavior tenaciously. In Kansas City's system, the anticipation of the civilian review of cases may have more to do with investigative thoroughness than does any other factor. It would seem, then, that the Kansas City system might somehow be considered "better" because it operates more independently of personal styles of management.

Berkeley's investigations, too, are professional and complete. The Berkeley City Manager confirms that the results are usually in agreement with internal review conclusions. Thus, the intuitive argument of those in law enforcement, that civilian investigators will be incompetent, seems to be unfounded. In fact, outcome decisions were found to be "objective," in a legalistic sense, in all three of the model systems. That is to say, that a removed observer would almost always concur with the decisional outcomes developed by each process, internal, external, and monitor.

Corroboration for this assertion can be gleaned from the consistent agreement between civilian and police reviewers as to outcome, in those locations where this and other studies have been able to make comparisons. However, these points about complaint statistics and agreement in outcome might appear to be inconsistent. It has been noted that city managers find that the results of internal and civilian review mechanisms usually agree when these bodies have investigated the same cases; in places where parallel systems operate, the systems' members almost universally come to the same conclusion when treating a given incident. (One must remember, however, that city managers usually concern themselves only with "major" cases, wherein police officers have been *found guilty* of misconduct.) Comparisons of these mechanisms tell us that (1) internal systems are rigorous and (2) civilian systems do not tend to find the police guilty of misconduct more often than do their internal counterparts.

Elsewhere this study has noted, however, that internal review systems almost universally find the police guilty of misconduct *more often* than do civilian systems. How can these statements both be correct? The answer is that *studies of overall caseloads tend to find that civilian review is easier on the police than is internal review.* That is, when the results of major cases, minor complaints, and "satisficing" practices are all put together into systemic "sustained rates," the police-operated systems find a higher percentage of officers guilty of misconduct.

This disparity is explained in several ways. The discussions of 233 "satisficing" point out that a significant number of minor cases are not investigated by the police. Concomitantly, as previously noted, in many civilian systems these cases *are* investigated, and this skews sustained statistics. This discussion has also noted the police system's interest in truthfulness. Police chiefs and their delegates in internal affairs pursue falsification as a major offense, but lying is usually considered rather unimportant, almost a "part of the game," by civilian systems. Thus, sustained rates will, again, tend to be higher for internal systems.

In civilian monitor systems, internal investigations are reviewed by external administrators or civilian commission members. In these systems, such as in Kansas City, Baltimore, or San Diego, this study found that the monitors' findings agree with the internal investigators' findings, again, almost universally. In fact, where statistics are kept, this agreement exceeds 95 percent of cases considered (such as in Baltimore).

One must also consider the impact of the complaints that are not sustained. When there is no independent evidence in a case and the review system has only the word of a police officer against the word of a citizen, there is no fair and just way to decide the outcome. "Not sustained" must be the finding in these cases. Such outcomes make up a huge portion of caseloads everywhere. In 1989, the Los Angeles Police Department found that 43 percent of its complaints were not sustained (1989). The much smaller Richmond, California, department finds cases not sustained at the rate of 56 percent (Richmond, California, Police Department 1990).

But this comparison must note that civilianized operations develop even higher numbers of outcomes that are not sustained than do police-operated systems. In Chicago, the civilian-run Office of Professional Standards finds that 81.5 percent of its cases are not sustained (1991). In New York City, the civilian monitor system there finds that 85 percent of its cases are thus categorized (NYCLU 1991).

If one puts these results together with the propensity for internal police systems to find outcomes sustained more often than do civilian ones, one reaches a disconcerting conclusion for proponents of civilian review; civilianized mechanisms are less likely to produce statistics that are in any way comforting to those outside the police experience. Furthermore, other profes-

234

sions are far more guilty of self-serving, defensive tactics where alleged misbehavior is concerned (American Bar Association 1970; Hanewicz 1985; McDowell 1991). Lawyers are particularly important in this regard, because they are often at the forefront of efforts to change police review systems. It is not irrelevant to the police that the legal profession's own internal disciplinary mechanism seldom finds fault with attorneys accused of misconduct. (In only slightly more than 1 percent of the cases that it investigates does the bar's own grievance-handling committee find fault with peer professionals [American Bar Association 1970; Carlin 1966].)

Thus, this study has found that in several modern, professional police organizations chiefs and police officers, in general, are tougher on cops than are civilians. Klockars nicely sums up this part of the discussion:

> The problem with outsider review of either police or medical practices is not that lay persons would demand too much of police or physicians, but that they do not possess the kind of knowledge of options and alternatives that would permit them to demand more. The only ones who have the detailed knowledge necessary to distinguish good policing from that which is merely not criminal, civilly liable or scandalous are experienced, skilled police officers. (1992: 12)

There is no answer to the dilemma of professional expertise versus external review. This study found both sides of the debate to be persuasive. Acceptance of the civilian monitor system, however, is predicated on the belief that professional expertise must be accepted and deferred to, while external perspectives are brought to bear in an advisory capacity. Combining the external and internal perspectives as it does, the monitor allows for the generation of the optimum amount of fairness, competence, and objectivity.

Analysis now focuses upon legitimacy, a more problematic criterion of evaluation.

LEGITIMACY

Internally operated mechanisms fair very well with respect to the first criterion. The externally perceived legitimacy of these systems is, of course, their major shortcoming. According to this study's examination, it is the completely in-house, police-operated system that seems to develop the least amount of acceptance in the community. In areas in which police-community relations suffer from significant tensions, usually with racial overtones, community acceptance is especially low.

In the inner city, unlike in suburban and rural areas, police departments have spent great amounts of time and money developing internal police review systems, in order to develop departmental legitimacy. However, the operational conventions of internal systems actually restrict the growth of citizen-based faith in them. The secrecy of the internal affairs process is particularly troublesome to the development of community faith.

That tenacious internal mechanisms may be developed for the wrong reasons is beside the point when one considers their effects on police behavior, but when one considers the basic reasons for the development of these systems, it is not irrelevant to be concerned with perceptions of legitimacy. The defensiveness inherent in internal police processes can help to develop more than rigorousness in investigations, it can produce in the police a dogged devotion to organizational secrecy, which can be counterproductive with respect to community-based legitimacy.

As Carlin notes in his study of the disciplinary systems of bar associations, "The organized bar through the operation of its formal disciplinary measures seems to be less concerned with scrutinizing the moral integrity of the profession than with forestalling public criticism and control" (1968: 62–65). Although this goal may still allow the development of rigorous review conventions, its legitimacy outside the organized bar will tend to be limited. The same could be said about the law enforcement profession. The defensiveness of the system can be perceived easily by observers who expect the worst.

As a reaction to external legitimacy problems, in Kansas City the police organization negotiated the inclusion of civilians in their process (Selznick 1966). A good rapport has developed, over time, between the police and the semiexternal monitoring structure.

The disparity of satisfaction that police officers and citizens obtain from the three types of review systems is quite striking.

The police tend to support local review systems no matter what form they take; whatever is familiar seems to be preferable. Even those cops subject to civilian review seem to have normalized it as simply a part of the "rules of the discipline game." (It must be remembered that in 80 percent of complaint investigations handled by internal review systems, the police do not find their fellow officers guilty of misbehavior.)

Citizen complainants, however, find almost all systems lacking in legitimacy. The majority of the respondents held negative perceptions of the thoroughness, fairness, and objectivity of the various systems to which they complained. Even those citizens whose cases were treated by civilians at Berkeley, where satisfaction levels were somewhat higher, found the system lacking. Since complainants "lose" 80 percent of the time, this feeling is understandable. If complainants "won" more often, undoubtably they would feel that police review mechanisms, of whatever form, were more legitimate.

The tendency of those in the survey sample to strongly correlate complaint outcome with evaluations of systemic integrity is confirmed by another study of citizen attitudes toward complaint mechanisms. Patricia Ward Crowe (1978) found the same dynamic operating with respect to the Massachusetts Commission Against Discrimination. Crowe found that complaint evaluations of review system fairness were directly related to investigative outcome. This evaluative dynamic places severe limitations on citizen acceptance of review systems. Because citizens file many complaints that cannot be substantiated and because police are usually legally and procedurally correct in their actions, a fair and objective system finds "for" police much more often than "for" citizens. And it *should* do so.

Although most review systems seem objective and thorough, two problems have been illustrated that severely limit complainants acceptance of these systems. First, legal requirements are imposed on review systems through codified law, administrative case law, and convention. These make some outcomes substantively unfair from the complainant's perspective. Second, complainants do not seem to be able to differentiate between outcome and integrity. Since this is so, and since review systems employ adversarial, legalistic processes, the overwhelming majority of complainants will be disappointed with their treatment by any review system.

It may seem that too much is being made of "potentials," goals that have not yet been realized. Indeed, there are critics of civilian involvement in police review systems who feel that the experiments with civilians in these systems have been shams, fooling the public into trusting internal mechanisms. Mike Meyers of the New York ACLU asserts that the New York civilianized system is not a real civilian review board because so few cases of abuse are sustained (ACLU 1991). Several points should be made about this.

For some, the substantive correctness of the accused police officer in the vast majority of cases means that no system will ever be considered legitimate. Thus discussions of the potential that a given system might have for developing "perceived legitimacy" or police officer acceptance are not wasted efforts. If, by their very nature, fair review systems *cannot* satisfy many complainants, their symbolic actions and images become of paramount importance. Also, the institutionalization of experimental systems takes time. The potential of civilianization to bridge the police-community communications gap, for example, may not be realized for a number of years in cities where civilian review is being attempted. In Berkeley and Kansas City, after a generation of effort, there is evidence that progress is being made. Yet, because a majority of America's civilian systems have only been founded in the past ten years, one is often forced to speculate about civilian review potentials. One must also consider the political impact of police officer professional organizations. Their constant attacks against the development of accountability mechanisms of any kind color the perceptions and understanding of the dynamics of civilianization.

One should not be too hasty to label concerns about "perceived legitimacy" as Machiavellian. After all, this study has shown many distinctive advantages to internal review that are simply not known or believed by the general public. Though externally perceived legitimacy is very important, it is not the only yardstick by which review mechanisms must be measured. One can envision a system of ad hoc, "kangaroo courts," that finds every accusation of police misconduct to have substance. To

238

some citizens, using a system whose members assume that police accused of misconduct are guilty may seem to be a legitimate method of dealing with allegations of police abuse. Yet this system could be so unfair to police officers that it could change the entire fabric of the criminal justice system. To be concerned with the symbolic meaning of a system, or its "front," is not to be unreasonably patronizing of the public. It is a rational exercise of political importance to the police and to local political elites. It speaks directly to the symbols of accountability.

Finally, with respect to external legitimacy, one must be reminded of the importance of publishing police review mechanisms' data and procedures. This kind of openness costs review organizations little; even so, some police review systems avoid publishing even the most basic complaint data (number of accusations, number sustained, and number of contacts, for example). Making these data available is a simple public relations action that can be an important tool in developing support for any kind of review process.

Lack of community faith in internal systems, then, seems to be a problem that is not limited to the police. The openness that civilian involvement in any kind of administrative review may generate can develop a faith in accountability mechanisms not normally existent. If only as symbols, civilians may be of considerable utility to police review systems and to police-community relations in general.

Because legitimacy is a two-edged sword, one must consider briefly the police officer's view of the various types of systems. This research endeavor began with the understanding that the overwhelming majority of police officers and police executives in America were prejudiced against civilian review. An examination of the data compiled in the seventeen years of this study has not changed that understanding. Where civilian review has not been attempted, this prejudgment still exists among law enforcement personnel. Yet one crucial finding of this study is that police officers in jurisdictions that *have* experienced civilian review are not opposed to it. The police officers who have been educated to the realities of civilian review will often take issue with some of the specifics of its application. They will argue with the politics of particular individuals and interest groups involved in civilian processes. But a majority of police officers who have direct experience with civilian review neither fear it nor believe it to be illegitimate. On the contrary, police officers educated to the potential legitimizing functions of civilian review believe it to be a viable, workable concept.

To recap, citizens' perceptions of the legitimacy of review systems depends on whether their complaints are sustained or not sustained. Citizens dislike the secrecy of internal systems and feel that openness is extremely important. Openness includes publishing data that citizens and review systems may examine. Finally, police that have participated in civilianized systems are more accepting of them than are police who have not participated.

It is now time to determine how citizens and police feel about the learning potential inherent in these models.

LEARNING

Internal police review systems are the most effective mechanisms for actually influencing the behavior of police officers on the street. The observations and interviews across all organizations studied indicate that police departmental review mechanisms are often in the minds of police officers when they make discretionary judgments. If there is a deterrent effect operating in a prospective manner between police review systems and the would-be errant officer, and this study concludes that there is, it is most fully realized in internal systems.

This is the case for several reasons. Internal systems have important influences on police officers' career goals. If a beat cop develops a troublemaker image in the eyes of the police chief, his or her peers, or with internal affairs itself, the officers' ability to operate effectively within the subculture can be limited. Whether one considers promotional potential, getting the transfer one covets, or specific beat and shift assignments, the errant cop can find a bad reputation to be problematic. As one Oakland cop confided, "You gotta learn who the real cowboys are. Then you stay away from them. Just bein' around the real clowns will get you in the s—— with 'em!"

Internal review systems can influence police officers' careers in another way, as well. The expertise of professional investigators produces thorough investigations and reports. The chances, then, of police officers avoiding being disciplined when wrong are slight in the internal systems. When motivated by a chief executive genuinely concerned with developing accountability, internal systems offer alternatives that answer the concerns about behavioral influence in a most positive way.

Concomitantly, external police review systems are less effective in influencing police behavior in several ways. Due process rights granted to officers by many external mechanisms impose limitations on the rigor of these external investigations. The price paid for procedural fairness is often a lessening of substantive thoroughness.

Also, the extra impetus that pushes the professional to seek out police malpractice does not drive the civilian investigator to the same lengths. Civil service commission experiences are apposite. Chiefs in Berkeley, San Jose, Contra Costa County, and Oakland are consistently more harsh on their police officers than the Civil Service Commissions think they should be. Despite what police officers intuit about civilian review, all of the evidence from this research indicates that civilians who sit on civilian review boards, civil service commissions, or juries are less tough on cops than are modern-day police chiefs.

In very recent history, the idea that civilian review would be a cure-all that stifles police misbehavior has been severely challenged. The existence of civilian review mechanisms did not deter the police officers who rioted at Tompkins Square in New York City in 1988 or police corruption in Cleveland in 1991 (*Cleveland Plain Dealer*, 30 May 1991). It did not control the police at the Berkeley People's Park riot in 1991 (*Berkeley Gazette*, 1–4 August 1991). And it did not impact the systematic abuse of suspects by police in Chicago during the 1980s (*Associated Press*, 8 February 1991). Though police-operated systems were also present, this study must take a hard line and acknowledge that these city's civilian systems failed to deter police misbehavior.

The consideration of the behavioral impact of civilian review systems has underlined another basic problem with many internal regulatory mechanisms. Most internal systems focus on in-

241

dividual complaint adjudication, to the exclusion of policy analysis. Thus the organizational learning of almost all of America's police review systems is very limited. "The essential focus is upon the individual incident. Rarely do individual incidents produce a serious analysis of aggregate performance" (Moore and Stephens, 1991: 61).

Even civilian review boards have problems in this area, because they sometimes confuse the two functions so much that individual cases can become platforms for political diatribes. Yet the review system of the Berkeley PRC, which holds regular hearings that focus on police policy, is a step in the right direction. If this type of system is accepted by the local police and, indeed, receives their cooperation and participation, the resultant open discussion of police policy can help to generate accountability. Review systems' policy development groups should be advisory to the chief, or as they are in Berkeley, to the city manager. With the participation of educated professionals, relevant interest groups, and representatives of the community in general, police policy formulation bodies can, in fact, achieve better police-community relations without in any negative way impacting the police chief's ability to run the department.

Another step forward in the direction of producing prospective behavioral control is the "no-fault" system of complaint consideration, operational in Contra Costa County. Whenever complaints are minor, such as those that relate to procedural questions, officer attitude, lack of action, and so forth, this process treats them as problems for "counseling and training." If other review systems employed this practice, they might be able to increase police officer cooperation, intelligent policy formulation, and organizational communication. This could, in the long run, lessen the influence of the "blue wall of silence," lower the numbers of complaints, and greatly increase citizen satisfaction. Klockars is illustrative here:

> The problem of getting skilled police officers to teach other officers to work in ways that minimize the use of force requires that such teaching be done under conditions in which the normal punitive and disciplinary orientation of police administration is suspended. Only under such conditions will officers be prepared to assume a

242

reasonably receptive, non-defensive posture, and only then will experienced, skilled supervisors be capable of offering constructive criticism of officer conduct. (1992: 12)

Police professional organizations could take a lead in this field. But because of the defensiveness that police unions have traditionally generated in the individual cop, their cooperation in the field of policy analysis and positive behavior control is wanting. What O. W. Wilson said in the past still holds true today. Professionalism among police officers differs from professionalism in other occupations "in that the primary function of the professional code will be to protect the practitioner from the client rather than the client from the professional" (Wilson and McLaren 1963: 201). This trend will be difficult to stem. It will only be exacerbated by review systems that continue to focus on specific complaints and on the culpability of individual officers.

Internal review systems are the most rigorous because they are operated by the police subculture and because internal investigators possess a "driven" nature. But these systems must also be reviewed with respect to their propensities to develop counterproductivity. Some police officers are cynical about internal review mechanisms. They feel that the police are inhibited on the street by overzealous review. It is paradoxical for proponents of civilian review that these police inhibitions were produced by internal review operations. What is more, police are not usually intimidated, abused, or frightened by external civilian police review. Most officers subject to civilian review feel it has no effect whatever on their behavior.

Here one sees the obverse of the strengths of internal review. Although internal review has the greatest impact on police behavior because of its rigor, it is also the system that is most prone to abuse police officers. On one hand, recent history is replete with examples of internal review run amuck, with internal affairs organizations that have produced counterproductive tendencies among the cops they police. On the other hand, this study has determined that in the entire history of civilian review there has never been so much as a hint in any jurisdiction that police officers have ever been abused by civilianization.

Generally, this study found that in none of the systems exam-   243 ined have police officers developed a deep enough cynicism to affect their day-to-day behavior in a negative way. Save in unusual crisis periods, police officers as a group accept police review systems of all sorts as part of the milieu within which they must operate. They may direct some of their traditional police officer cynicism toward review systems, but, in practice, cops are quite conservative in their acceptance of whatever is familiar.

This analysis of counterproductivity has outlined most persuasively the lack of problems associated with civilian review or civilian monitor systems. It has also illustrated the limits of judicialization of complaint processes. It puts in perspective perfectly the balancing act that review system construction involves. More concern for due process means less behavioral impact. More judicialization means less learning by young cops. More secrecy means less legitimacy. There is no system that can make the paradoxes of police review magically disappear.

Thus, although internal review systems seem to have the most powerful deterrent effect on police of the systems examined, perhaps because internal systems are tougher on cops than are external systems, the organizational learning is limited in internal police review systems. External review systems may have less of a deterrent effect on police, but their focus on setting policy that the citizens, the police, and the department can all benefit by may provide an important learning tool for all concerned.

The evaluation of these review systems and the very nature of comparative study begs the question, Which is best?

THE BEST POLICE REVIEW SYSTEM

This discussion has taken great pains to point out the limited utility of considering police review systems as truly comparable. As is often true in the field of public administration, this discussion is underwritten by the question, "Whose ox is gored?" Because of the dual nature of administrative accountability outlined at the beginning of this volume, the question of how the police should be held accountable has never quite been completely resolved. The police argue that "democratic accountability" requires them to be answerable only to the law, interpreted through their professional expertise. Interest groups profess that "democratic accountability" requires the police to answer to their constituencies in a direct fashion. But which is the best system? The theoretical potential of civilian police review to generate legitimacy is persuasive, and the operational utility of the civilian monitor system is appealing in this era of fiscal constraints.

The multiple systems of Berkeley, however, offer a "something-for-everyone" approach to police review. As Goldsmith points out, having numerous avenues available can generate an optimum amount of accountability; to wit:

> An "interpolable balance" perspective takes as its starting point a need to identify "self-policing" mechanisms which are already present in any system, and to build on those. . . . [It] does not assume that "control" is necessarily to be exercised from any fixed place in an institutional system, but can contemplate a network of complementary and overlapping detectors and effectors (that is, "redundant channels," in information-processing language) with mobility—even lability—in the seat of the checking mechanism. (1991: 51)

In Berkeley, those with no faith in police departmental structures can go to a completely external civilian organization to press a complaint. That system offers an open hearing process and a civilianized decision-making perspective. The internal review system is also available to those who wish the police department to handle their own processes. One must remember that some citizens—19.7 percent of all respondents in this study's collective surveys—prefer to bring complaints to the police directly. Thus a parallel system like that of Berkeley might be well received by citizen complainants of both persuasions.

The Berkeley Police Review Commission, however, spends a great deal of time and money duplicating procedures that are also performed by the internal mechanism. As long as police are legally required to investigate complaints, chiefs desire to have direct control over their officers, and municipalities feel threatened by the potential of civil litigation, internal police review systems will exist. But duplication is costly, and this problem is

245

theoretically tantalizing to the discussion because it responds to so many of the concerns about balance. The cost of parallel systems may be prohibitive in most jurisdictions.

The Berkeley PRC's operations carry a $320,000 price tag. This is what civilian review costs in a city of only 104,000. The parallel internal affairs budget at the Berkeley Police Department is $214,000. Other costs for the police review process are covered elsewhere in the city budget (time spent by the city manager, for example). The total expense of more than a half-million dollars covers 140 cases; therefore, the taxpayers of Berkeley spend almost $4,000 ($534,000 divided by 140) for every complaint filed against the police.

The budget for San Francisco's Office of Citizen Complaints is $1.4 million for a city of 750,000 (*San Francisco Chronicle*, 29 May 1990). In Minneapolis, the new civilian board there spent over $350,000 in 1991 for a system that only held four formal hearings and handled eleven complaints (Minneapolis Civilian Police Review Authority 1992). Honolulu's budget seems more fiscally conservative, but that city spent over a quarter-million dollars on 159 complaints (Honolulu Police Commission 1988–1989). In Canada, the Royal Canadian Mounted Police Public Complaints Commission typically spends over US$3 million to monitor about 2,400 complaints per year, and this process has formal hearings so infrequently (nine hearings in the past three years) that virtually all of this expenditure is aimed at monitoring investigations already done by the police (RCMP 1990–1991). To translate this kind of price tag to a city the size of Los Angeles, for example, would result in a cost totaling tens of millions of dollars. One must remember that these monies are being spent *in addition to those spent to support in-house, police-operated systems.* Such a financial obligation to police review is simply unrealistic in most locations in America today. It would be both fiscally irresponsible and politically suicidal for most municipal administrators to contemplate such fiscal commitments.

Alternately, the duplication of the civilian monitor system's practices at Kansas City are limited. Input expenditures for the city are born by the OCC, money for investigative budgets is found in the Internal Affairs Department, and outcome expenses are handled in the OCC. With no parallel investigations to underwrite, Kansas City is billed only once for each part of its system, and, as noted above, the relative costs of civilian analysts versus sworn police investigators actually makes the OCC's operations less expensive. The overall cost of the civilian monitor mechanism thus approximates that of internal review, $1,000 per case at Kansas City, the same as the cost at Oakland.

The theoretical utility of this system has been well illustrated in Chapter 6. It allows the police to police themselves to a certain extent and, therefore, plays on the strengths of both internal investigative systems and informal subcultural peer review. The system amalgamates the strengths of internal and external review in a commonsense manner; it neither sanctifies nor vilifies police-operated internal review mechanisms.

What is more, in terms of police officer acceptance the civilian monitor system speaks to the concern that the population policed must accept a review mechanism in order for the system to be effective. This study found that the 150 officers from Berkeley and Oakland were defensive of internal investigators. They felt that the civilian investigative staff was less competent than police officers to carry on the difficult task of policing the police. These findings seem to support the idea that the police feel that only they can effectively police their own operations.

But this survey went further to reveal some startling information about officer attitudes toward civilianization. When asked to reflect on the ideal system, 64 percent of the police officers surveyed felt police investigators should populate review mechanisms, but an unexpected 35 percent opted for a combination of police and civilian investigators. The data were even more surprising when this study asked these officers who they thought should populate a hearing board for the purposes of adjudicating cases of significant gravity. *Sixty-two percent of the police officers surveyed said that they thought a formal hearing board should be made up of a combination of cops and civilians!*

This finding was not expected at all. It seems to fly in the face of all conventional wisdom about police acceptance of civilian review. One must remember that these officers are working in jurisdictions where they experience civilian review every day. These are not the feelings of police officers who are ignorant of

247

the exigencies of civilianized systems. On the contrary, these police are educated to what civilian review means in practice. Their limited acceptance of the idea of combined civilian- and police-handled investigations and their overwhelming agreement with the concept of civilianized hearing processes is testimony to the fact that police officers feel that civilian review does *not* abuse them or interfere with police organizations' interests.

Gellhorn sums up many of the strengths of a monitor approach. He writes that the discharge of disciplinary responsibility in

> all instances must be subject to an outsider's examination . . . with the object of publicly disclosing slipshod administration or adoption of wrong attitudes. That course should be acceptable to the police as well as to the public. It does not remove from police hands the power to direct, judge, and discipline the staff members whose actions have been challenged, but, as in the case of other departments, leaves to the professionals the job of appraising fellow professionals (1966: 193).

The monitor system, then, leaves intact the behavioral impact and investigatory expertise of the police. It also can generate the external legitimacy and removed perspective of the civilian review board. As in the Toronto monitor system, "initial police investigation of a complaint was intended as a means of giving the police a stake in the system, thereby encouraging their acceptance of it and preserving an important management role. The monitoring and review power of the public complaint commissioner, together with the commissioner's extraordinary right of initial investigation, was intended to ensure that initial investigation and adjudication by police would be thorough and impartial" (Lewis 1991: 159). Its strengths, taken together with its fiscal responsibility, make Kansas City's OCC the best system of those that were studied. The civilian monitor mechanism come closest to answering all of the concerns of police review interest groups at once.

But this study is not limited to a discussion of only the operational systems. Each model has important strong suits. Oakland's system obtained very high marks in several areas, particularly with respect to its willingness to experiment with behavioral modification strategies, and I would like to laud that internal system for its rigor. This study's examination of civilian police review systems found that the increase in citizens' perceptions of legitimacy there are a paramount achievement.

This comparative analysis suffers from limitations of its own. The discussion of the best system must include more than this balancing act, thus, the final chapter deals with a treatment of an "ideal" police review system.

An Ideal Police Review System

Police review systems can teach attitudes and behavior patterns to police officers, and, after wrestling with the problems and paradoxes of police review, it is this study's conclusion that police officer learning is *the* most important mission of any review mechanism. The retroactive punishment of specific offenders can be a necessary function of a review mechanism, but exercising a proactive influence over the behavior of all police officers is a far more critical endeavor.

This educational focus will not comfort the individual complainant. As is true in the criminal justice system, the victims of violence and unfairness of the law enforcement system cannot be expected to take the long view. But in both systems, the long view is precisely what practitioners, politicians, and analysts must take. Due process norms may free the substantively guilty criminal, but these occurrences do not dissuade us from understanding that the system must have integrity for it to remain effective. Similarly, in an individual case of police misconduct it might be important to chastise, discipline, or even fire an errant officer. But the individual incident has only transient importance to those who are concerned with review system effectiveness.

This research has made it obvious that effective police accountability is accomplished through multiple avenues. A system that receives complaints of errant behavior and treats them as cases for adjudication cannot stand alone. This is an important part of a police accountability system, but it is only a *part*. Effective accountability is generated by creating several information loops around the operations of the complaint review apparatus. These loops channel administrative review mechanism findings in several directions, and in a symbiotic way they then receive feedback and, in turn, call for responses.

One loop involves police policy development. It is clear that policy must be created with an eye toward the strict requirements of the law and with an understanding of the opinions and desires of the community policed. It also must be created with an understanding of the pragmatic exigencies of police work on the street. This study has discussed at length why these various perspectives are important for accountability. Whoever formulates police policy, the City Council and the Police Commission, or the chief, the city attorney, and the city manager together, the process must include feedback from review systems. Knowledge developed from studying complainant statistics, individual police officer behavior patterns, collective officer behavior patterns, review system outcomes and dynamics, and so on must be used in a prospective manner in the adaptation and formulation of policy. Policy formulators must be expected to learn from members of police review systems and vice versa.

A second key area of information transfer and feedback is the training loop. Police officer training systems, both police academy and in-service, must be constantly updated with regard to complaint dynamics and patterns. Substance and process are equally important. That is, it is legitimate for this information loop to focus both on changing police officer behavior and on changing citizen perceptions of police officer behavior.

Certainly those in the police training system will want to find out what review systems can teach about errant police officer behavior patterns, but they should also focus on the citizen perceptions that help to cause complaints. This study found severe limitations to complainant acceptance of any type of review system, no matter how fair and objective. It is appropriate, therefore, for those running police training mechanisms also to study how to avoid citizens' complaints, irrespective of police officer behavior. An information loop must include more than just the police department's training personnel. It involves communication between review mechanism personnel, line supervisors, executive decision makers, and those in peer review programs (if these programs exist), so that genuine, substantive learning can be generated.

The third loop of police review is the complaint investigation and adjudication loop itself. As the focus of almost all work done heretofore in the field, it is only one critical tool that operates to hold the police accountable for their actions. It impacts on and is influenced by both loops mentioned above. It began as the sole focus of this research seventeen years ago, but it ends as merely a part of an integrated whole.

A police review mechanism must, therefore, (1) develop information for the purposes of future policy development, (2) convey information and learning to training mechanisms and supervisors for their use and dissemination, and (3) investigate and adjudicate specific complaint incidents. If they can do all of this, police review mechanisms will then be operating in formal and informal modes. They will be concerned with subcultural, organizational, and legal dynamics. They will be taking the "short view" in focusing on the individual incident, complainant, and officer, the "intermediate view" in focusing on patterns of individual officers and groups of officers, and the "long view" in concerning themselves with the police organization in toto and future police officer behavior in general. Finally, they will be interacting with and learning from a variety of actors involved inside, outside, and on the edge of the municipal structure.

In this discussion of an ideal review system, it is important to illustrate some of this study's points using one of the incidents mentioned in the beginning of this volume. It is therefore appropriate to consider, for example, the Rodney King beating incident as it might have been handled by an ideal police review system. Not all of these ideas will be transferable to the Los Angeles political and administrative mediums; nevertheless, real-life examples may help to focus this discussion. Thus, in the next section of this chapter the examination focuses on the effects of police departmental policy and on the leadership role of the chief of police when both are faced with serious challenges. It considers how an ideal system should function under similar circumstances.

LEADERSHIP AND POLICY FORMULATION

An ideal police review system is one that is situated within a political and administrative framework that is supportive and realistic in its expectations of the police. The local officials, the press, and the power elites must be willing to support the police when they are professional and responsive to community expectations. That is hardly a problem, either in Los Angeles or anywhere else. Supporting the local police is a regular part of the operational life styles of these actors. Yet there must be a concomitant willingness to hold the police (and the chief) accountable when malpractice, scandal, or political unresponsiveness occurs. If a police organization (or a chief) becomes uncontrollable, in the sense that it begins to answer only to itself, these other actors bear a direct responsibility to generate accountability pressures in any way they can. An administrative police review system cannot by itself be responsible for the behavior of law enforcement personnel who are under the kind of stress that is involved in modern-day policing. Police review mechanisms must have political support and moral sustenance from without if they are to properly balance the conflicting requests they receive daily from their constituencies.

In Los Angeles, there is no doubt that the mayor, City Council, Police Commission, press, and power elite missed the chance to take some responsibility for change after the Dalton Avenue raid. In an ideal review system, all of these actors would have demanded and then supported any sort of effort police management made toward positive change. Similarly, they would have born a direct responsibility to press for a change of leadership if reform was not attempted.

In sum, an ideal system cannot be created without these players taking two responsibilities seriously: (1) They must demand intelligent, honest, creative management from police executives and must support this management with the necessary resources; these include, but are not limited to, money, legal expertise, help in developing modern management systems, and political support; and (2) they must demand accountability from police leadership. If creative management is not forthcoming, they must push for a change of leadership. If change involves charter revision, as it did in Los Angeles, these actors must support it wholeheartedly. If a police chief has significant political support, the battle must be joined in an effort to wrestle control of the police from the chief and give it back to the community.

Asking for this kind of political responsibility may seem unre-   253 alistic, but asking for police accountability to be generated spontaneously is equally unrealistic. Remember the assertion in Chapter 7 that a city gets the police it desires. Similarly, a power elite gets the sort of police accountability it desires.

In an ideal system, if it is supported as illustrated above, the police chief will find it possible to exercise the type of leadership that genuine accountability requires. The chief will be able to develop responsive, rational policy in partnership with the political elite and community groups. As noted in Chapter 7, policy can impact police behavior in many ways. It can help to create an atmosphere that supports tough law enforcement at the same time that it demands restraint and civility from individual police officers. Creative selection, training, management, discipline, and police officer learning, in general, can all be produced by such a partnership.

The key word, of course, is "partnership." Such a relationship works both ways. In Los Angeles, for example, after a scandalous incident like the Dalton Avenue raid, local elites should have demanded change from the chief. These political elites bear an equal responsibility, however, to support honest efforts at reform. If, for example, police chiefs need more training in advanced, cutting-edge management principles for police middle managers, they should get it. If actions such as these are not supported, local elites may expect more incidents in the future akin to the Rodney King beating.

Police chiefs, therefore, should embrace several concepts. First, no chief can remain a viable leader unless he or she understands the unacceptability of scandalous behavior. A chief cannot only be "personally appalled" (Gates 1992) at malpractice. He or she must stand up *in public* to decry it. Second, no chief can be an effective manager unless he or she understands how to work within the organization to avoid this type of behavior in the future. Police chiefs must be willing to use whatever formal and informal channels exist to influence police behavior to avoid the repetition of such incidents. Third, and, in the long run, most important, no one who professes to believe that he or she is not a political actor can operate in the high pressured role of chief of police. Arguing, as Chief Gates of Los Angeles often did, that the head of the police department is above the political fray and should not be responsive to elected officials is silly and irresponsible. It is counterproductive for the city administration, for the community, and for the police themselves.

How might all of this have impacted Rodney King? Remember that high-speed chases ending in beatings by police had been a problem for the Los Angeles Police Department for several years before the famous incident. Ideally, the mayor, City Council, Police Commission, press, and elites should all have exerted pressure on the police chief to do something about this behavior. Such pressure need not have been applied openly; in fact, anyone experienced in the realities of politics knows that it would have been better to apply it informally and quietly. Allowing the police chief to respond without appearing to "back down" would have better served the people of Los Angeles (and King, in particular).

The chief should have taken positive steps to end police abusive behavior. What could he have done? He could have employed specific training aimed at police officers' responses to high-speed chases and their aftermath. As at the Sacramento, California, Police Academy, he could have instituted role-playing exercises that put officers through similar situations. The police chief could have advised sergeants that they were to be held personally responsible for misbehavior at arrest scenes. Academy classes, in-service training, informal communications channels, and direct messages from the Los Angeles chief himself (using existing video technology) could have been used to approach the problem head on. Thus, instead of waiting for them to "go away" or hoping that nothing terrible would happen, such festering problems need to be attacked prospectivly.

To expect a review mechanism by itself to deal retroactively with such tacitly accepted patterns of police abuse is to expect the impossible. The reactive review mechanism, however, does have a role in helping the police chief control this misbehavior. In advance of the King beating, the police chief could have sent out a straightforward, "no nonsense" warning to his officers through the operations of the internal review mechanism. In Los Angeles, investigators and command personnel from the Internal Affairs Section openly bemoaned the fact that Chief Gates was not strong enough in supporting the application of stern sanctions for those found guilty of using excessive force. There can be no doubt that this message made its way to the street and into the minds of the police officers involved in the King beating incident.

All of these ideas must be woven together in an ideal system to form an environment within which police officers can learn proper behavior patterns. Support for restraint and civility can and must come from within the municipal administration, from outside the department, from the police chief's office, and from police supervisors. Within such an atmosphere, an administrative police review mechanism can operate effectively to adjudicate complaints and to teach police officers. Without a supporting environment, the police review mechanism is left to fend for itself.

From the initial paragraphs of this discussion, this study has made use of the analogy between the criminal justice system and police review systems, and this is apposite again here. A broad spectrum of politicians and academicians agree on one idea with respect to the contemporary American criminal justice system; it is unrealistic to expect the police to control crime without the support of traditional institutions such as the church, the family, the local school, and the media. If the police are not supported in their endeavor by honest, consistent, role models and positive images of acceptable, moral behavior, their efforts at behavioral control are doomed.

So too it is with police review systems. Their efforts at controlling errant police behavior are doomed to failure if they are not supported by local power elites, "no nonsense" chiefs, and creative, problem-solving supervisors. Intelligently formulated policy must be developed of, by, and for the partnership between police management and community leadership. Ideally, all of the above produces police officer learning. Policy is formed through a partnership between police executives, police management, community representatives, and interest groups. This policy reflects curbside realities and complaint trends because of the communication of the first information loop. Furthermore, the operation of retroactive police review systems also develops information about particular police officers with problems and communicates this to supervisors and training managers. But what is the role of training with respect to the ideal review system?

TRAINING

Police accountability mechanisms must use this information concerning problem officers in several ways: (1) They must educate new police officers through the operations of academy training systems; (2) allow mediation and conciliation programs to proceed with as little interference as is legally possible; (3) communicate policy changes and complaint trends to line officers in service; (4) "get out of the way" of subcultural training processes and genuinely collegial approaches to behavior modification (that is, peer review and informal teaching mechanisms must be allowed to operate to teach both errant police officers and would-be errant officers how to avoid complaints and complaint-producing behavior); and (5) communicate to police officers and citizens alike the strict disciplinary standards to which truly abusive police officers have been and will be held.

Academy training throughout the police world has improved remarkably in the past several decades. In response to the prodding of many actors, not the least of which included the U.S. Supreme Court, modern police academy training is now lengthy and sophisticated in its treatment of the specifics of criminal law and search and seizure regulations. But it now must take a different direction. In order to breathe life into this training, academies must back up a step to include basic study in the nature of limited government and the principles of due process. This may include the consideration of police officer bills of rights as an important "coloring" device to add interest for the rookie cop.

Current training tends either to avoid the subject of citizens' complaints or to treat it in an unrealistic manner. The academies that approach the subject do so in a sort of "Dragnet," "only the facts ma'am" manner. Going along with this study's discussions of paramilitarism and management attempts to control police officer discretion, some academies attempt to intimidate the rookie with a kind of "fear of God" speech from a representative of internal affairs. Instead, a frank discussion of complaints is in order. Rookie cops should hear how citizens

257

complain and what they tend to complain about. Experienced officers who possess this sort of knowledge should teach rookies a few "tricks of the trade" in avoiding complaints. This study has shown that time spent this way is not wasted. It can produce better police-community relations, save the police review system time and money, and, in the long run, help the young officer to develop into a more seasoned professional in a shorter time.

Similarly, law enforcement academy classes on police ethics should be discussion-oriented. Diatribes full of sanctimony, again given by members of internal affairs, tend to plug into subcultural cynicism, which rookie cops pick up all too early in their experience. Realistic considerations of gratuities, corruption opportunities, and ethical responsibility would be far more productive than that currently directed "at" rookies in the academy. For example, the Sacramento Academy involves rookies in role-playing, wherein they learn to become agents that limit the application of excessive force by fellow officers. The Los Angeles Academy, known for its militaristic "haircuts and shoeshines" perspective, would be well rid of some of its officiousness in the name of more informal, interactive training.

The mediation and conciliation procedures offered by police departments in many locales should be expanded to most jurisdictions. These informal complaint procedures do more than help police avoid official complaints and save time. They should, if operated properly, keep avenues open between the young officer (in particular) and the citizen. One must remember that all police officers begin their adult lives as civilians, and they lose touch with the perspective of civilians for a number of reasons (outlined in Chapter 2). To use any complaint-handling format that allows learning (or in this case "relearning") about the citizen's perspective is a positive step for community relations. It can teach the police officer complaint-avoidance techniques on a first-hand basis. It is not a panacea, but an important part of an overall strategy to limit complaints and change behavior. If the Los Angeles Police Department moves to a genuine "community-based policing" format, it may find that the accompanying decentralization could facilitate this type of informality, even in such a large organization.

As in the Oakland Police Department, complaint trends should be communicated to line officers on a regular basis. Statistics are fine; they can actually be productive, on occasion. But specific training should be undertaken that periodically focuses the police officer's attention on complaints and their avoidance. When this training is taken seriously by supervisors, as it is in Oakland, it can be perhaps the most effective element of the official training loop. When done in a prospective manner, training is far less deleterious to officer attitudes than are complaint-system operations. Once this is understood—and good supervisors can facilitate that development—the training will be taken seriously, as it is in Oakland. Not wishing to appear less "macho" than subcultural necessity demands, police officers may make fun of tips from more experienced personnel. But, in fact, they will listen to expert analysis of how they may avoid career-influencing complaints. This focus can be generated, in Los Angeles, for example, by leadership that takes police officer training seriously and leads by example.

Perhaps most important, informal police counseling and training must be allowed to operate wherever and whenever possible. In terms of teaching restraint and civilized citizen treatment, advice from a trusted police sergeant, practical examples illustrated by a veteran officer, or words of encouragement from a peer may be the most important tools of a police officer's education. Police review systems, official training mechanisms, and formalized supervisorial chains of command must all make as much room as they can for informal subcultural training.

In the space of a generation, American policing has progressed from the Dark Ages of the "dumb flatfoot." It is now on the verge of a Golden Age of genuine police professionalism. Subcultural dynamics in many police organizations now operate in favor of restraint, civility, and legality. Neither the formal administrative structures that this study has examined nor those actors outside the subculture can be allowed to get in the way of the further development of this new brand of honesty and professionalism.

Peer review systems and no-fault complaint-handling procedures have much more to offer the community in the future than do punitive sanctions. Whenever it is legally possible, these informal systems should be allowed to use the strengths of the subculture to change errant police behavior. In the long run, they hold the most potential to develop police officers who are aggressive in the pursuit of their missions yet restrained in their use of force.

The Oakland Police Department is actually slightly smaller than are each of the Los Angeles Police Departments' substations. Yet the size is comparable enough that it is not unreasonable for those in power to expect this type of informal problem-oriented policing to develop at the grass-roots level.

Thus to improve the role of training in an ideal police review system police departments should concentrate on the following: changes in police academy training, support for mediation, communication between supervisors and street officers, informal teaching of complaint-avoidance, and, finally, an emphasis on high standards for police officers.

REVIEW SYSTEM STRUCTURES

In addition to concerns about leadership, policy development, and training, those interested in developing an ideal review system must also take into account how that mechanism deals with input, investigations, outcomes, discipline, and confidentiality. Analysis turns to consider these procedural elements of the structure of an ideal review system.

Input

The debate surrounding input structures is, in reality, more a discussion of fiscal limitations than it is one of the substantive differences between police and civilian-operated systems. It is quite clear that civilian-operated systems are, at the very least, no worse than those manned by sworn police officers. In addition, there can be no question that using physical locations removed from police departmental buildings are preferable to citizens filing complaints. These conventions may not produce significantly more freedom of access to complainants; nevertheless, when combined with access to the front desk at the police station itself, allowing "neutral" sites for complaint-reception is always better. Whether a municipality can afford to do so is quite another question.

In the current atmosphere of fiscal crisis, only those municipal administrations that can add reception locations at little or

no cost will be prone to do so. Whether it is "worth it" to spend additional taxpayer monies to open alternate input facilities is to be determined by those municipalities. Suffice it to say that establishing multiple locations for filing complaints would be ideal.

Los Angeles, however, has a municipal administration that operates so many facilities and offers so many services to its constituents that it can easily open up alternate complaint-filing locations. This endeavor involves logistical problems, but subsuming the costs into a multimillion dollar budget is a relatively painless operation. All that is required in a complaint-acceptance site, as in San Diego, California, is a desk or small office in a civic building.

Of course, to Rodney King, having alternate avenues available for complainants may very well have been irrelevant. But openness in the input procedures may be relevant in the future because it can impact police behavior over time. Thousands of complaints that the Christopher Commission found were quashed by the Los Angeles Police Department at its station houses might have been effectively filed at nonpolice locales. The consequent caseload for the Los Angeles internal review mechanisms might indeed have changed the attitudes of the department, Police Commission, chief, police supervisors, and rank-and-file officers toward complaints and complainants over the years.

The best policy to follow is to require the acceptance of complaints by any and all personnel, at the office, over the phone, in the mail, or on the street, as is done in Oakland and in many other modern police departments. No reasonable defense can be made for procedures that allow a system to ignore anonymous complaints, that require complainants to sign and notorize their statements, or that intimidate citizens with admonitions about prosecution for untruthfulness. These procedures belong more properly to a time when cops were referred to as "flatfoots" and when the rule of law gave way to the rule of the nightstick. Insuring inclusiveness would also require that any municipality that could do so would allow neutral, nonpolice personnel for this purpose.

In Los Angeles, as noted above, it is certain that such a large-scale municipal administration could do this kind of civilian-complaint reception in a fiscally conservative manner. In fact, given how much less expensive it is to hire civilian clerks than it is to pay for sworn police officers, a large municipality may actually *save* money by civilianizing its initial input mechanism. Thus one can see that the initial acceptance of a complaint is important to all concerned, but even more important is the investigation of that complaint.

Investigations

A fascinating set of trade-offs come to light when complaint investigations are examined. From a removed perspective, the police review systems studied all appear to do a thorough job of investigating alleged police malpractice. Oakland and Kansas City's investigations are done in a thorough and competent manner by professional police investigators. The Berkeley system, operating on the strength of investigations done by civilians without experience in police work, also appears to operate in a competent manner. Berkeley's PRC investigations usually include the same sorts of statements, compiled from the same sorts of sources, as the Berkeley Internal Affairs Section reports. Their substantive direction and composition rarely differs from those of the police system.

Sometimes citizens are so frightened or disgusted with the police that they will not talk to police investigators. In those instances, the reports done by a civilian investigatory body might appear to be more thorough. But the growing propensity of police officers to be truthful about misconduct tends to be stifled by interactions with civilian investigators and augmented by contact with police investigators.

Of course, the real paradox of this debate is sometimes brought home to the analyst by the Berkeley parallel review system. Although it does not occur often, there are times in Berkeley's system when one is confronted by an investigation in which the two bodies have outdone each other on their respective home fields. In such instances, the IA Section's investigator is able to develop information from police sources that the PRC's investigator has missed. Concomitantly, the PRC has sometimes obtained statements from civilians that IA has not seen.

What, then, is the answer with respect to populating investigatory bodies? Two options seem to possess great potential. The first is being tried on an experimental basis in several jurisdictions, including Cleveland and Pittsburgh; it combines the investigatory forces of civilians and police officers. The strengths of each group can be used in appropriate arenas. The sworn police investigators can interrogate police officers, and the civilians can obtain statements from complainants. This, in theory, allows for the optimum potential of cooperation from these separate groups of individuals.

The cross-pollination of ideas that can result may also have positive side-effects. Investigators with police experience, under such a team concept, may be forced to explain to nonpolice personnel some of the underlying principles they use to rationalize seemingly inappropriate behavior. In short, investigators having to explain the realities of beat number twenty-one to those who have not policed it can be an important check on the free-wheeling power of the police subculture to operate in an unaccountable manner. Concomitantly, civilians without sworn police officer experience may tend to bring an external perspective to each case, interrogation, and hearing that requires such explanation.

The ombudsman office may work even better for most jurisdictions. The ombudsman setup may be especially appropriate for smaller municipalities in which the cost of multiple investigators is prohibitive. It requires the same type of explanation and accountability to nonpolice perspectives, yet it does not develop an administrative mechanism that might, because of its civilian-police makeup, create unwieldy personnel problems for supervisors. It can allow the professional investigatory expertise of the police to operate in an unfettered manner while it holds that professional group to standards of conduct that it might otherwise avoid. This kind of review mechanism essentially performs ongoing investigations about internal affairs' investigations. Thus it is a sort of continuously operating auditing mechanism.

In Los Angeles, the size of the municipality is such that either of these options may be pursued. Most persuasive, on balance, is the idea that the Police Commission might operate a monitor-type of body that systematically audits internally generated investigations. Because of the size of the Los Angeles Police Department and the potentiality for corruption as well as malpractice to flourish there, it is entirely appropriate that a monitor body possess a limited, extraordinary capacity to proceed with its own investigations where that is appropriate. Going outside of the internal police review structure should be eschewed under normal circumstances. But the availability of this avenue of redress can insure that the internal system operates with complete integrity and that an optimum amount of legitimacy attaches to the system in its entirety.

The long-term impact of such a process might have been enough to avoid the Rodney King incident altogether. Such an expectation may be too expansive, but it may very well be that the legitimacy gained by the operation of a civilian monitor system might be so great as to negate the necessity for violent protest about police abuses. This discussion does not in any way wish to rationalize the riot in March 1992 that followed the first trial of the police officers accused of beating King. Nevertheless, police review systems in operation in some locations *have* generated enough legitimacy to be given the benefit of the doubt with regard to incidents of police malpractice. The fact is that police shootings and the use of excessive force has not led to violent protest in some urban areas, and this may, at least partially, be traceable to the deference that local civil liberties groups and minority community leaders have given to some police review systems.

Related to concerns of appropriate and thorough investigations are those of deciding the final outcomes of these complaint investigations.

Outcomes

This study observed numerous police chiefs who are rigorous and stern in their disciplinary decisions. However, it also observed police organizations in which chiefs and other administrators were not serious about their disciplinary decisions (witness the examples of San Francisco or Boston in 1991–1992). When complaints are of such gravity that they allege conduct involving brutality, racism, or corruption, they usually cannot be handled informally. They cannot be dealt with out of view of the public. Under these circumstances, accusations of police misconduct must necessarily be brought out from under the umbrella of the police organization. Only by opening the investigation of these types of incidents to some form of an external, removed perspective can objective evaluations of culpability be developed.

Here one arrives at a critical dilemma for review systems. How far should a system go toward understanding the police officer's lot? How much cognizance should a review mechanism take of the pressures of being out on the street? A system may be unfair to complaining citizens if it allows too much deference toward the police subcultural wisdom of how policing should be done. Yet it can be unfair to cops if it does not take the time to understand the reality of the pressures that build on the beat cop day-by-day. Balancing these concerns is by no means an easy task. In the interests of fairness and long-term accountability, it does no good to throw up our collective hands and decide that the interests of one group (cops) or another (complainants) should be controlling. Neither of these alternatives is acceptable, for reasons already discussed.

For the types of incidents that are of major importance, hearings are essential, for several reasons. First, formalized hearings allow complaining citizens a direct avenue of redress for their grievances. No matter what may be argued and analyzed about the competence of investigators, both internal and external, the ability of complainants to present evidence, to cross-examine witnesses (especially police officers), and to argue cases for themselves is one guarantee, albeit limited, that misconduct by public agents will not go unaccounted for.

Second, the hearing process avails accused officers of a forum within which to directly refute accusations and clear their names. Some police officers accuse internalized systems of abusing the rights of cops. Many in police work bemoan the fact that internalized systems do not allow the accused officer the right to confront complainants directly. Formalized hearing processes avail the cop of such rights so that the officer may attempt to absolve him- or herself of the taint of accusations of wrongdoing.

But hearings do more than this for the accused police officer. They allow a variety of due process protections to become guaranteed through the openness of the proceedings. Internal departmental tensions caused in some organizations by overzealousness may be lessened by open hearings. Individual officers may have their due process rights observed under the watchful eyes of the public and the press. An additional benefit for the criminal justice system, in general, may develop from a mechanism that occasionally puts police officers "on trial" in this manner. If police officers understand their own due process rights when accused of misconduct, they may develop a better understanding for the due process rights afforded citizens accused of criminal conduct.

Of course, in terms of time and money, the cost of hearings is significant. This study has already noted that the Berkeley civilian board's expenditures would be considered exorbitant in most places. Given the availability of civil litigative redress, this option to hold hearings should be reserved for only the most serious allegations.

Finally, one must confront the problem of perspective regarding outcome decisions. Police officers fear that civilians will not understand their perspective and experiences and will not be objective. Complainants fear that police officers will not understand *their* perspective and will not be objective. Both groups tend to feel that the other will not understand the law and will act intuitively instead of in a rational, legal manner. The solution to these perceptual problems is that which is proposed by the surveyed police officers.

Hearing boards should be composed of experienced police officers, civilian representatives of the community, and legal experts. Each of these agents' critical perspectives need not completely control the outcome. As in Toronto, three hearing board members may be chosen from rosters of individuals representing each group (Lewis 1991). One roster is composed of civilian review board–type citizens from the community. A second roster is composed of experienced police officers, always chosen from another jurisdiction or from a list of retired officers. A third is made up of retired lawyers and judges, so they are not currently involved in litigation as a profession.

Such caveats have been operational in Toronto for over fifteen years. This method of gathering board members from the police, the legal profession, and the community brings to the hearing process an understanding of police work and of the exigencies of the job. It brings an understanding of the law and the specifics of criminal procedure. And, finally, it infuses the mechanism with community input that, though sometimes ignorant of the law and police practice, is nevertheless allowed to impact police accountability.

While no magical solution exists, the Toronto system comes the closest to drawing together the concerns of the various interest groups. It responds to each perspective with equal deference. It makes certain that the legal, the police, or the citizen perspective alone does not completely control police review outcomes. It is a particularly persuasive answer to the paradoxical balancing of the interests involved. It essentially represents the formula suggested by police officers experienced with both internal and external review systems.

In Los Angeles, a system similar to Toronto's could be constructed. Together, local political leaders, civil liberties lobbies, and police leadership should analyze the situation. If they believe that the trouble and expense of this kind of system needs to be avoided, they may use the body that Los Angeles already has in place to hear cases. As in San Francisco and Kansas City (to name only two examples), the Police Commission itself is a completely appropriate body for review hearings. As was pointed out with regard to the chief of police, if the people populating the Police Commission are not the type of individuals that can fairly and objectively rule on the issues, they should be replaced with those who can.

What happens to those officers who, in fact, have been found guilty of misconduct? The discussion next moves to a consideration of how discipline is meted out in an ideal police review system.

Discipline

Some observers have called for the disciplinary process to be external to police systems. The San Francisco example shows evidence that some police executives may not be trusted with this responsibility, but one cannot allow emotion to interfere with sound management principles. It is axiomatic that responsibility be linked to authority where discipline is concerned. This principle is not limited to public organizations, but finds its roots in private-sector management principles, as well (Griffin and Moorhead, 1986: 566).

As considered in Chapter 4, police executives must be held directly responsible for the actions, both macroscopic and microscopic, of their review systems. To apply this accountability to the police chief fairly, one must entrust the chief to impose sanctions on those who have been found guilty of misconduct. If the police executive cannot be trusted with this responsibility, then the solution for the municipality is clear; get a new chief.

For disciplinary systems to be effective in the long term, it is essential that those who apply discipline understand the population of police officers being policed. Important to disciplinary decisions are specific organizational dynamics, citywide and particularized beat problems, training practices, supervisorial histories, and so on. All relate to how sanctions may be applied. It is equally important that the individual disciplinary decision be fairly related to the disciplinary history and experience of the police officer involved. It is critical to the effectiveness of disciplinary processes to infuse these decisions with a feeling for the equity of the specific situation as well as for the overall interests of the police officer population of the department.

As a "politician" responsible to a constituency, the police executive must be allowed latitude within which to develop accountability processes that respond to the concerns of the public. If the police chief does not develop these measures, it is clear that he or she should be replaced in favor of someone who will. The failure of particular chiefs to do this job with integrity should not be used as an excuse to circumvent good management principles. It should not be used to create irrational systems that place disciplinary authority in the hands of those who are not directly responsible for the actions of police officers.

When one applies these ideas to Los Angeles, one comes to several interesting conclusions. First, because of the lack of seriousness with which Chief Gates approached discipline over time (for use of excessive force in particular) Los Angeles *had* to take the step it took in the June 1992 elections and change its charter. This change now allows the chief of police to have a limited tenure and to be held more accountable for his or her actions.

Second, this bad experience with a particular chief should not blind local leaders to the principles outlined here. In general, the police chief should be given room within which to work. Unless there exists specific evidence indicating that the chief has a lax attitude toward the use of force such as that uncovered by the Christopher Commission, local police review systems should be operated under the direction of the chief without interference.

It should be made clear to all, and the Police Commission and local political leaders bear a direct responsibility for this education, that the chief of police is hired specifically for the purpose of setting organizational direction, operating quality control systems, and proscribing discipline where appropriate. There are hard times coming for police organizations if this message is not accepted. Part of the responsibility to sell this idea belongs to the political elites, who will benefit from the good work that the police and the chief do.

The final review system facet to be discussed is that of confidentiality. How important is the privacy of police records to an ideal police review system?

Confidentiality

Although complete access to all departmental documents *could* be allowed in the name of civilian oversight, city attorneys and city managers all over the country (except, of course, in Kansas City) are adamantly opposed to this suggestion. This opposition is self-serving for the city; nevertheless, it is a problem that must be considered when cities are engineering police review systems that must fit into today's era of fiscal conservatism at all levels. As has been true so often in this discussion, a compromise solution seems to be in order.

Citizen access to complaint information may be made available in the form of investigative conclusions and statement summaries. This would allow the complainant a more definitive picture of the rationale behind complaint case outcomes, and it

269

would open up the process, albeit in a limited way, to external scrutiny. It may also help to develop increased legitimacy. Moreover, if done properly, providing access to information will not impact the municipality by expanding civil litigative exposure.

As noted, such summary findings are made available in Kansas City, Missouri, without significant drawbacks. Yet, Kansas City possesses some limited immunity from civil litigation, which is not afforded to other municipalities. Similarly, there are places (in California, for example) in which complaint investigations must be kept secret by law. Here is an area that requires the type of legislative responsibility and intestinal fortitude called for above. Local- and state-level legislators can help to develop increased police accountability. They could put together legislative packages that at the same time allow access and limit civil litigative awards.

Such limits have been proposed for some time. But given the lobbying power of the legal profession, they may be far off. Their institution would require of many individuals the type of commitment to police accountability and personal chance-taking that everyone expects of police chiefs everywhere. It will be interesting to see how well such suggestions fair in the near future.

In California, legislation seems to be headed in the opposite direction. Several suggestions under consideration are aimed at legally limiting the powers of civilianized review systems. With this as the political backdrop, one would be hard-pressed to expect of Los Angeles much in the way of progress in this direction. Such a municipality cannot unilaterally take these steps.

SUMMATION

What sort of police review system should a municipality create if it has the ability to develop one from the beginning? Aside from the fiscal and political realities of a particular jurisdiction, how should a city engineer an ideal police review system? It should begin by establishing civilian- and police-operated input structures. Both physical sites and personnel should be mixed. Police professionals would handle investigations, and they would be monitored by civilian analysts, as in Kansas City.

The civilian staff would have the extraordinary power to investigate specific complaints, if situations warranted, yet this would be a seldom-used avenue.

An ideal system should allow great latitude to the police professional and subcultural structure for dealing with minor complaints. The system would attempt mediation and conciliation whenever possible. Furthermore, for minor police transgressions, an ideal system would use no-fault disciplinary methods, such as positive counseling and training, in the interests of police officer learning.

Outcomes for serious cases should be decided by hearings before three panel members, chosen, as in Toronto, from rosters of individuals representing the three critical perspectives that this study has outlined. The final implementation of discipline should be left to the police chief; that is the chief's job, and it should remain so. If the chief cannot perform this task, he or she is the wrong person for the job. A municipality should expect no more and no less of its chief executive law enforcement officer than the prudent, honest, educated exercise of intelligence in disciplinary decisions.

It might seem that this analysis has landed too heavily in the camp of the police. But in support of their viewpoint, this study has taken great pains to emphasize that many complaints are minor. In the discussion, readers have been asked to accept peer review, mediation, and other forms of informal complaint resolution, "whenever possible." The police subculture, slowly moving in the direction of professionalization, should be entrusted with much of the responsibility for behavior modification of errant police officers. This discussion must not be construed to mean that police abuse is not a real problem. It is. In fact, there are places in this country where it is considered the most weighty problem faced by citizens. It should not, it cannot, be ignored. It also cannot be wished away by well-meaning expectations that "the police will change."

But this study has found that police malpractice is a problem largely of society's own creation. America has taken great pains to develop a criminal justice system that appears to be consistent, knowable, rational, and equitable. These are laudable goals. They are necessary to the legitimation of any legal system (Fuller

1964). Yet human beings and social life are so complex that our codifications fall far short of actually ordering behavior. People, and not laws, must do that.

The people who take up the charge of doing this job must be pragmatists. Society requires this of them. Yet society also asks that they adhere to a rigid set of legalistic norms; we want to "have our cake and eat it too!" To maintain order, police officers must cleave to the rule of law (which often does not work well for this purpose) and eschew abusive and coercive tactics (which usually *do* work well). This nation has created a role expectation for the police officer that is unrealistic; therefore, one should not be surprised when the cop becomes frustrated, and one should not react too indignantly when that frustration spills over into abusive behavior.

If the last thirty years of studying the police have taught us anything, it is the powerful significance of the working experience of being a street cop. Through education, reeducation, and modern training systems, a "new breed" of police officer has been developed. Yet the problem of police abuse is still with us. One must realize that abuse, and perceived abuse, does not stem from the intellectual or moral failings of "police types." Modern police officers are more intelligent, better educated, more rational, and more civilized than are most of the people they meet on the street. (Anyone who does not believe this is indeed ignorant of the realities of the contemporary police experience.) Abuse is a natural product of the situation in which police officers are placed.

Of course, all administrators must deal with the limits of the rule of law. The police may simply generate more hostility and controversy because they are licensed to take away the personal liberty of citizens. Society is attempting to regulate administrative behavior, but what can it do to improve existing mechanisms?

This study found that the involvement of external dilettantes or community representatives hamper neither the operations of review systems nor those of police organizations generally. The inclusion of such perspectives may be useful to all involved. It can allow administrative professionals to obtain feedback from those who are not so close to the problems of everyday administration that they lose sight of the obvious. It can serve to educate the public about both substantive and procedural problems in administration. And the inclusion of nonprofessionals can require the organization to explain the assumptions that underwrite its police review mechanisms.

This study found that the real-life exigencies of administration are such that great deference must be given to the professional expertise of the practitioner. Law has tremendous limitations. But it is the personal moralities, competencies, and power of citizens that determine the informal sets of relationships that actually maintain order. Law has a role in the process, a critical role, but a limited one.

In the long run, no system, no rigid, formalized regulatory scheme, will control police abuse, administrative discretion, or criminal behavior, for that matter. Within the general confines of such systems, people will control each other through action and exhortation. In the end, one must trust the integrity and competence of people. To depend too much on systems, to focus on them as an end, is to be dangerously shortsighted. Police review systems, police departments, criminal justice systems, or even governmental systems of "checks and balances" will not be effective unless they are populated by honest and diligent people.

A significant amount of time has been spent arguing the nature of the relationship between humankind and its institutions. Some hold that institutions are merely reflections of human development; that they are after-the-fact constructs that cleave to people's requirements. Others point out that social institutions can be liberating agents that allow humankind to develop to its fullest potential, that they can have positive influences on social progress.

This study of police accountability mechanisms shows that both assertions are correct. Systems can be constructed that influence behavior and develop more conscientious, responsible individuals. Yet, in developing institutions of behavioral control, it must be kept uppermost in mind that their rigid conventions are of limited utility. People, with all of their failings, will populate behavioral control institutions, and they will subject such systems to the same sorts of problems that the systems themselves are designed to monitor.

Society must, at some point, allow that such limitations exist. We must make realistic demands of our accountability mechanisms and place a great deal of trust in the integrity of people. Such systems will always fall short of the expectations of some, for they can only attempt to balance the numerous interests outlined in these pages.

APPENDIXES, BIBLIOGRAPHY, NEWSPAPER REFERENCES, CASE REFERENCES, AND INDEX

Appendix A: Methodology

So much has been espoused in favor of and against the idea of civilian review of police conduct that a search for genuine "study" in the field is almost embarrassing. Little more than intuitive rhetoric exists. No one has even attempted to weigh the strengths and weaknesses of civilian and internal review in a measured manner. In 1977 a comparative study of the topic began to intrigue me. I chose five police review systems for the project. They each seemed to offer interesting alternatives.

The Oakland, California, Police Department had an internal affairs organization that was well respected in police and academic circles. As a well-respected internal review system, it appeared that its shortcomings would be the least that one would expect to observe in a police-operated process. San Jose, California, had an ombudsman's system. A preliminary review of police accountability literature indicated a broad-based feeling among scholars that this type of system held great potential for dealing adequately with the trade-offs inherent in police review. Berkeley, California, had the only civilian review board in the country. Given the topical nature of civilian review and the volatility of the idea among the police, the inclusion of the Berkeley Police Review Commission was basic to the study.

The Chicago, Illinois, and Kansas City, Missouri, systems, hybrid forms that used civilians and police together, were added to the study. Finally, the Contra Costa County, California, organization, which had no systematized approach to police review at all, would be the closest I could come to a "nonsystem." I thus added this large sheriff's department to the study's list of organizations as a control group, to answer the question, "What if you did nothing?" Contra Costa County's organization was the null set.

Through academic and police organizational contacts I was able to obtain introductions to the chiefs of police and civilian administrators of all of these systems. Though they exhibited some reservations, I was able to gain access to each review body, internal and external. I spent several months in direct observation of each system so that I might intelligently direct my efforts. It was during this preliminary phase of research that the study became funded (by CETA) as the Comparative Police Review Systems Project.

Supported by the grant, I centered the study in Oakland. I took research trips to Chicago, Los Angeles, and Kansas City. At the Oakland Police Department, I was allowed complete access to complainants' files, to the Patrol Division, and to the Internal Affairs Section. This complete access to complainants' files afforded to the project was, and still is, to my knowledge, unprecedented for such studies.

The other systems also allowed me to observe input mechanisms, investigators working in the field, witness and suspect officer interviews, and hearings. At each organization one hundred cases (or more) were randomly pulled for my perusal. I spent several thousand hours on these endeavors over the years. During the course of this study I conducted hundreds of interviews with beat cops, police middle managers, chiefs, police commissioners, civilian board members, civilian investigators and staff, hearing officers, civil service commissioners, "police beat" reporters, civil rights attorneys, police officer professional organization attorneys, and activists championing various perspectives.

Since the initial two years of work, I have undertaken additional studies at San Diego, San Francisco, and Richmond, California, funded by Skyline College in San Bruno, California. Along the way the study has monitored, and has looked into, operations in dozens of locations. It has examined scandals involving calls for civilian review in Sacramento, Rochester, San Diego, and Boston. Follow-up has been ongoing in Oakland, Berkeley, San Francisco, Kansas City, and Contra Costa County.

The study's written surveys of complainants' attitudes were conducted initially in 1978 in Oakland, Berkeley, San Jose, Kansas City, Chicago, and Contra Costa County. In-depth interviews with randomly selected street officers, followed by written questionnaires, were done at the same time in the same locations. In 1991 complainants' attitudes were again surveyed, through the same written questionnaire, in Oakland and Berkeley. One hundred and eighty police officers' attitudes about civilian and internal review were surveyed in Oakland and Berkeley (in 1991). Both of these survey tools were developed by the Survey Research Center at the University of California at Berkeley.

The decade of study that followed the intensive investigation period from 1977–1978 was accomplished from outside the existing organizations.

REVIEW SYSTEM OBSERVATION

Oakland Police Department

As previously noted, the Oakland internal review system is known throughout the law enforcement and academic worlds as the most rigorous internal operation; thus, I made it the center of the initial investigation. I spent a great deal of time monitoring the Oakland Police Department's Internal Affairs Section. Over one hundred hours were spent in preliminary observation and police officer interviews, and, over the course of the study, several thousand hours were spent at the Oakland Police Department. Thus, at Oakland, the role that I chose for myself was different from the one I assumed at other organizations. I had time to develop a rapport and a trust with Oakland Police Department officers and investigators that I could not obtain elsewhere. These people were subject to all sorts of pressures because of their constant interactions with antagonistic police officers and citizens alike. A sympathetic ear was at times greatly appreciated.

Since I studied Oakland's Internal Affairs Section at close range for approximately twenty months, I was able to observe its operations under two deputy chiefs of police and under two Internal Affairs Section commanders. I saw a turnover of the entire investigative staff, via transfers out of the section. I am thus confident that the dynamics I observed during this initial period are truly indicative of the system's operations.

279

This begs the question of how my presence affected the people in Internal Affairs. It might seem that the presence of a civilian observer would change their behavior in a way that would mask from me their true natures. But over the course of the twenty months, often observing in IA for eight hours each day, five days each week, there is no doubt in my mind that my presence was normalized. I was, after a while, "one of the boys." I was one of those few people who understood the IA investigator's difficult lot and that they were precariously perched between the complainants, the cops, and the police chief.

So much did I gain acceptance that a small experiment was devised by the deputy chief of police. After I had been around the organization for about a year, he felt that, for my own edification and in order to try out the idea of civilian involvement in IA, I should handle a few complaints. I thus spent some time interviewing complainants, taking statements, and short-circuiting complaints when appropriate. This experience was invaluable. It enabled me to understand the investigator's position, and it gave me a closer look at complainants than I had obtained from previous observations.

Other Organizations

When I studied all of the other internal organizations during the initial grant period, I represented myself to them as an "Oakland analyst." My project was clearly outlined as being of great interest to the Oakland chief, however. Because of direct requests from Police Chief George Hart himself, I was able to obtain access to police personnel and systems with relative ease. Thus, because I was labeled as a "police-type," I was usually able to avoid suspicion regarding my motives as a "researcher from Berkeley."

The effects of this particular role construction when dealing with police organizations were obvious. On one hand, taking such a posture helped me to develop a significant amount of trust from police officers and administrators because I was seen as a member of the police subculture; thus, operations would not have been likely to change for appearances sake when I was present. As a police person, I could be entrusted with "the real story" of how these in-house systems operated.

On the other hand, being a member of the police subculture would hardly have been an asset when dealing with civilian review structures. Therefore, I took a somewhat different approach to these civilian systems. Although I did not hide my project's affiliation with Oakland's chief, I emphasized that I was a "social scientist from Berkeley."

My dual approach to the study of police review has been quite successful now for almost seventeen years. I find myself slipping rather easily from being "Dr. Perez who went to Berkeley in the 1960s," to being "former police officer Perez who worked for the Oakland chief." Given the emotion involved in police review, this dual role has been an important tool, though not always an effective one, that has helped me to find access for the ongoing study in a variety of environments.

My interviews with local academicians, administrators, and interest group members are the only sources I have to check on my observations at Chicago, Los Angeles, and Kansas City. Because of the distance of these cities from the study's base, I allowed myself only several weeks of direct observation of their review systems. While communication has been maintained for over a decade, and return visits have been possible intermittently, the study must hesitate to extrapolate too much from this available data. Unlike the Oakland experience, I have only perused the information from those organizations studied "on the road" from a removed, "researcher's" perspective.

San Jose and Contra Costa County presented middle cases. I was not housed near these areas and thus was not as close to the research situation as I was in Oakland. But I was able to monitor their ongoing investigations over the course of several years. Unlike in Chicago, Los Angeles, and Kansas City, I spent much time cross-referencing findings and interviews in San Jose and Contra Costa County.

POLICE OFFICER SURVEYS

When I was surveying attitudes of police officers, I restricted myself to those in uniform. Statistics from many police departments suggest that patrol officers are the subject of an overwhelming majority of all of the citizen complaints filed. For the initial 1978 studies, I chose twelve police officers at random from each of the four police departments that I could observe over protracted periods of time (Oakland, Berkeley, San Jose, and Contra Costa County). Kansas City and Chicago police officers had to be chosen less systematically. There, owing to time pressures, I was only able to interview officers working shifts convenient for my purposes. Although I interviewed the same number of police officers as in the other four locations, the representativeness of these officers is unknown. They were simply chosen by chance, because they were on the street and in uniform when I was at the Chicago and Kansas City Patrol Divisions.

I wished to control these samples for several demographic variables. Given my initial studies, I felt that a police officer's race, age, sex, and seniority might all affect that officer's propensity to generate complaints and influence his or her attitudes about review procedures. Happily, my randomly taken samples were fairly representative all around. (See Appendix B.) San Jose's Police Department is an exception to this. I was unable to obtain information regarding the racial, sexual, age, and seniority distributions for the Patrol Division, as a whole. Therefore, I do not know if these police officers are representative. Since the procedures for selection were always the same, and since the officers selected were representative elsewhere, I have assumed that this sample, too, is a good one.

Because of resignations and transfers, only a total of forty-six officers were interviewed at length and were sent follow-up questionnaires. They were asked a series of questions about internal and civilian review systems. My extended interviews with these police officers took place out on their beats, in their patrol cars. The follow-up questionnaires were used only as a check on my interview results (in 1977–1978). Though the feedback was essentially the same, some officers indicated more liberal and accepting attitudes, toward civilian review in particular, on their written surveys.

In 1991, after the Berkeley PRC had existed for eighteen years and the Oakland civilian board for almost ten, I decided to survey a larger group of officers in those jurisdictions. I used the same questions about internal review, civilian review, and ideal review systems that I had used in 1978. I attempted to contact 280 police officers. One hundred and fifty surveys were filled out and returned. I checked the demographic profiles and (happily again) I had a representative sample. (The officer demographics for the 1991 sample are included in Appendix C.)

COMPLAINANT ATTITUDINAL SURVEYS

In Oakland, Chicago, Kansas City, and San Jose, I selected one hundred complainants at random for contact. At Contra Costa County and Berkeley less people were contacted because less than one hundred complaints were received in the entire year. I sent out a total of 465 questionnaires, and 163 were returned. When, in particular, one considers the transience of many complainants, this rate of 35 percent is better than one might expect.

Again, the questionnaire was developed with the help of the Survey Research Center. I compiled and refined preliminary tests of the questions, and I performed a pretest using Oakland complainants. Two researchers each contacted five complainants, a task of great difficulty—indicative of the transient nature of complainants. These complainants were given the proposed questionnaire and asked to fill it out. They were then interviewed regarding the clarity of questions and the ease of filling out the form. After some minor changes, the survey went out to the randomly drawn samples.

Because complainant confidentiality is of concern to most organizations, checking the demographic representativeness of our samples was impossible. Most organizations do not allow race, age, or sex statistics to be kept about complainants.

I did the resurveying of complainants at Oakland and Berkeley in 1991 in a similar fashion. Questionnaires included the same questions asked in 1978. This time the response rate was 30 percent. (It is interesting to note that 40 percent of the surveys were returned as undeliverable because complainants had given faulty addresses.)

Appendix B: Interviewed Officer Demographics

TABLE B-1. BERKELEY POLICE DEPARTMENT COMPARISONS

	Patrol Division	Sample
Average Age	29.4	28.8
Average years of service	5.5	4.8
Sex		
Male	94.5%	91.7%
Female	5.5%	8.3%
Race		
White	64.6%	66.8%
Black	22.8%	16.6%
Hispanic	6.3%	8.3%
Other	6.3%	8.3%

TABLE B-2. CONTRA COSTA COUNTY SHERIFF'S DEPARTMENT COMPARISONS

	Patrol Division	Sample
Average Age	32.9	33.5
Average years of service	6.2	6.4
Sex		
Male	97.9%	100.0%
Female	2.1%	0.0%
Race		
White	94.8%	91.7%
Black	2.1%	8.3%
Hispanic	1.0%	0.0%
Other	2.1%	0.0%
Total minority (by race and sex)	5.2%	8.3%

TABLE B-3. OAKLAND POLICE DEPARTMENT COMPARISONS

	Patrol Division	Sample
Average Age	30.8	30.6
Average years of service	5.9	5.5
Race	63.2%	58.3%
White		
Black	21.9%	25.0%
Hispanic	8.6%	8.3%
Other	6.3%	8.3%
Marital status		
Married	72.5%	83.4%
Single	16.4%	8.3%
Divorced	11.2%	8.3%
Education		
High school	23.1%	16.6%
Some college	38.5%	50.0%
A.A. degree	21.8%	8.3%
B.A. or beyond	16.6%	25.0%
Military experience	66.0%	58.3%

Appendix C: Officer Attitudinal Questionnaire Demographics

TABLE C-I. OAKLAND POLICE DEPARTMENT COMPARISONS

	Department	Sample
Race		
White	54.5%	49%
Black	25.1%	23%
Hispanic	10.8%	11%
Other	9.6%	17%
Total race minority	45.5%	51%
Sex		
Male	92.0%	91%
Female	8.0%	9%
Rank		
Captain	1.4%	1%
Lieutenant	3.2%	3%
Sergeant	18.9%	28%
Officer	75.8%	67%

TABLE C-2. BERKELEY POLICE DEPARTMENT COMPARISONS

	Department	Sample
Race		
White	60.4%	74.7%
Black	20.9%	15.7%
Hispanic	6.6%	1.2%
Asian/Pacific Is.	11.0%	3.6%
Native American	1.1%	4.8%
Total race minority	39.6%	25.3%
Sex		
Male	87.9%	91.6%
Female	12.1%	8.4%
Rank		
Captain	2.2%	1.2%
Lieutenant	4.9%	7.2%
Sergeant	19.7%	16.9%
Officer	73.2%	74.7%

Bibliography

ACLU. *See* American Civil Liberties Union.

Aitchison, Will. 1990. *The Rights of Law Enforcement Officers*. Portland, Ore.: Labor Relations Information Systems.

American Bar Association. 1970. "Problems and Recommendations on Disciplinary Enforcement." Report of the Special Committee on Evaluation of Disciplinary Enforcement. Chicago, Ill.: American Bar Association.

American Civil Liberties Union. 1991. 27 June. Biannual Conference. Burlington, Vt.

Americans for Effective Law Enforcement. 1982. "Police Civilian Review Boards." Chicago, Ill.: Law Enforcement Legal Defense Center.

Anderson, Stanley V. 1969. *Ombudsman Papers: American Experience and Proposals*. Berkeley, Calif.: Institute for Governmental Studies.

Anderson, Stanley V., and John F. Moore, eds. 1971. *Establishing Ombudsman Offices: Recent Experience in the United States*. Berkeley, Calif.: Institute for Governmental Studies.

Andrews, Allen H., Jr. 1985. "Structuring the Political Independence of the Police Chief." In *Police Leadership in America. See* Geller 1985.

Annotated Codes of Maryland. "Crime and Punishment." Articles 27, 728.

Associated Press. 1991. 8 February.

Banton, Michael. 1964. *The Policeman in the Community*. London: Tavistock.

Barker, Thomas, and Julian Roebuck. 1973. *An Empirical Typology of Police Corruption: A Study in Organizational Deviance*. Springfield, Ill.: Thomas.

Barry, Dave. 1983. "So What's News? A Visit to the Nine O'Clock Eyewitness News Center Studios." *Chicago Tribune Magazine*. 4 December, p. 34.

Bartol, Curt R. 1982. "Psychological Characteristics of Small Town Police Officers." *Journal of Police Science and Administration* 10: 58–63.

Bayley, David H. 1985. *Patterns of Policing: A Comparative International Analysis*. New Brunswick, N.J.: Rutgers University Press.

_____. 1988. Cited in Andrew J. Goldsmith, "New Directions in Police Complaints Procedures: Some Conceptual and Comparative Departures." *Police Studies* 11, no. 12 (Summer): 60–71.

Bayley, David H., and Harold Mendelsohn. 1968. *Minorities and the Police.* New York: Macmillan.

Berkley, George. 1969. *The Democratic Policeman.* Boston: Beacon.

Betz, Joseph. 1985. "Police Violence." In: *Moral Issues in Police Work,* edited by Frederick Elliston and Michael Feldberg. Totowa, N.J.: Rowman & Allenheld.

Bittner, Egon. 1970. *The Functions of the Police in Modern Society.* Chevy Chase, Md.: National Institute of Mental Health.

_____. 1990. *Aspects of Police Work.* Boston: Northeastern University Press.

Black, Algernon D. 1968. *The People and the Police.* New York: McGraw-Hill.

Black, Donald J. 1972. "The Social Organization of Arrest." In *Deviance: The Interactionist Perspective,* edited by Earl Rubington and Martin S. Weinburg. New York: Macmillan.

Bogdanich, Walt. 1992. *The Great White Lie: How America's Hospitals Betray Our Trust and Endanger Our Lives.* New York: Simon & Schuster.

Bouza, Anthony. 1985. "Police Unions: Paper Tigers or Roaring Lions?" In *Police Leadership in America. See* Geller 1985.

_____. 1990. *The Police Mystique.* New York: Plenum.

Box, Steven. 1983. *Power, Crime, and Mystification.* London: Tavistock.

Bray, Robert J. 1962. "Philadelphia's P.A.B.: A New Concept in Community Relations." *Villanova Law Review* 7 (Summer): 656–73.

Brown, D. 1991. "Civilian Review of Complaints Against the Police: A Survey of the United States Literature." Cited by Andrew J. Goldsmith in *Complaints Against the Police.* New York: Clarendon.

Brown, Jill. 1992. "Defining 'Reasonable' Police Conduct: *Graham v. Connor* and Excessive Force During Arrest." *UCLA Law Review* 38: 1257–86.

Brzeczek, Richard J. 1985. "Chief-Mayor Relations: The View from the Chief's Chair." In *Police Leadership in America. See* Geller 1985.

Buckner, Hubbard T. 1967. *"The Police: The Structure of a Social Control Agency."* Ph.D. diss., University of California, Berkeley.

Burke, Edmund. [1790] 1985. *Reflections on the Revolution in France,* edited by F. P. Locke. London: George Allen & Unwin.

Burnham, David. 1989. *A Law unto Itself.* New York: Random House.

California Evidence Code. Sections 1101, 1102, 1103.

California Peace Officers' Association. 1970. "Berkeley Review Board Clears More Cops than Departmental Internal Affairs Bureau." March.

California Penal Code. Section 832.5.

Cardozo, Benjamin N. 1921. *The Nature of the Judicial Process.* New Haven: Yale University Press.

Carey, Carl. President of the Deputy Sheriff's Association. 1991. Interview conducted at Contra Costa County Sheriff's Department, 24 May.

Carlin, Jerome E. 1966. *Lawyer's Ethics: A Survey of the New York City Bar.* New York: Russell Sage.

————. 1968. "Lawyer's Ethics: Formal Controls." In *The Federal Judicial System,* edited by Thomas P. Johnige and Sheldon Goldman. Hinsdale, Ill.: Dryden.

Carter, David L. 1990. "Drug-Related Corruption of Police Officers: A Contemporary Typology." *Journal of Criminal Justice* 18, no. 2: 85–98.

Cashmore, Ellis, and Eugene McLaughlin. 1991. *Out of Order: Policing Black People.* London: Routledge.

CBS. *See* Columbia Broadcasting System.

Chafee, Zecharial. 1931. Preface. E. J. Hopkins. *Our Lawless Police.* New York: Viking.

Chevigny, Paul. 1969. *Police Power.* New York: Vintage.

Chicago Commission on Race Relations. 1922. *The Negro in Chicago: A Study of Race Relations.* Chicago: University of Chicago Press.

Chigwada, Ruth. 1991. "The Policing of Black Women." In *Out of Order: Policing Black People. See* Cashmore and McLaughlin 1991.

Christopher Commission. 1991. "Report to the Mayor of Los Angeles." 9 July. Unpublished.

Clark, Ramsey. 1970. *Crime in America.* New York: Simon & Schuster.

Cohen, Howard S., and Michael Feldberg. 1991. *Power and Restraint: The Moral Dimension of Police Work.* New York: Praeger.

Cole, George F. 1988. *Criminal Justice: Law and Politics.* Pacific Grove, Calif.: Brooks/Cole.

Columbia Broadcasting System. 1991. "60 Minutes" Television Program. 15 June.

Comber, Edward, and Richard H. Blum. 1964. *Police Selection.* Springfield, Ill.: Charles C. Thomas.

Commission on Civil Disorders. 1968. *To Secure These Rights.* Washington, D.C.: U.S. Government Printing Office.

Contra Costa County Sheriff's Department. 1975. Internal Memo. October.

Coxe, Spencer. 1961. "Police Advisory Board." *Connecticut Law Review* 35: 138–55.

———. 1965. "The Philadelphia Police Advisory Board." *Law in Transition Quarterly* 2: 179–93.

Crowe, Patricia Ward. 1978. "Complainant Reactions to the Massachusetts Commission Against Discrimination." *Law and Society Review* 12, no. 2 (Winter): 217–36.

Dahl, Robert. 1989. *Democracy and Its Critics.* New Haven: Yale University Press.

Daley, R. E. 1980. "The Relationship of Personality Variables to Suitability for Police Work." *DAI* 41: 1551–69.

Daley, Robert. 1971. *Target Blue.* New York: Dell Books.

Davis, James R. 1990. "A Comparison of Attitudes Toward the New York City Police." *Journal of Police Science and Administration* 17, no. 4: 233–43.

Davis, Kenneth Culp. 1969. *Discretionary Justice.* Baton Rouge: Louisiana State University Press.

Deal, A. 1986. "The Pennsylvania State Police: Findings and Recommendations." Philadelphia: Pennsylvania House of Representatives.

Delattre, Edwin J. 1989. *Character and Cops.* Washington, D.C.: American Enterprise Institute for Public Policy Research.

de Tocqueville, Alexis. 1968. *Democracy in America.* New York: Washington Square Press.

Donner, Frank. 1989. *Protectors of Privilege.* Berkeley and Los Angeles: University of California Press.

Douglas, Jack D., and John M. Johnson. 1977. *Official Deviance.* New York: Lippincott.

Dugan, John R., and Daniel R. Breda. 1991. "Complaints about Police Officers: A Comparison among Types and Agencies." *Journal of Criminal Justice* 19: 165–71.

Durkheim, Emile. 1933. *The Division of Labor in Society.* Toronto, Ontario, Canada: Macmillan.

Ehrmann, Henry W. 1976. *Comparative Legal Cultures.* Englewood Cliffs, N.J.: Prentice-Hall.

FBI. *Law Enforcement Bulletins.* 1970. Washington, D.C.: U.S. Government Printing Office.

FBI. *Uniform Crime Reports.* 1960, 1970, 1980, 1990. Washington, D.C.: U.S. Government Printing Office.

Fletcher, Connie. 1990. *What Cops Know.* New York: Random House.

Foner, Philip S., ed. 1970. *The Black Panthers Speak.* New York: Lippincott.

Fraser, Donald M. 1985. "Politics and Police Leadership: The View from City Hall." In *Police Leadership in America. See* Geller 1985.

Fuller, Lon. 1964. *The Morality of Law.* New Haven: Yale University Press.

Galvin, Raymond, and Louis Radelet. 1967. *A National Survey of Police and Community Relations.* East Lansing: Michigan State University.

Garmire, Bernard L. 1982. *Local Government Police Management.* Washington, D.C.: International City Management Association.

Gates, Daryl. 1992. *Chief.* New York: Bantam Books.

Geller, William A., ed. 1985. *Police Leadership in America.* New York: Praeger.

Gellhorn, Walter. 1966. *When Americans Complain.* Cambridge: Harvard University Press.

――――. 1969. *The Ombudsman and Others.* Cambridge: Harvard University Press.

Germann, A. C. 1971. "Changing the Police: The Impossible Dream?" *The Journal of Law, Criminology, and Police Science* 62, no. 1: 57–71.

Glazer, Myron Peretz, and Penina Migdal Glazer. 1989. *The Whistleblowers.* New York: Basic Books.

Goldsmith, Andrew J. 1988. "New Directions in Police Complaints Procedures: Some Conceptual and Comparative Departures." *Police Studies* 11, no. 2 (Summer): 60–71.

――――. 1991. "External Review and Self-Regulation: Police Accountability and the Dialectic of Complaints Procedures." In *Complaints Against the Police,* edited by Andrew Goldsmith. Oxford: Clarendon.

Goldstein, Herman. 1967. "Administrative Problems in Controlling the Exercise of Police Authority." *Journal of Criminal Law, Criminology, and Police Science* (June): 160–72.

――――. 1977. *Policing A Free Society.* Cambridge: Ballinger.

――――. 1990. *Problem-oriented Policing.* Philadelphia: Temple University Press.

Government Code of California. Section 3307.

Governor's Commission on the Los Angeles Riots. 1965. "Violence in the City: An End or a Beginning?" (2 December).

Governor's Committee to Investigate Riots Occurring in Detroit, 21 June 1943. 1943. *Final Report.* (11 August). Detroit, Michigan.

Griffin, Ricky W., and Gregory Moorhead. 1986. *Organizational Behavior.* Boston: Houghton Mifflin.

Guyot, Dorothy. 1991. *Policing as Though People Matter.* Philadelphia: Temple University Press.

Halpern, Stephen C. 1974. "Police Employee Organizations and Accountability Procedures in Three Cities: Some Reflections on Police Policy Making." *Law and Society Review* 8, no. 4 (Summer): 561–82.

293

Hanewicz, Wayne B. 1985. "Discretion and Order." In: *Moral Issues in Police Work,* edited by Frederick Elliston, and Michael Feldberg. Totowa, N.J.: Rowman & Allanheld.

Hoffman, Paul, and John Crew. 1991. "On the Line." American Civil Liberties Union. San Francisco, Calif.

Honolulu Police Commission. 1988–1989. *Annual Reports.* City of Honolulu, Hawaii.

Huberman, John. 1964. "Discipline Without Punishment." *Harvard Business Review* 42 (July–August): 62–68.

Hudnut, William H. III. 1985. "The Police and the Polis: A Mayor's Perspective." 1985. In *Police Leadership in America,* edited by William Geller. New York: Praeger.

Hunt, Morton. 1972. *The Mugging.* New York: Signet Books.

Huntington, Samuel P. 1957. *The Soldier and the State.* Cambridge: Belknap.

IACP. *See* International Association of Chiefs of Police.

International Association of Chiefs of Police. N.d. *A Survey of the Police Department: Chicago, Illinois.* Chicago: IACP.

International City Management Association. 1971. *Municipal Police Administration.* Washington, D.C.

Jaffe, Louis. 1973. "The Illusion of the Ideal Administration." *Harvard Law Review* 86: 1183–99.

Jefferson, Tony. 1990. *The Case Against Paramilitary Policing.* Milton Keynes, England: Open University Press.

Johnston, David. 1983. "The Cop Watch." *Columbia Journalism Review* 22 (Winter): 51–54.

Jowell, Jeffrey. 1973. "The Legal Control of Administrative Discretion." *Public Law* (Autumn): 178–220.

Kansas City, Missouri, Police Department. 1990. General Order 90–1. 17 February.

Kelling, George L. 1985. "Order Maintenance, the Quality of Urban Life, and Police: A Line of Argument." In *Police Leadership in America. See* Geller 1985.

Kerstetter, Wayne A. N.d. "Citizen Review of Police Misconduct." Chicago: Chicago Bar Association.

————. 1985. "Who Disciplines the Police? Who Should?" In *Police Leadership in America. See* Geller 1985.

Kieselhorst, Daniel. 1974. "A Theoretical Perspective of Violence Against Police." Norman, Okla.: Bureau of Government Research, University of Oklahoma.

Klockars, Carl. 1985. "The Dirty Harry Problem." In *Moral Issues in Police Work,* edited by Frederick Elliston and Michael Feldberg. Totowa, N.J.: Rowman & Allanheld.

————. 1992. "The *Only* Way to Make any Real Progress in Controlling Excessive Force by Police." *Law Enforcement News* 15 (May).

Lane, Roger. 1967. *Policing the City of Boston.* Cambridge: Harvard University Press.

Lea, John, and Jock Young. 1984. *What Is to Be Done about Law and Order?* New York: Penguin.

Lee, Melville. 1971. *A History of the Police in England.* Montclair, N.J.: Patterson-Smith.

Leinen, Stephen. 1984. *Black Police, White Society.* New York: New York University Press.

Leuci, Robert. 1989. "The Process of Erosion: A Personal Account." In *Police and Policing: Contemporary Issues. See* Kenney 1989.

Lewis, Clare E. 1991. "Police Complaints: Metropolitan Toronto." In *Complaints Against the Police. See* Goldsmith 1991.

Lindberg, Richard. 1991. *To Collect and Serve.* New York: Praeger.

Lipset, Seymour Martin. 1974. "Why Cops Hate Liberals . . . and Vice Versa." In *Before the Law,* edited by John J. Bonsignore, et al. Boston: Houghton Mifflin.

Lohman, Joseph D., and Gordon E. Misner. 1966. *The Police and the Community.* Berkeley: University of California School of Criminology.

Los Angeles, California, Police Commission. 1993. Public Relations Office. 30 August.

Los Angeles, California, Police Department. 1989. *Internal Affairs Report for 1989.* Los Angeles, Calif.

Lundman, Richard. 1980. *Police Behavior.* New York: Oxford University Press.

McDowell, Banks. 1991. *Ethical Conduct and the Professional's Dilemma.* New York: Quorum.

McLaughlin, Vance, and Robert Bing. 1989. "Selection, Training, and Discipline of Police Officers." In *Police and Policing: Contemporary Issues. See* Kenney 1989.

Madison, James. [1789] 1961. Essay 51. *The Federalist Papers.* New York: Mentor.

Mailer, Norman. 1968. *Miami and the Siege of Chicago.* New York: Signet.

Major, Victoria L. 1991. "Law Enforcement Officers Killed: 1980–89." *FBI Law Enforcement Bulletin* (May). Washington, D.C.: U.S. Government Printing Office.

Malouff, J. M., and N. S. Schutte. 1986. "Using Biographical Information to Hire the Best New Police Officers." *Journal of Police Science and Administration* 14: 256–77.

Manning, Peter K. 1977. *Police Work: The Social Organization of Police Work.* Cambridge: M.I.T. Press.

Martin, Susan Ehrlich. 1980. *Breaking and Entering: Policewomen on Patrol.* Berkeley and Los Angeles: University of California Press.

Mayo, Louis A. 1985. "Leading Blindly: An Assessment of Chiefs' Information about Police Operations." In *Police Leadership in America. See* Geller 1985.

Mayor's Commission on Conditions in Harlem. 1935. "The Negro in Harlem: A Report on Social and Economic Conditions Responsible for the Out-Break of March 19, 1935." New York Municipal Archives. Unpublished.

Merryman, John. 1969. *The Civil Law Tradition.* Palo Alto, Calif.: Stanford University Press.

Merton, Robert. 1957. *Social Theory and Social Structure.* New York: Glencoe.

Mill, John Stuart. 1961. *On Liberty.* New York: Doubleday.

Minneapolis, Minnesota, Civilian Police Review Authority. 1992. *Statistical Report.*

Minneapolis, Minnesota, Police Department. Internal Affairs Division. 1990. *Monthly External Case Reporting Comparison.* City of Minneapolis, Minn.

————. 1992. *External Case Reporting Comparison.*

Moore, Mark, and George Kelling. 1983. "To Serve and Protect: Learning from Police History." *The Public Interest* 70: 49–65.

Moore, Mark H., and Darrel W. Stephens. 1991. *Beyond Command and Control: The Strategic Management of Police Departments.* Washington, D.C.: Police Executive Research Forum.

Moss, Larry E. 1977. "Black Political Ascendancy in Urban Centers and Black Control of the Police." San Francisco: R & E Research Associates.

Muir, William K., Jr. 1977. *Police: Streetcorner Politicians.* Chicago: University of Chicago Press.

New York Civilian Complaint Investigative Bureau. 1989. *Annual Report.* City of New York.

New York Civil Liberties Union. 1990. "Police Abuse: The Need for Civilian Investigation and Oversight" (June).

Niederhoffer, Arthur. 1969. *Behind the Shield.* New York: Anchor.

NYCCIB. *See* New York Civilian Complaint Investigative Bureau.

NYCLU. *See* New York Civil Liberties Union.

Oakland, California, Police Department. 1978. *General Order Manual,* M–3.

Oakland Citizens' Complaint Board. *Annual Reports.* 1981–1991. City of Oakland.

OCCB. *See* Oakland Citizens' Complaint Board.

Office of Citizen Complaints. 1990. *Annual Report*. City of Kansas City, Mo.

Office of Professional Standards. 1991. *Report to the Superintendent of Police*. 4 January. Chicago, Ill. Unpublished.

Olson, Robert. 1969. "Grievance Response Mechanisms for Police Misconduct." *Virginia Law Review* 55: 909–33.

Packer, Herbert L. 1968. *The Limits of the Criminal Sanction*. Palo Alto, Calif.: Stanford University Press.

Petterson, Werner E. 1991. "Police Accountability and Civilian Oversight of Policing: An American Perspective." In *Complaints Against the Police*. See Goldsmith 1991.

Philadelphia Police Advisory Board. 1965. *Annual Report*. City of Philadelphia, Pa.

Phillips, Kevin. 1989. *The Politics of Rich and Poor*. New York: Harper Perennial.

Pickl, Viktor J. 1983. "Investigating Complaints: A Comment." In *International Handbook of the Ombudsman*, edited by Gerald E. Caiden. Westport, Conn.: Greenwood Press.

Pinkele, Carl F., and William C. Louthan. 1985. *Discretion, Justice, and Democracy*. Ames, Ia.: Iowa State University Press.

Platte, Anthony. 1971. *The Politics of Riot Commissions*. New York: Macmillan.

Potts, Lee W. 1983. *Responsible Police Administration*. Huntsville: University of Alabama Press.

Pringle, Patrick. 1955. *Hue and Cry*. London: Museum Press.

Radano, Gene. 1968. *Walking the Beat*. Cleveland, Ohio: World.

Rainey, Richard, and John Quartolo. 1978. "Correction Without Punishment." *Police Chief* (January).

RCMP. *See* Royal Canadian Mounted Police.

Reiner, Robert. 1985. *The Politics of the Police*. New York: St. Martin's Press.

Reiss, Albert J., Jr., 1971. *The Police and the Public*. New Haven: Yale University Press.

———. 1985. "Shaping and Serving the Community: The Role of the Police Chief Executive." In *Police Leadership in America*. See Geller 1985.

Reiss, Albert J., Jr., and David J. Bordua. 1967. "Environment and Organization: A Perspective on the Police." In *The Police*, edited by David J. Bordua. New York: John Wiley.

Richmond, California, Police Commission. 1990. *Quarterly Report to the Mayor and Members of the City Council*. Fall. Richmond, California.

Richmond, California, Police Department, 1988, 1989, 1990. *Internal Affairs Statistics.*

Ricker, Darlene. 1991. "Behind the Silence." *American Bar Association Journal* (July).

Rossi, Peter, Richard Berk, and Bettye K. Eidson. 1975. *The Roots of Urban Discontent.* New York: Wiley.

Royal Canadian Mounted Police. 1990–1991. Public Complaints Commission. *Annual Report 1990–1991.* Ottawa, Ontario, Canada: Ministry of Supply and Services.

Rubenstein, Jonathan. 1973. *City Police.* New York: Ballantine.

Rueschemeyer, Dietrich. 1964. "Doctors and Lawyers: A Comment on the Theory of the Professions." *Canadian Review of Sociology and Anthropology* 1964: pp. 17–30.

St. Clair, James D. 1992. "Report of the Boston Police Department Management Review Committee." Submitted to the mayor, 14 January. Boston, Mass. Unpublished.

Schlesinger, Steven R. 1977. *Exclusionary Injustice.* New York: Marcel Dekker.

Schmidt, Wayne W. 1985. "Section 1983 and the Changing Face of Police Management." In *Police Leadership in America. See* Geller 1985.

Schuck, Peter H. 1983. "Organization Theory and the Teaching of Administrative Law." *Journal of Legal Education* 33: 79–92.

Schur, Edwin M. 1969. *Our Criminal Society.* Englewood Cliffs, N.J.: Prentice-Hall.

Schwartz, Louis B. 1970. "Complaints Against the Police: Experience of the Philadelphia D.A.'s Office." *University of Pennsylvania Law Review* 118: 1023–35.

Selznick, Philip. 1966. *TVA and the Grass Roots.* New York: Harper Torchbook.

———. 1969. *Law, Society, and Industrial Justice.* New York: Russell Sage.

Sherman, Lawrence. 1978. *Scandal and Reform.* Berkeley and Los Angeles: University of California Press.

———, ed. 1974. *Police Corruption: A Sociological Perspective.* New York: Anchor Books.

Simon, Herbert. 1957. *Administrative Behavior.* New York: Macmillan.

Skolnick, Jerome H. 1967. *Justice Without Trial.* New York: John Wiley & Sons.

———. 1969. *The Politics of Protest.* New York: Simon & Schuster.

Skolnick, Jerome H., and David H. Bayley. 1986. *The New Blue Line.* New York: Macmillan Free Press.

Skolnick, Jerome H., and James J. Fyfe. 1993. *Above the Law*. New York: Macmillan Free Press.

Skolnick, Jerome H., and Candace McCoy. 1985. "Police Accountability and the Media." In *Police Leadership in America. See* Geller 1985.

Sparrow, Malcolm K., Mark H. Moore, and David M. Kennedy. 1990. *Beyond 911*. New York: HarperCollins.

Speilberger, C. D., H. C. Spaulding, M. T. Jolley, and J. C. Ward, Jr.. 1979. "Selection of Law Enforcement Officers: The Florida Police Standards Research Project." In *Police Selection and Evaluation*, edited by C. D. Speilberger.

Spiotto, James. 1973. "Search and Seizure: An Empirical Study of the Exclusionary Rule and Its Alternatives." *Journal of Legal Studies* 2: 243–53.

Stalzer, Benjamin. 1961. "Press Portrayal of the New York City Police Department." Unpublished Master's Thesis, Bernard M. Baruch School of Business and Public Administration, City College of New York.

Stamper, Norman H. "Organizational Audit and an Agenda for Reform," San Diego Police Department, April 1991 (unpublished).

Stark, Rodney. 1972. *Police Riots*. Belmont, Calif.: Wadsworth Publishing.

Starr, Paul. 1982. *The Social Transformation of American Medicine*. New York: Basic Books.

Steer. 1985. *Uncovering Crime*. (Royal Commission on Criminal Procedure Research Study 7, London: HMSO.) Quoted in *The Politics of the Police. See* Reiner 1985.

Stephens, Otis H. 1973. *The Supreme Court and Confessions of Guilt*. Knoxville: University of Tennessee Press.

Stoddard, E. R. 1983. "Blue Coat Crime." In *Thinking about Police*, edited by Carl Klockars. New York: McGraw-Hill.

Talley, Joseph E., and Lisa D. Hinz. 1990. *Performance Prediction of Public Safety and Law Enforcement Personnel*. Springfield, Ill.: Charles Thomas.

Terrill, Richard. 1982. "Complaint Procedures: Variations on the Theme of Civilian Participation." *Journal of Police Science and Administration* 10, no. 4: 398–406.

———. 1990. "Alternative Perceptions of Independence in Civilian Oversight." *Journal of Police Science and Administration* 17, no. 2: 77–83.

Thompson, James D. 1967. *Organizations in Action*. New York: McGraw-Hill.

Tigar, Michael, and Madeline R. Levy. 1974. "The Grand Jury as the

New Inquisition." In *Before the Law,* edited by John J. Bonsignore et al. Boston: Houghton Mifflin.

Time. 1991. 1 April.

Toch, Hans, J. Douglas Grant, and Raymond T. Galvin. 1975. *Agents of Change: A Study in Police Reform.* Cambridge, Mass.: Schenkman.

Toffler, Alvin. 1971. *Future Shock.* New York: Bantam.

Toronto Public Complaints Commissioner. 1989. "Eighth Annual Report of the Office of the Public Complaints Commissioner: 1989." Toronto, Ontario, Canada.

Trojanowicz, Robert C. 1980. *The Environment of the First Line Supervisor.* Englewood Cliffs, N.J.: Prentice-Hall.

Tyre, Mitchell, and Susan Braunstein. 1992. "Higher Education and Ethical Policing." *FBI Law Enforcement Bulletin* (June). Washington, D.C.: U.S. Government Printing Office.

Uglow, Steve. 1988. *Policing Liberal Society.* New York: Oxford Press.

U.S. Civil Rights Commission. 1981. *Who Is Guarding the Guardians?* Washington, D.C.: U.S. Government Printing Office.

U.S. Congress. House. 1981. "Report of the Special Committee Authorized to Investigate the East St. Louis Riots." 35th Cong., 2d sess., 15 July 1981. H. Doc. 1231.

————. 1991a. "Police Brutality Accountability Act of 1991." 102d Cong., 1st sess., 17 April 1991, H. Doc. 1914.

————. 1991b. "Police Accountability Act of 1991." 102d Cong., 1st sess., 23 July 1991, H. Doc. 2972.

U.S. Department of Justice. 1989. *Building Integrity and Reducing Drug Corruption in Police Departments.* Washington, D.C.: International Association of Chiefs of Police (IACP).

Vick, C.F.J. 1982. "Ideological Responses to the Riots." *Police Journal* 55: 1–27.

Waddington, P.A.J. 1991. *The Strong Arm of the Law.* Oxford: Clarendon.

Wagner, Allen E. 1980. "Citizen Complaints Against the Police: The Complainant." *Journal of Police Science and Administration* 8, no. 3: 247–52.

Walker, Samuel. 1977. *A Critical History of Police Reform: The Emergence of Professionalism.* Lexington, Mass.: Lexington Books.

————. 1990. *In Defense of American Liberties.* New York: Oxford Press.

Walker, Samuel, and Vic Bumphus. 1991. "Civilian Review of the Police: A National Survey of the 50 Largest Cities, 1991." Department of Criminal Justice, University of Nebraska. Omaha, Nebr.

Weisburd, David, Jerome McElroy, and Patricia Hardyman. 1989.

"Maintaining Control in Community-Oriented Policing." In *Police and Policing: Contemporary Issues. See* Kenney 1989.

West, Paul. N.d. "PERF Investigation of Complaints Against the Police: Survey Summary Report of Results." Police Executive Research Forum. Washington, D.C.

Westley, William A. 1970. *Violence and the Police.* Cambridge: M.I.T. Press.

Whitaker, Gordon P., and Charles David Phillips. 1983. *Evaluating Performance of Criminal Justice Agencies.* Beverly Hills, Calif.: Sage.

White, Susan O. 1973. "Controlling Police Behavior." In *Police: Perspectives, Problems, Prospects,* edited by Donald E. J. MacNamara and Marc Riedel. New York: Praeger.

Wickersham Commission on Law Observance and Law Enforcement. 1931. Washington, D.C.: U.S. Government Printing Office.

Wilson, James Q. 1968. "The Police and the Delinquent in Two Cities." In *Controlling Delinquents,* edited by S. Wheeler. New York: John Wiley & Sons.

———. 1972. *Varieties of Police Behavior.* New York: Atheneum.

Wilson, James W. 1963. "The Police and Their Problems: A Theory." *Public Policy* 12: 189–216.

Wilson, O. W., and Roy C. McLaren. 1963. *Police Administration.* New York: McGraw-Hill.

Wyner, Alan J. 1973. *Executive Ombudsmen in the United States.* Berkeley: Institute for Governmental Studies.

Yarmey, Daniel. 1990. *Understanding Police and Police Work.* New York: New York University Press.

Zagoria, Sam. 1988. *The Ombudsman: How Good Governments Handle Citizen's Grievances.* Washington, D.C.: Seven Locks Press.

Newspaper References

Berkeley Gazette. 1966. 29 May.

———. 1973. 8 January; 16 April; 19 April.

———. 1991. 1–4 August.

Boston Globe. 1991. 28 July; 2–5 August.

———. 1992. 18 January; 19 July.

Burlington Free Press. 1993. 17 February; 2 September.

Cleveland Plain Dealer. 1991. 30 May.

Detroit Free Press. 1992. 7 November; 12 December.

Los Angeles Daily News. 1991. 10 July; 16 July; 19 July.

Los Angeles Times. 1991. 5 March; 26 June; 10 July; 12 July; 17 July.

———. 1992. 2–5 May.

New York Times. 1966. 29 May.

———. 1967. 4 March.

———. 1992. 25 June; 8 July; 29 July.

Philadelphia Inquirer. 1960. 13 October.

Sacramento Bee. 1991. 18 September.

San Diego Union. 1991. 14 August; 16 August.

San Francisco Chronicle. 1978. 6 July.

———. 1990. 9 May; 29 May.

San Francisco Progress. 1977. 27 April.

Case References

Allen v. Murphy, 322 N.Y. 2d 435 (1971).

Bence v. Breier, 501 F.2d 1185, 1190 (7th Cir.).

Boulware v. Battaglia, 344 F. Supp. 899, D. Del. (1972).

Cleveland Board of Education v. Laudermill, 470 U.S. 532 (1985).

Elkins v. United States, 364 U.S. 206 (1960).

Farmer v. City of Fort Lauderdale, 427 So. 2d 187, 190 Fla.

Garrity v. New Jersey, 385 U.S. 493 (1967).

Glass v. Town Board, 329 N.Y.S. 2d 960 (1972).

Kammerer v. Board of Fire and Police Commissioners, 256 N.E. 2d 12, Ill. (1970).

Kannisto v. City and County of San Francisco, 541 F.2d 841 (9th Cir.).

Miranda v. Arizona, 384 U.S. 436 (1966).

People v. Curtis, 70 Cal. 2d 347 (1969).

Pitchess v. Superior Court, 11 Cal. 3d 531 (1974).

Rinderknecht v. Maricopa County, 520 P.2d 332, 335 (Ariz. App.).

Stone v. Powell, 44 U.S. 5313, 5334 (1976).

Index

Accountability, 2, 241, 263, 265, 270; administrative, 10, 229; "democratic," 244–45; judicial, 9, 10; legal standards of, 211; legislative, 9, 211; limitations upon, 273; mechanisms, 11, 51, 53, 136–89, 274; police, 8, 13, 14, 16, 42–44, 48, 57–58, 62–63, 65, 82, 141, 196, 199, 201, 213, 217, 219, 221, 223, 250, 252–53, 257; of police to chief, 268; of sergeants, 206

Accusatorial systems. *See* Adversary

ACLU. *See* American Civil Liberties Union

Acton, Lord John, 9

Adjudication, 15, 74, 250; type of review systems, 77. *See also* Complaints: adjudication

Administrative review systems, 35, 57, 253; and hearing rules, 58; legal limitations of, 133

Administrators, 54, 76; authority of, 78; constituencies of, 10

Adversary: situations for police, 203; systems, 7, 101, 190, 237

Affirmative action, 204

Aitchison, Will, 57–58, 95, 171

Albuquerque, New Mexico, civilian monitor system, 166

Allen v. Murphy, 59

American Bar Association, 152; grievance committee, 235; self-policing of, 222, 235–36

American Civil Liberties Union, 51, 74, 76, 87, 114, 212, 238; conflict of interest for attorneys involved in

civilian review, 187, 222–23; history of, 222; suggested marketing techniques for, 223–24. *See also* New York Civil Liberties Union

Americans for Effective Law Enforcement, 125

Anderson, Stanley V., 166, 184, 186, 189, 190

Andrews, Allen H., Jr., 27, 196, 217

Annotated Codes of Maryland, 60

Anomie, in police officers, 38

Anonymity, in American society, 36

Arbitrariness, 10

Arrest, 12, 13, 14, 26, 67, 68, 95, 120

Assault under color of authority, 11, 146

Associated Press, 241

Atlanta, Georgia, civilian monitor system, 166

"Attitude test," 12

Attorneys, 76, 187, 221, 227; insensitive, 199

Balances of police review, 13, 14, 65, 68, 69, 72–73, 84, 137, 148, 163, 189, 218, 253, 265, 267, 274. *See also* Comparative review systems

Baltimore, Maryland, civilian monitor system, 166

Banton, Michael, 36, 116

Barker, Thomas, 23

Barry, Dave, 56

Bartol, Curt R., 202

Bayley, David H., 26, 35, 46, 88, 90, 112, 149–51, 165, 232

321